SQUADRON

SUPREME

BY ANY MEANS NECESSARY!

LO, AND THERE CAME AN END OF DAYS, WHEN REALITIES CRASHED AND WORLDS FELL.
WHEN ENTIRE UNIVERSES WERE AS CANDLE FLAMES, BURNING BRIGHTLY ONE
MOMENT AND THEN SNUFFED OUT, GONE, WITH DARKNESS IN THEIR PLACE.
BUT THERE WERE SURVIVORS...

OF THE UNTOLD BILLIONS WHO PERISHED, THERE WERE BUT A FEW — FIVE
AMAZING BEINGS — THE LAST OF THEIR KINDS WHO LIVED TO REMEMBER.

8 MONTHS LATER...

COLLECTION EDITOR:
MARK D. BEAZLEY

ASSOCIATE EDITOR:
SARAH BRUNSTAD

ASSOCIATE MANAGER, DIGITAL ASSETS:
JOE HOCHSTEIN

ASSOCIATE MANAGING EDITOR:
ALEX STARBUCK

EDITOR, SPECIAL PROJECTS:
JENNIFER GRÜNWALD

VP, PRODUCTION & SPECIAL PROJECTS:
JEFF YOUNGQUIST

SVP PRINT, SALES & MARKETING:
DAVID GABRIEL

BOOK DESIGNER:
JAY BOWEN

EDITOR IN CHIEF:
AXEL ALONSO

CHIEF CREATIVE OFFICER:
JOE QUESADA

PUBLISHER:
DAN BUCKLEY

EXECUTIVE PRODUCER:
ALAN FINE

SQUADRON SUPREME VOL. 1: BY ANY MEANS NECESSARY! Contains material originally published in magazine form as SQUADRON SUPREME #1-5 and AVENGERS #0. First printing 2016. ISBN# 978-0-7851-9971-7. Published by MARVEL WORLDWIDE, INC., a subsidiary of MARVEL ENTERTAINMENT, LLC. OFFICE OF PUBLICATION: 135 West 50th Street, New York, NY 10020. Copyright © 2016 MARVEL No similarity between any of the names, characters, persons and/or institutions in this magazine with those of any living or dead person or institution is intended, and any such similarity which may exist is purely coincidental. **Printed in Canada.** ALAN FINE, President, Marvel Entertainment; DAN BUCKLEY, President, TV, Publishing & Brand Management; JOE QUESADA, Chief Creative Officer; TOM BREVOORT, SVP of Publishing; DAVID BOGART, SVP of Business Affairs & Operations, Publishing & Partnership; C.B. CEBULSKI, VP of Brand Management & Development, Asia; DAVID GABRIEL, SVP of Sales & Marketing, Publishing; JEFF YOUNGQUIST, VP of Production & Special Projects; DAN CARR, Executive Director of Publishing Technology; ALEX MORALES, Director of Publishing Operations; SUSAN CRESPI, Production Manager; STAN LEE, Chairman Emeritus. For information regarding advertising in Marvel Comics or on Marvel.com, please contact Vit DeBellis, Integrated Sales Manager, at vdebellis@marvel.com. For Marvel subscription inquiries, please call 888-511-5480. **Manufactured between 4/22/2016 and 5/30/2016 by SOLISCO PRINTERS, SCOTT, QC, CANADA.**

10 9 8 7 6 5 4 3 2 1

SQUADRON SUPREME

JAMES ROBINSON
⊣ WRITER ⊢

LEONARD KIRK
⊣ PENCILER ⊢

PAUL NEARY
WITH *SCOTT HANNA* (#3)
& *MARC DEERING* (#4-5)
⊣ INKERS ⊢

FRANK MARTIN
WITH *GURU-eFX* (#5)
⊣ COLOR ARTISTS ⊢

VC'S TRAVIS LANHAM
⊣ LETTERER ⊢

CHRIS ROBINSON &
CHARLES BEACHAM
⊣ ASSISTANT EDITORS ⊢

MARK PANICCIA
& KATIE KUBERT
⊣ EDITORS ⊢

ALEX ROSS WITH *ALEX GARNER* (#5) AND *KENNETH ROCAFORT* & *RICHARD ISANOVE* (AVENGERS #0)
⊣ COVER ARTISTS ⊢

DEDICATED IN LOVING MEMORY TO THOSE WE'VE LOST.

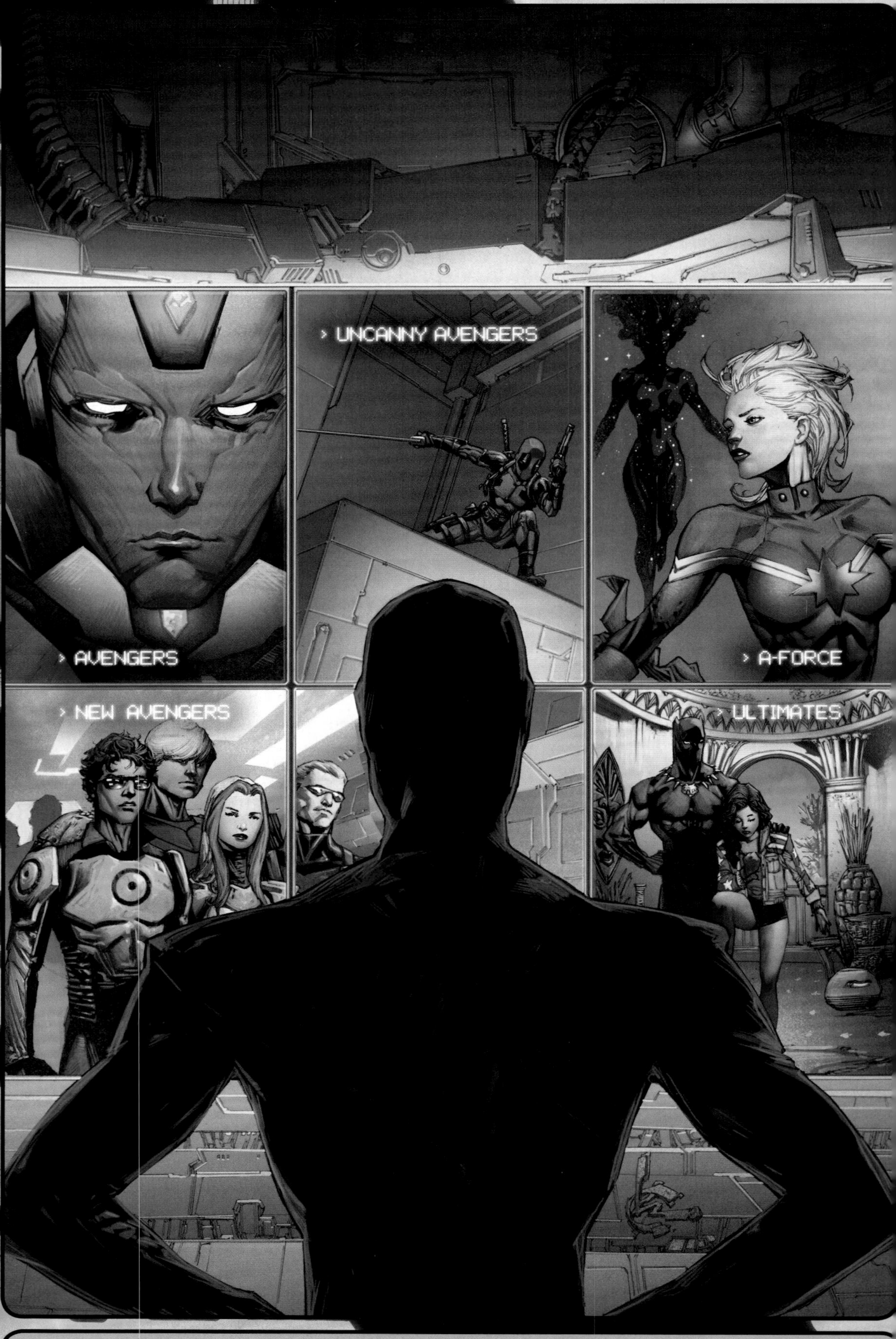
> UNCANNY AVENGERS
> AVENGERS
> A-FORCE
> NEW AVENGERS
> ULTIMATES

AVENGERS #0

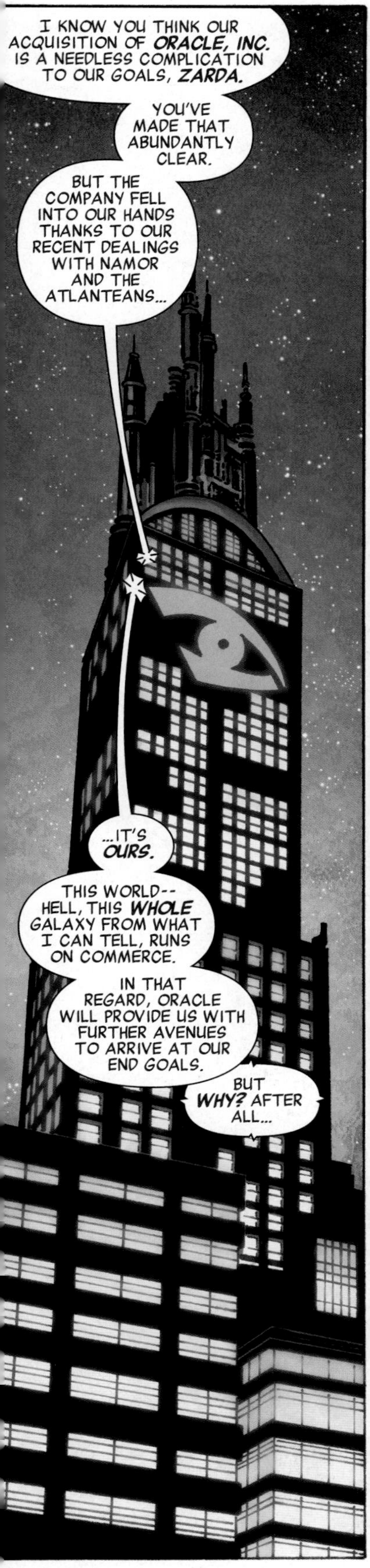
I KNOW YOU THINK OUR ACQUISITION OF ORACLE, INC. IS A NEEDLESS COMPLICATION TO OUR GOALS, ZARDA.
YOU'VE MADE THAT ABUNDANTLY CLEAR.
BUT THE COMPANY FELL INTO OUR HANDS THANKS TO OUR RECENT DEALINGS WITH NAMOR AND THE ATLANTEANS...
...IT'S OURS.
THIS WORLD-- HELL, THIS WHOLE GALAXY FROM WHAT I CAN TELL, RUNS ON COMMERCE.
IN THAT REGARD, ORACLE WILL PROVIDE US WITH FURTHER AVENUES TO ARRIVE AT OUR END GOALS.
BUT WHY? AFTER ALL...

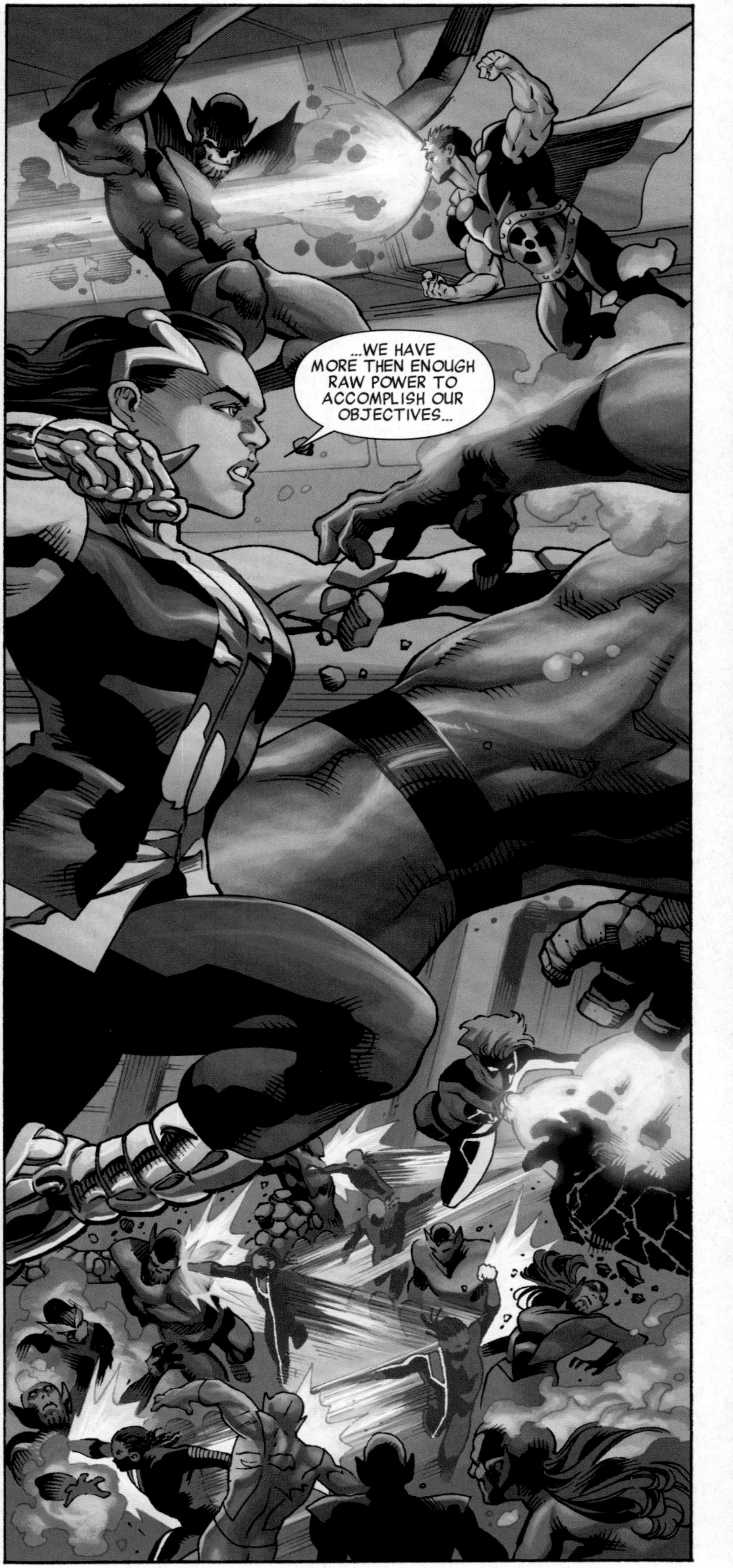
...WE HAVE MORE THEN ENOUGH RAW POWER TO ACCOMPLISH OUR OBJECTIVES...

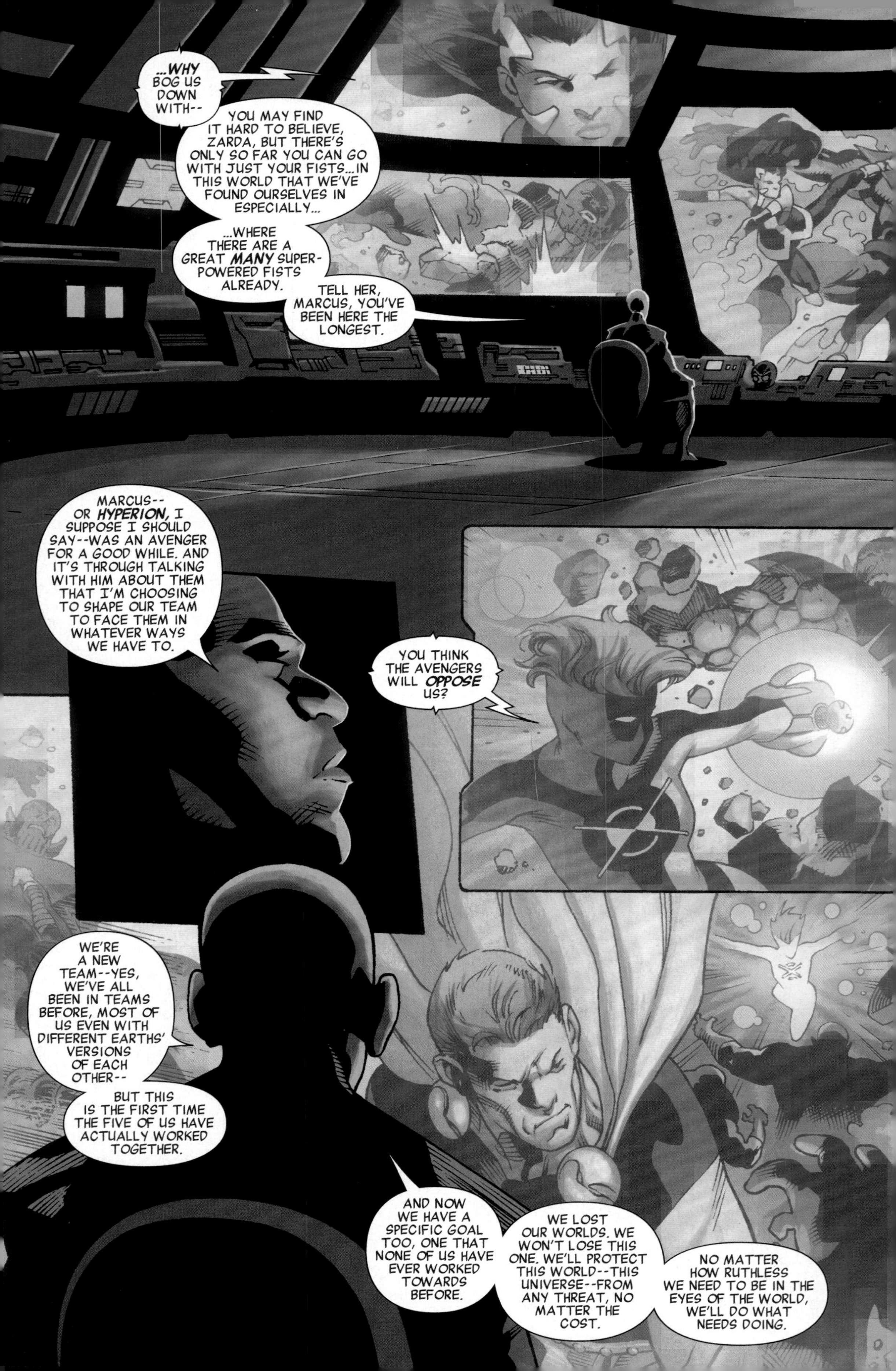
...WHY BOG US DOWN WITH--
YOU MAY FIND IT HARD TO BELIEVE, ZARDA, BUT THERE'S ONLY SO FAR YOU CAN GO WITH JUST YOUR FISTS...IN THIS WORLD THAT WE'VE FOUND OURSELVES IN ESPECIALLY...
...WHERE THERE ARE A GREAT MANY SUPER-POWERED FISTS ALREADY.
TELL HER, MARCUS, YOU'VE BEEN HERE THE LONGEST.
MARCUS--OR HYPERION, I SUPPOSE I SHOULD SAY--WAS AN AVENGER FOR A GOOD WHILE. AND IT'S THROUGH TALKING WITH HIM ABOUT THEM THAT I'M CHOOSING TO SHAPE OUR TEAM TO FACE THEM IN WHATEVER WAYS WE HAVE TO.
YOU THINK THE AVENGERS WILL OPPOSE US?
WE'RE A NEW TEAM--YES, WE'VE ALL BEEN IN TEAMS BEFORE, MOST OF US EVEN WITH DIFFERENT EARTHS' VERSIONS OF EACH OTHER--
BUT THIS IS THE FIRST TIME THE FIVE OF US HAVE ACTUALLY WORKED TOGETHER.
AND NOW WE HAVE A SPECIFIC GOAL TOO, ONE THAT NONE OF US HAVE EVER WORKED TOWARDS BEFORE.
WE LOST OUR WORLDS. WE WON'T LOSE THIS ONE. WE'LL PROTECT THIS WORLD--THIS UNIVERSE--FROM ANY THREAT, NO MATTER THE COST.
NO MATTER HOW RUTHLESS WE NEED TO BE IN THE EYES OF THE WORLD, WE'LL DO WHAT NEEDS DOING.

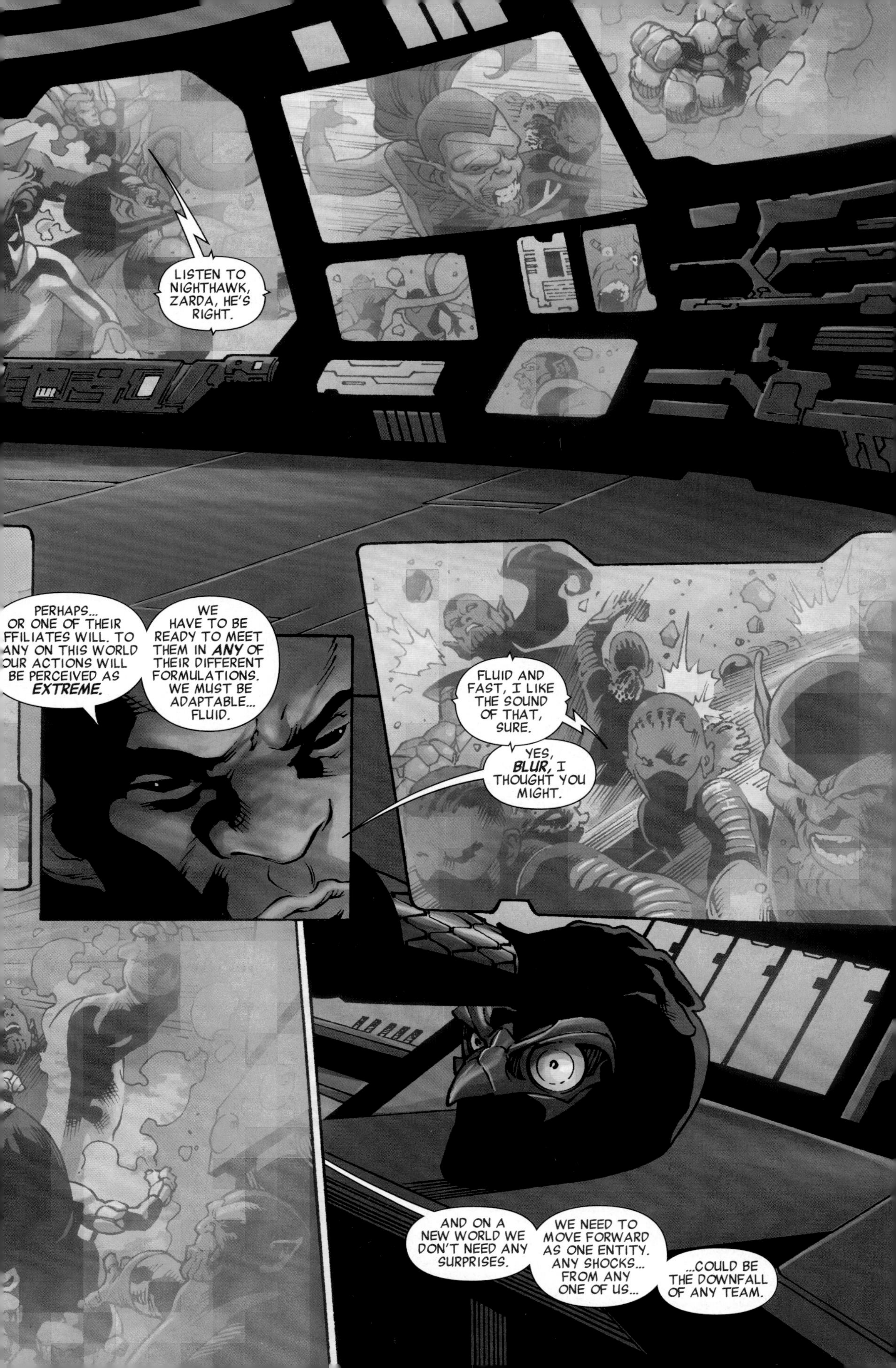
LISTEN TO NIGHTHAWK, ZARDA, HE'S RIGHT.
PERHAPS... OR ONE OF THEIR FFILIATES WILL. TO ANY ON THIS WORLD OUR ACTIONS WILL BE PERCEIVED AS EXTREME.
WE HAVE TO BE READY TO MEET THEM IN ANY OF THEIR DIFFERENT FORMULATIONS. WE MUST BE ADAPTABLE... FLUID.
FLUID AND FAST, I LIKE THE SOUND OF THAT, SURE.
YES, BLUR, I THOUGHT YOU MIGHT.
AND ON A NEW WORLD WE DON'T NEED ANY SURPRISES.
WE NEED TO MOVE FORWARD AS ONE ENTITY. ANY SHOCKS... FROM ANY ONE OF US...
...COULD BE THE DOWNFALL OF ANY TEAM.

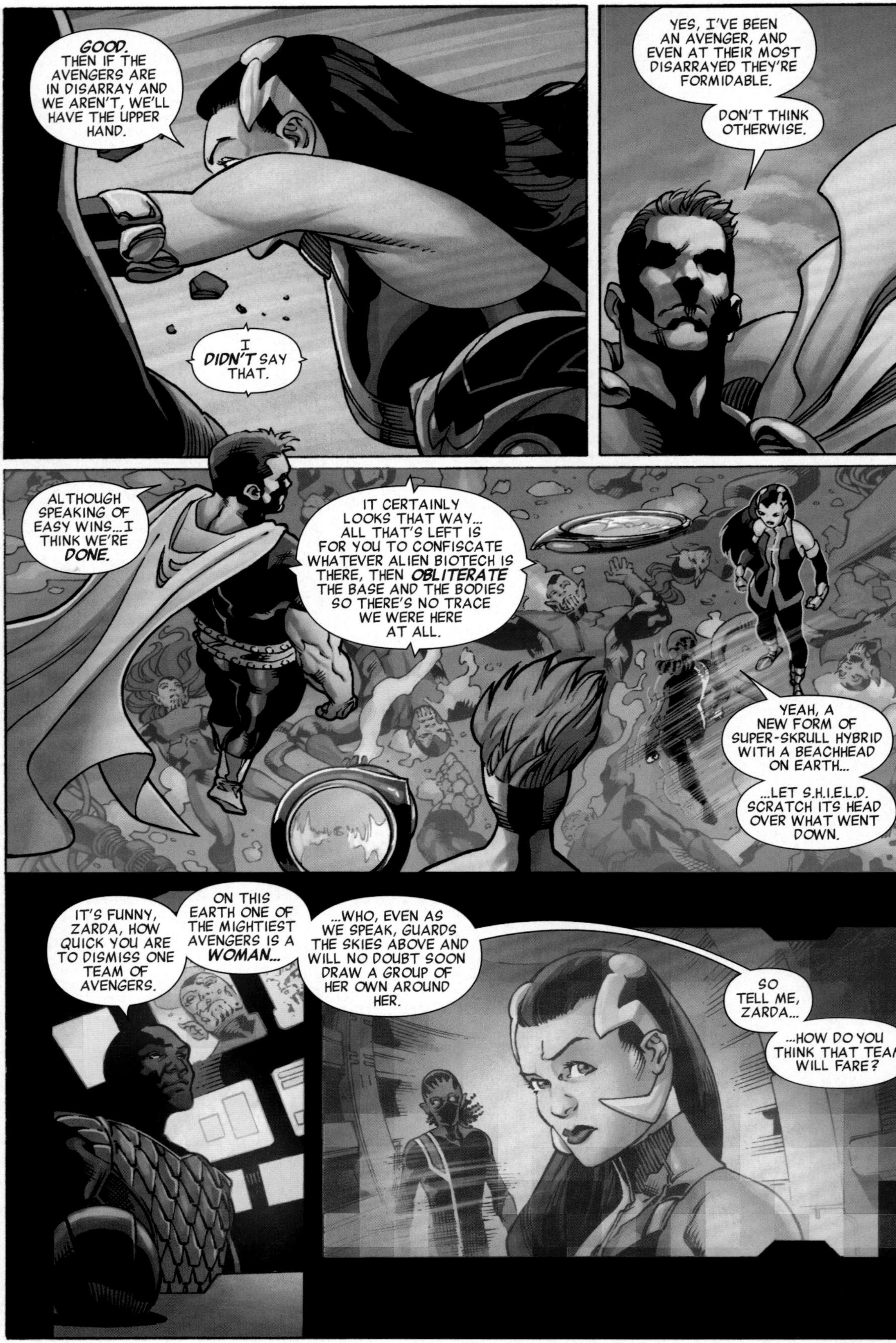
GOOD. THEN IF THE AVENGERS ARE IN DISARRAY AND WE AREN'T, WE'LL HAVE THE UPPER HAND.
I DIDN'T SAY THAT.
YES, I'VE BEEN AN AVENGER, AND EVEN AT THEIR MOST DISARRAYED THEY'RE FORMIDABLE.
DON'T THINK OTHERWISE.
ALTHOUGH SPEAKING OF EASY WINS...I THINK WE'RE DONE.
IT CERTAINLY LOOKS THAT WAY... ALL THAT'S LEFT IS FOR YOU TO CONFISCATE WHATEVER ALIEN BIOTECH IS THERE, THEN OBLITERATE THE BASE AND THE BODIES SO THERE'S NO TRACE WE WERE HERE AT ALL.
YEAH, A NEW FORM OF SUPER-SKRULL HYBRID WITH A BEACHHEAD ON EARTH...
...LET S.H.I.E.L.D. SCRATCH ITS HEAD OVER WHAT WENT DOWN.
IT'S FUNNY, ZARDA, HOW QUICK YOU ARE TO DISMISS ONE TEAM OF AVENGERS.
ON THIS EARTH ONE OF THE MIGHTIEST AVENGERS IS A WOMAN...
...WHO, EVEN AS WE SPEAK, GUARDS THE SKIES ABOVE AND WILL NO DOUBT SOON DRAW A GROUP OF HER OWN AROUND HER.
SO TELL ME, ZARDA...
...HOW DO YOU THINK THAT TEAM WILL FARE?

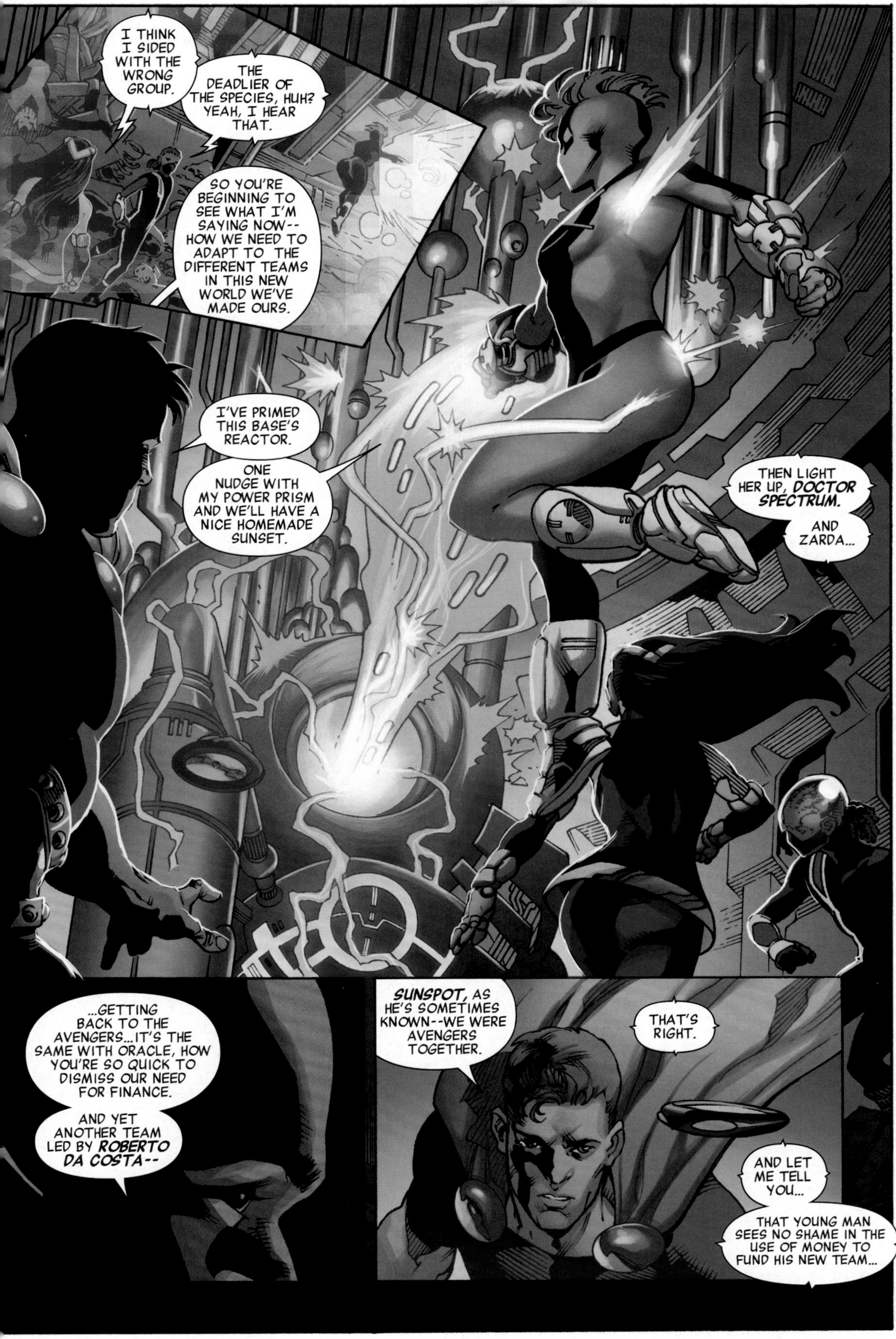

I THINK I SIDED WITH THE WRONG GROUP.
THE DEADLIER OF THE SPECIES, HUH? YEAH, I HEAR THAT.
SO YOU'RE BEGINNING TO SEE WHAT I'M SAYING NOW--HOW WE NEED TO ADAPT TO THE DIFFERENT TEAMS IN THIS NEW WORLD WE'VE MADE OURS.
I'VE PRIMED THIS BASE'S REACTOR.
ONE NUDGE WITH MY POWER PRISM AND WE'LL HAVE A NICE HOMEMADE SUNSET.
THEN LIGHT HER UP, DOCTOR SPECTRUM.
AND ZARDA...
...GETTING BACK TO THE AVENGERS...IT'S THE SAME WITH ORACLE, HOW YOU'RE SO QUICK TO DISMISS OUR NEED FOR FINANCE.
AND YET ANOTHER TEAM LED BY ROBERTO DA COSTA--
SUNSPOT, AS HE'S SOMETIMES KNOWN--WE WERE AVENGERS TOGETHER.
THAT'S RIGHT.
AND LET ME TELL YOU...
THAT YOUNG MAN SEES NO SHAME IN THE USE OF MONEY TO FUND HIS NEW TEAM...

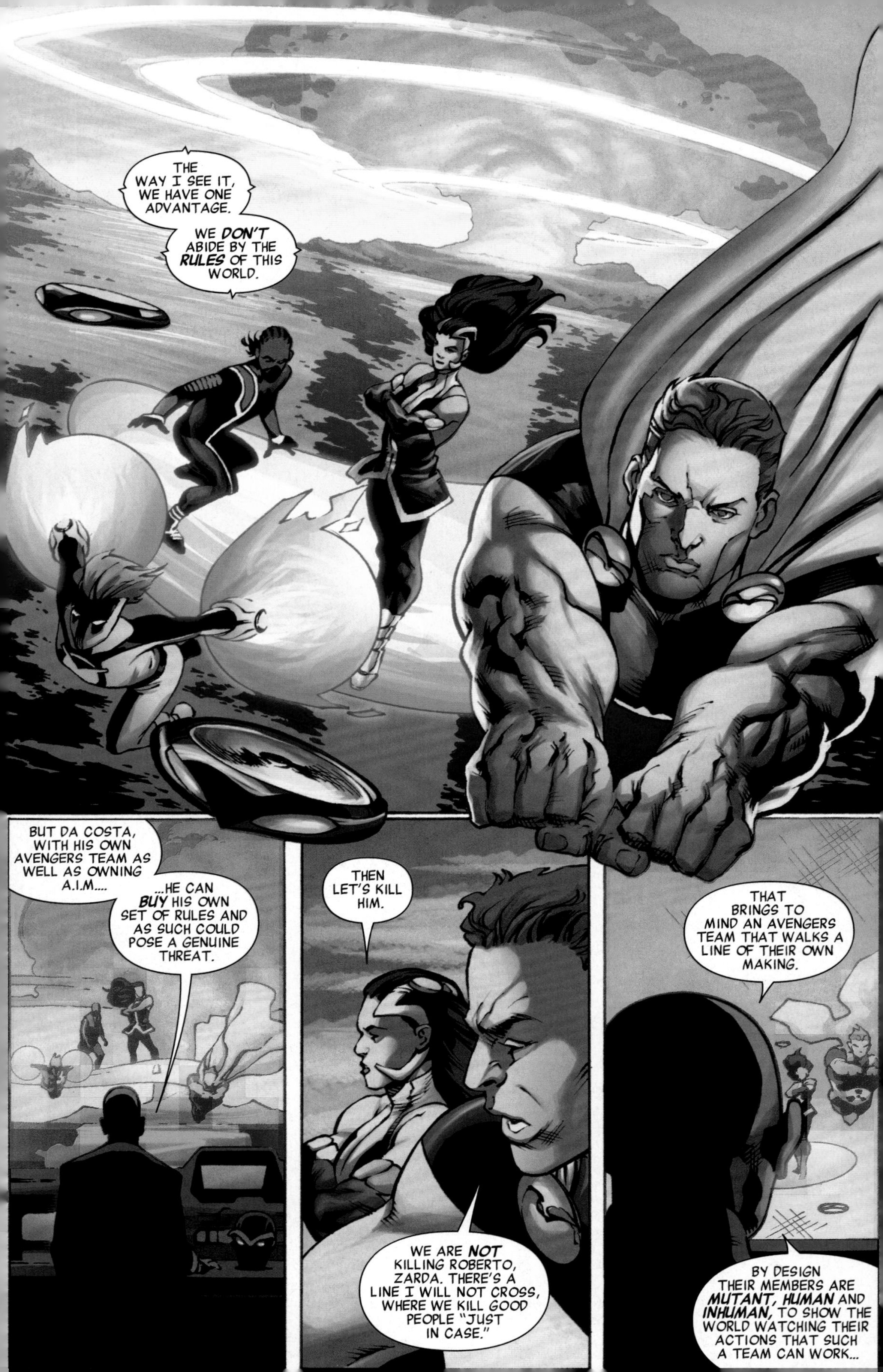
THE WAY I SEE IT, WE HAVE ONE ADVANTAGE.
WE DON'T ABIDE BY THE RULES OF THIS WORLD.
BUT DA COSTA, WITH HIS OWN AVENGERS TEAM AS WELL AS OWNING A.I.M....
...HE CAN BUY HIS OWN SET OF RULES AND AS SUCH COULD POSE A GENUINE THREAT.
THEN LET'S KILL HIM.
WE ARE NOT KILLING ROBERTO, ZARDA. THERE'S A LINE I WILL NOT CROSS, WHERE WE KILL GOOD PEOPLE "JUST IN CASE."
THAT BRINGS TO MIND AN AVENGERS TEAM THAT WALKS A LINE OF THEIR OWN MAKING.
BY DESIGN THEIR MEMBERS ARE MUTANT, HUMAN AND INHUMAN, TO SHOW THE WORLD WATCHING THEIR ACTIONS THAT SUCH A TEAM CAN WORK...

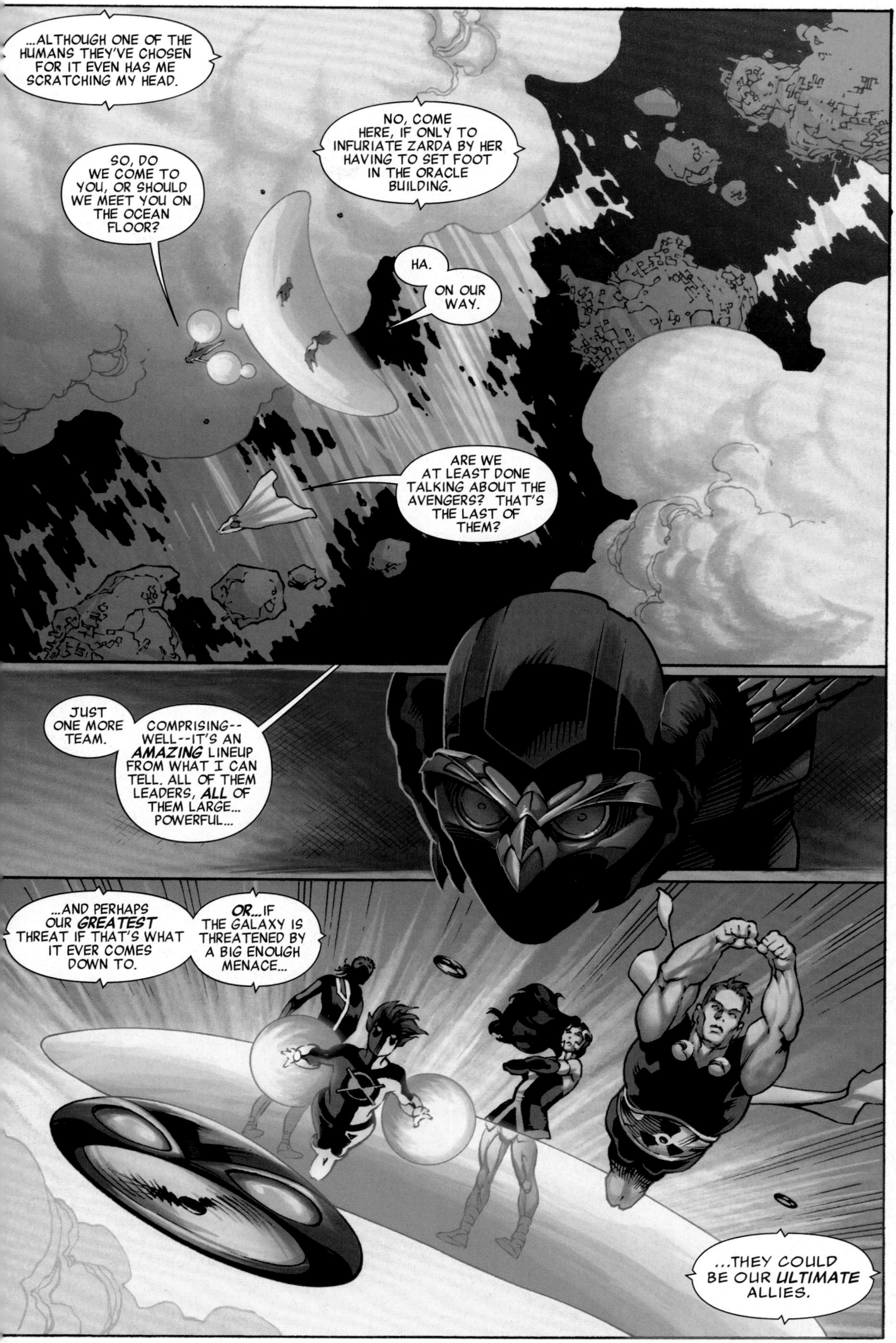
...ALTHOUGH ONE OF THE HUMANS THEY'VE CHOSEN FOR IT EVEN HAS ME SCRATCHING MY HEAD.
SO, DO WE COME TO YOU, OR SHOULD WE MEET YOU ON THE OCEAN FLOOR?
NO, COME HERE, IF ONLY TO INFURIATE ZARDA BY HER HAVING TO SET FOOT IN THE ORACLE BUILDING.
HA.
ON OUR WAY.
ARE WE AT LEAST DONE TALKING ABOUT THE AVENGERS? THAT'S THE LAST OF THEM?
JUST ONE MORE TEAM.
COMPRISING--WELL--IT'S AN AMAZING LINEUP FROM WHAT I CAN TELL. ALL OF THEM LEADERS, ALL OF THEM LARGE... POWERFUL...
...AND PERHAPS OUR GREATEST THREAT IF THAT'S WHAT IT EVER COMES DOWN TO.
OR...IF THE GALAXY IS THREATENED BY A BIG ENOUGH MENACE...
...THEY COULD BE OUR ULTIMATE ALLIES.

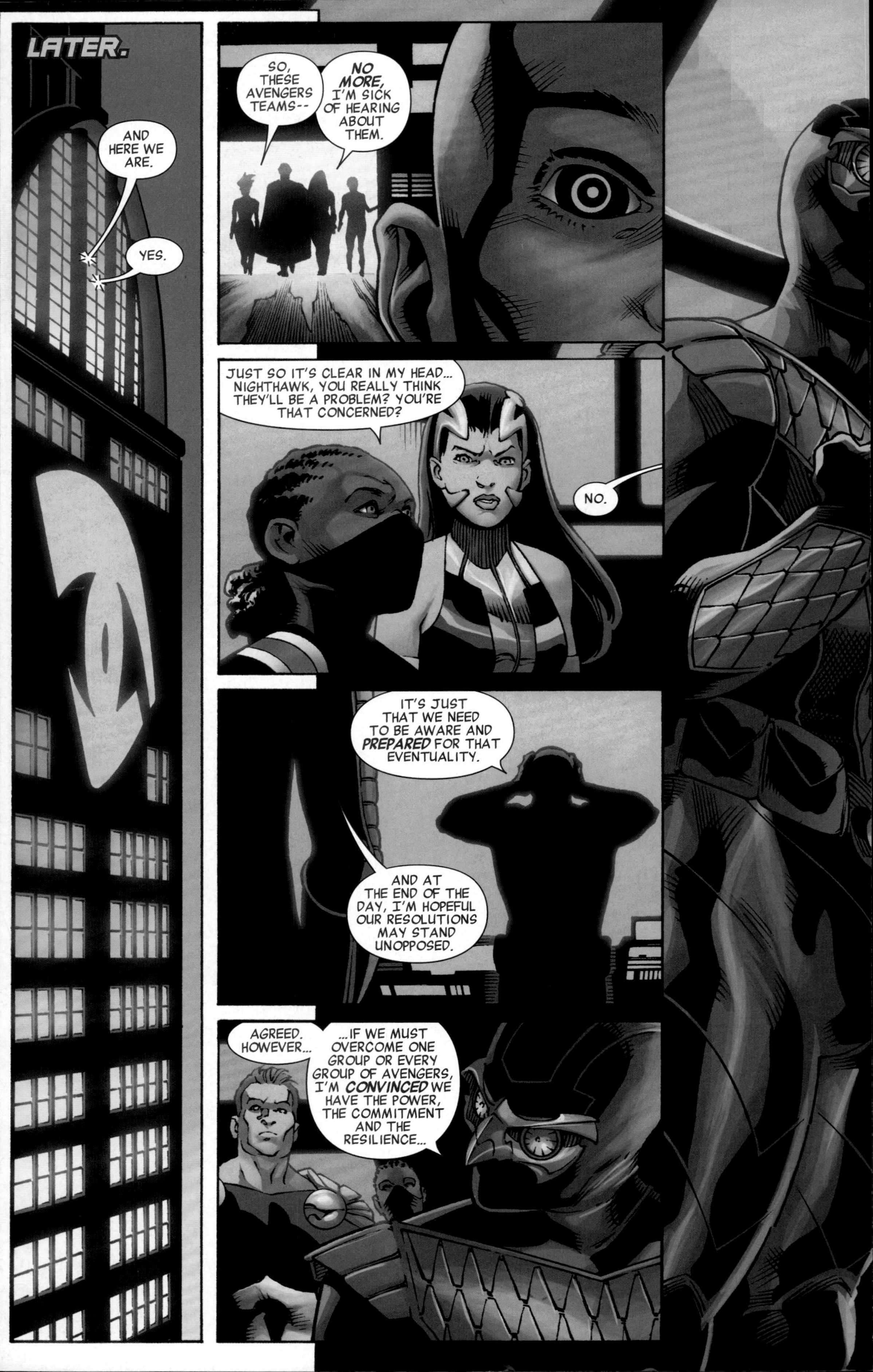
LATER.
AND HERE WE ARE.
YES.
SO, THESE AVENGERS TEAMS--
NO MORE, I'M SICK OF HEARING ABOUT THEM.
JUST SO IT'S CLEAR IN MY HEAD... NIGHTHAWK, YOU REALLY THINK THEY'LL BE A PROBLEM? YOU'RE THAT CONCERNED?
NO.
IT'S JUST THAT WE NEED TO BE AWARE AND PREPARED FOR THAT EVENTUALITY.
AND AT THE END OF THE DAY, I'M HOPEFUL OUR RESOLUTIONS MAY STAND UNOPPOSED.
AGREED. HOWEVER...
...IF WE MUST OVERCOME ONE GROUP OR EVERY GROUP OF AVENGERS, I'M CONVINCED WE HAVE THE POWER, THE COMMITMENT AND THE RESILIENCE...

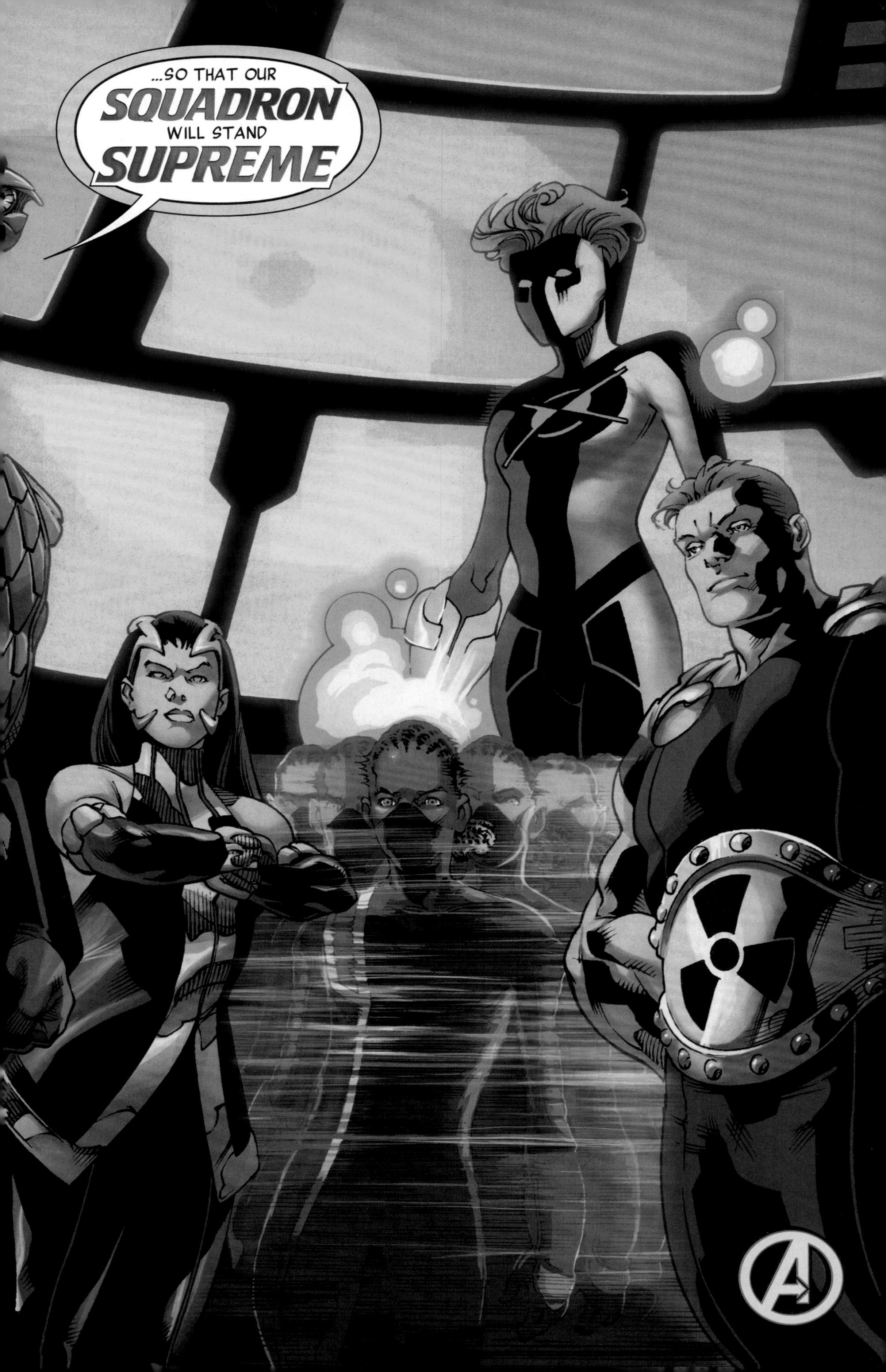
...SO THAT OUR SQUADRON WILL STAND SUPREME

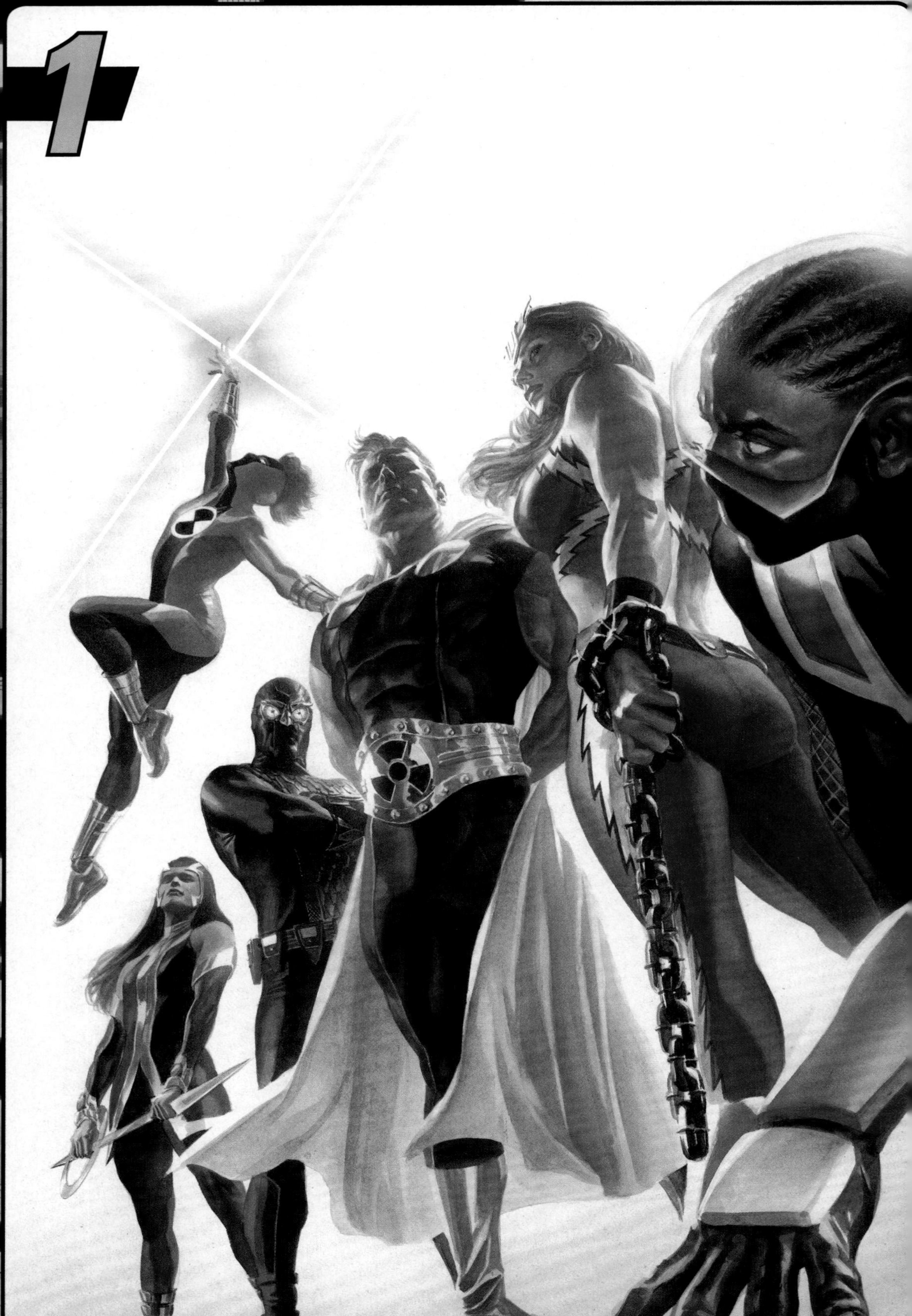
1

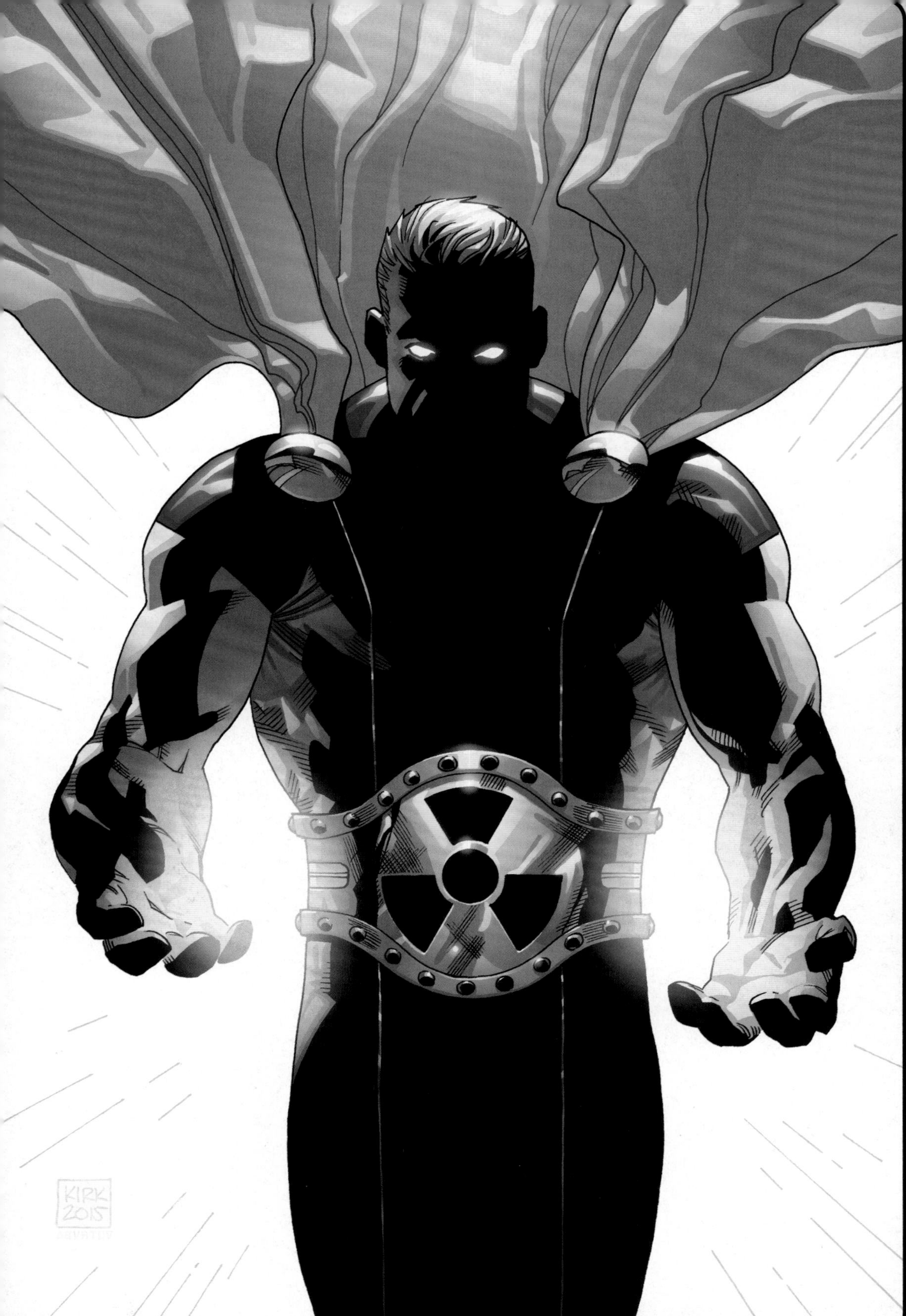
KIRK
2015

#1 VARIANT BY LEONARD KIRK & JESUS ABURTOV

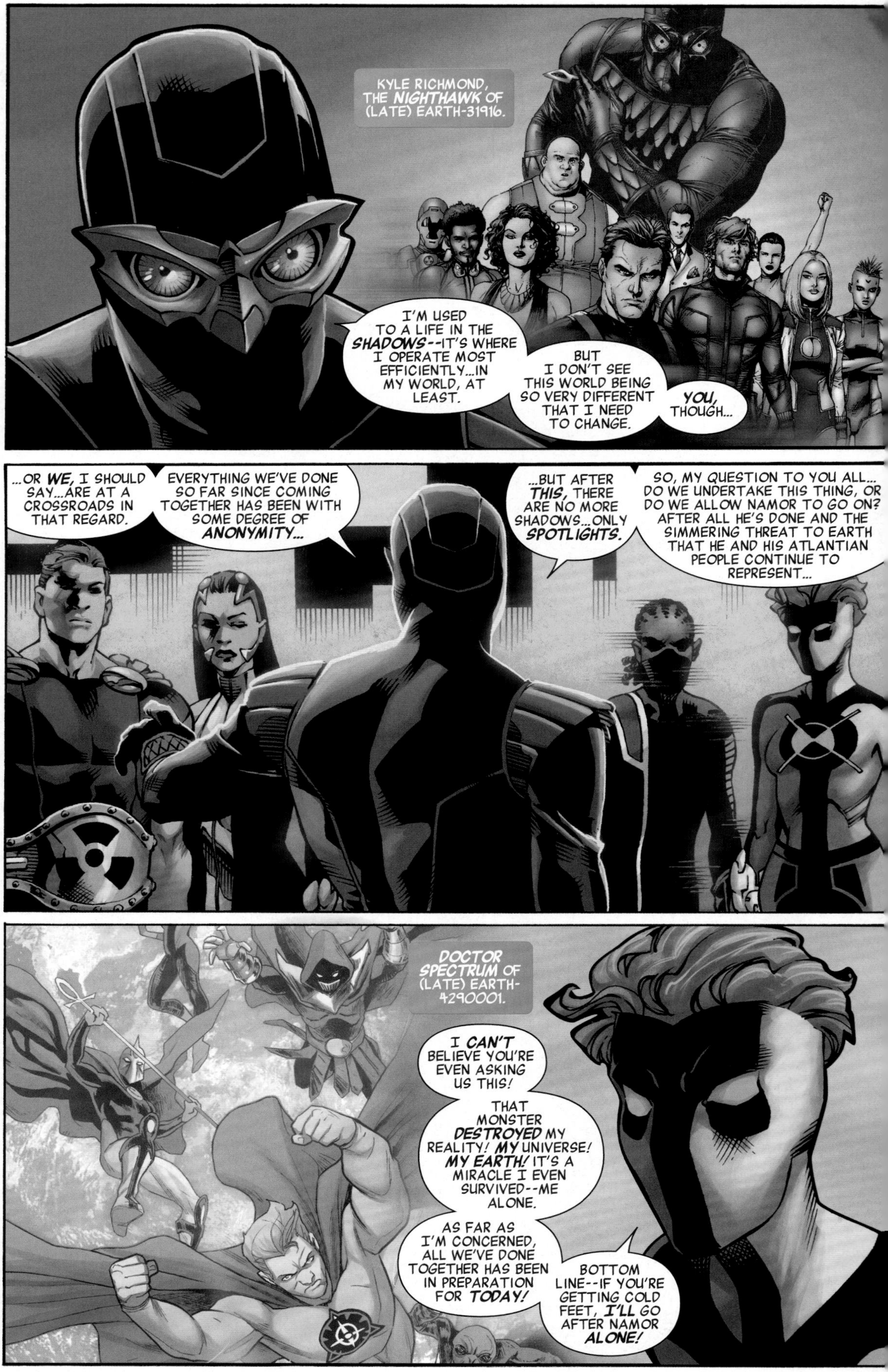
KYLE RICHMOND, THE NIGHTHAWK OF (LATE) EARTH-31916.
I'M USED TO A LIFE IN THE SHADOWS--IT'S WHERE I OPERATE MOST EFFICIENTLY...IN MY WORLD, AT LEAST.
BUT I DON'T SEE THIS WORLD BEING SO VERY DIFFERENT THAT I NEED TO CHANGE.
YOU, THOUGH...
...OR WE, I SHOULD SAY...ARE AT A CROSSROADS IN THAT REGARD.
EVERYTHING WE'VE DONE SO FAR SINCE COMING TOGETHER HAS BEEN WITH SOME DEGREE OF ANONYMITY...
...BUT AFTER THIS, THERE ARE NO MORE SHADOWS...ONLY SPOTLIGHTS.
SO, MY QUESTION TO YOU ALL... DO WE UNDERTAKE THIS THING, OR DO WE ALLOW NAMOR TO GO ON? AFTER ALL HE'S DONE AND THE SIMMERING THREAT TO EARTH THAT HE AND HIS ATLANTIAN PEOPLE CONTINUE TO REPRESENT...
DOCTOR SPECTRUM OF (LATE) EARTH-4290001.
I CAN'T BELIEVE YOU'RE EVEN ASKING US THIS!
THAT MONSTER DESTROYED MY REALITY! MY UNIVERSE! MY EARTH! IT'S A MIRACLE I EVEN SURVIVED--ME ALONE.
AS FAR AS I'M CONCERNED, ALL WE'VE DONE TOGETHER HAS BEEN IN PREPARATION FOR TODAY!
BOTTOM LINE--IF YOU'RE GETTING COLD FEET, I'LL GO AFTER NAMOR ALONE!

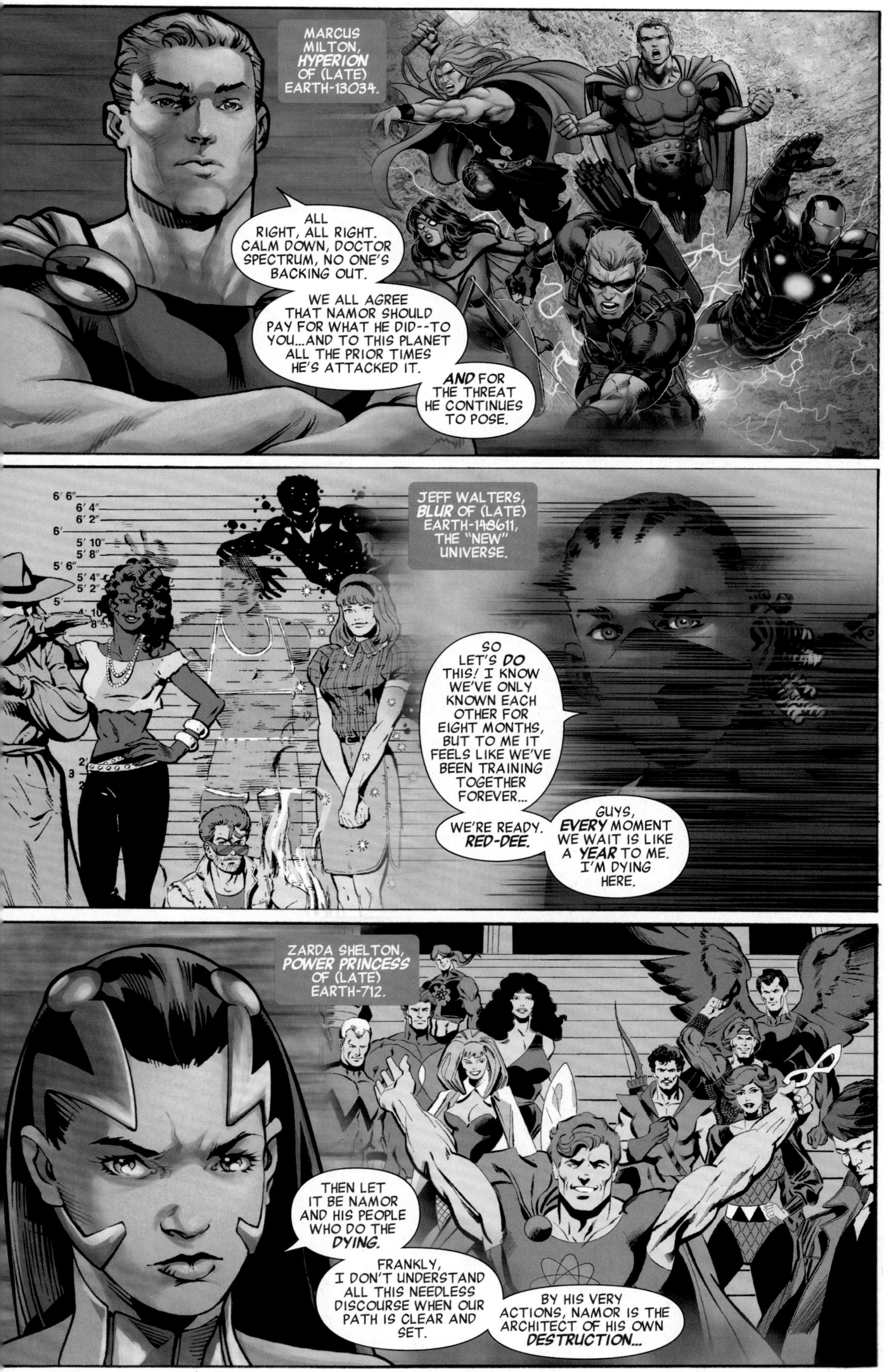
MARCUS MILTON, ***HYPERION*** OF (LATE) EARTH-13034.
ALL RIGHT, ALL RIGHT. CALM DOWN, DOCTOR SPECTRUM, NO ONE'S BACKING OUT.
WE ALL AGREE THAT NAMOR SHOULD PAY FOR WHAT HE DID--TO YOU...AND TO THIS PLANET ALL THE PRIOR TIMES HE'S ATTACKED IT.
AND FOR THE THREAT HE CONTINUES TO POSE.
6' 6"
6' 4"
6' 2"
6'
5' 10"
5' 8"
5' 6"
5' 4"
5' 2"
5'
JEFF WALTERS, ***BLUR*** OF (LATE) EARTH-148611, THE "NEW" UNIVERSE.
SO LET'S ***DO*** THIS! I KNOW WE'VE ONLY KNOWN EACH OTHER FOR EIGHT MONTHS, BUT TO ME IT FEELS LIKE WE'VE BEEN TRAINING TOGETHER FOREVER...
WE'RE READY. ***RED-DEE.***
GUYS, ***EVERY*** MOMENT WE WAIT IS LIKE A ***YEAR*** TO ME. I'M DYING HERE.
ZARDA SHELTON, ***POWER PRINCESS*** OF (LATE) EARTH-712.
THEN LET IT BE NAMOR AND HIS PEOPLE WHO DO THE ***DYING.***
FRANKLY, I DON'T UNDERSTAND ALL THIS NEEDLESS DISCOURSE WHEN OUR PATH IS CLEAR AND SET.
BY HIS VERY ACTIONS, NAMOR IS THE ARCHITECT OF HIS OWN ***DESTRUCTION...***

MARVEL COMICS

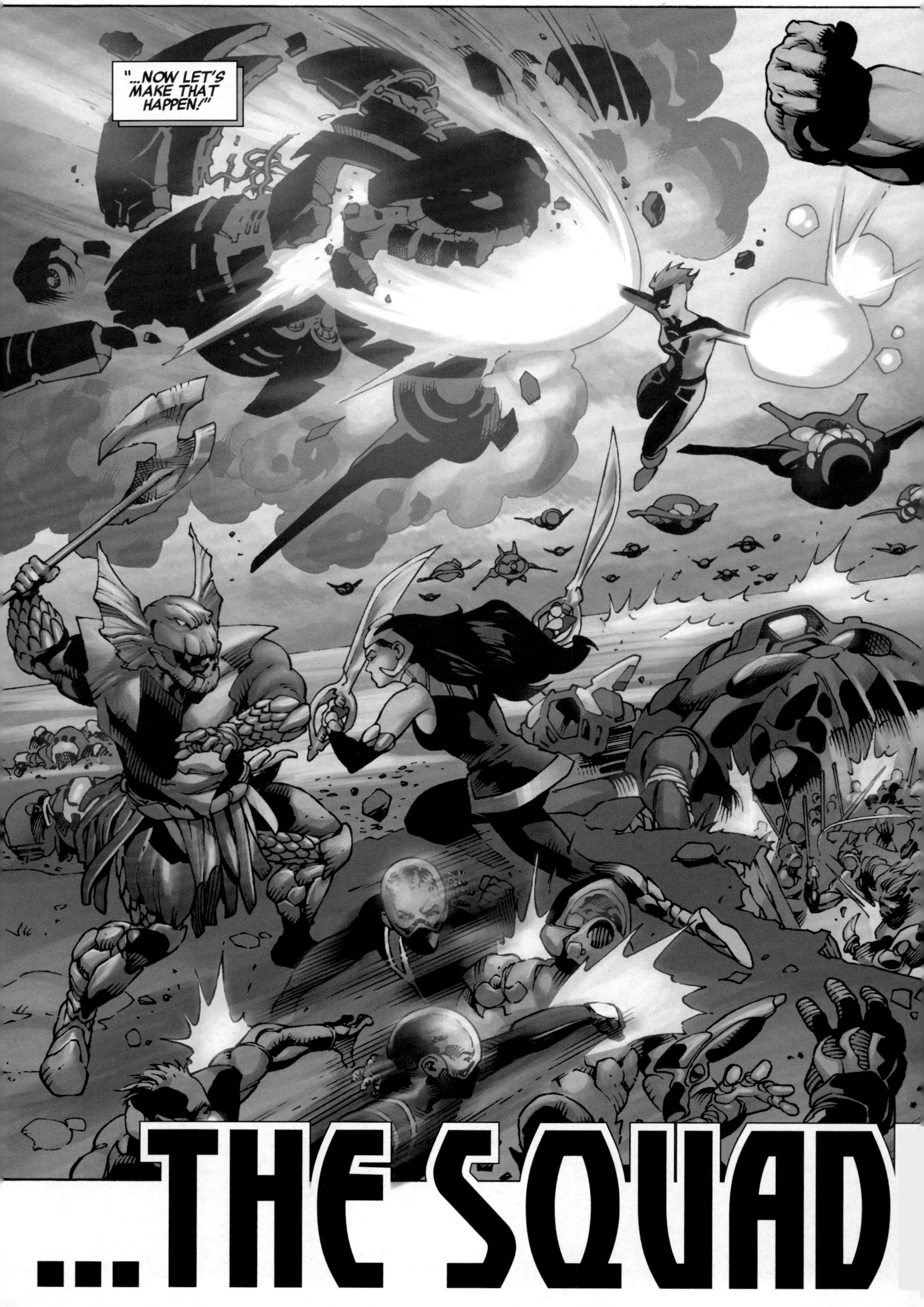
"...NOW LET'S MAKE THAT HAPPEN!"
...THE SQUAD

PROUDLY PRESENTS...

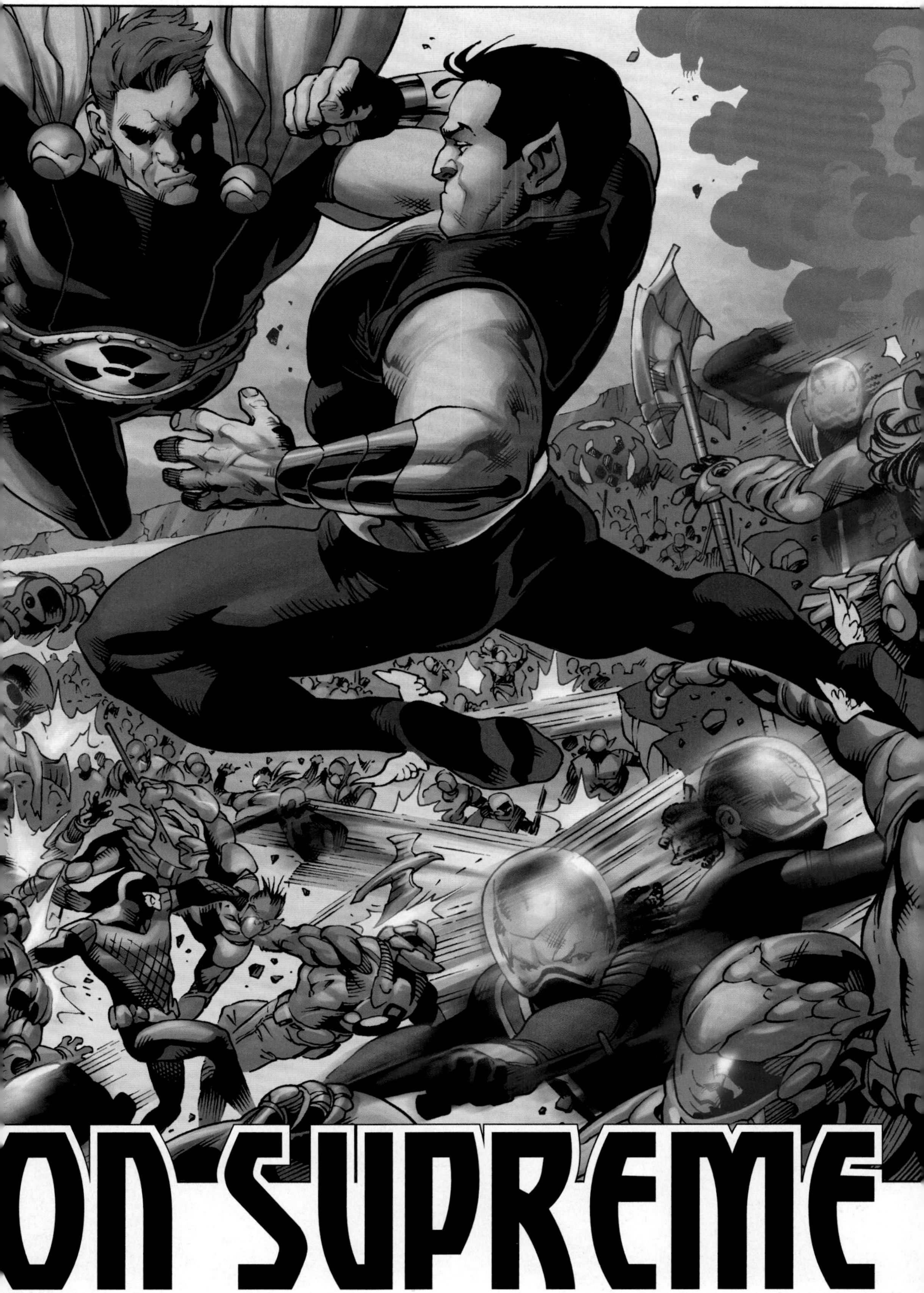

ON SUPREME

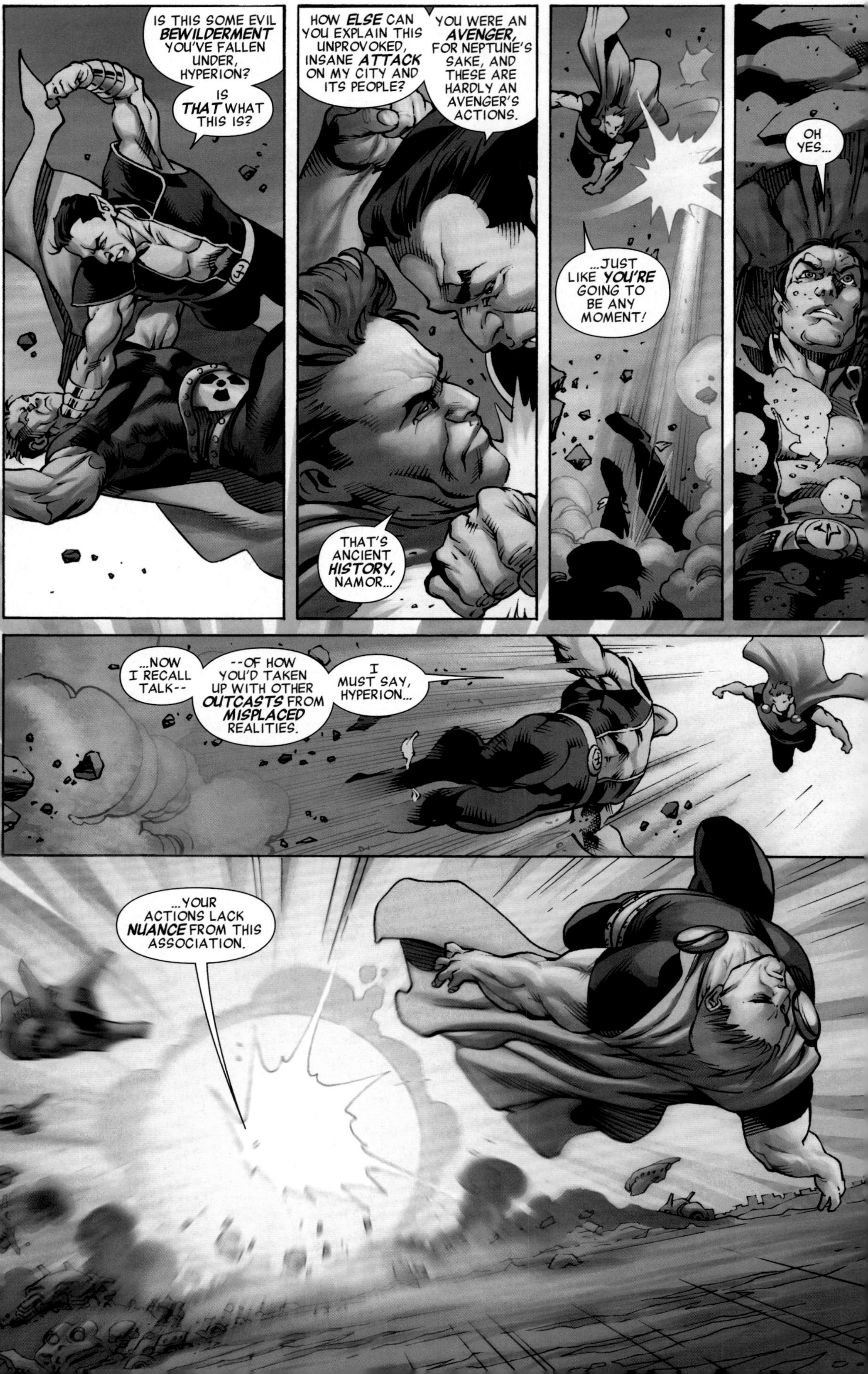
IS THIS SOME EVIL BEWILDERMENT YOU'VE FALLEN UNDER, HYPERION?
IS THAT WHAT THIS IS?
HOW ELSE CAN YOU EXPLAIN THIS UNPROVOKED, INSANE ATTACK ON MY CITY AND ITS PEOPLE?
YOU WERE AN AVENGER, FOR NEPTUNE'S SAKE, AND THESE ARE HARDLY AN AVENGER'S ACTIONS.
THAT'S ANCIENT HISTORY, NAMOR...
...JUST LIKE YOU'RE GOING TO BE ANY MOMENT!
OH YES...
I MUST SAY, HYPERION...
...NOW I RECALL TALK--
--OF HOW YOU'D TAKEN UP WITH OTHER OUTCASTS FROM MISPLACED REALITIES.
...YOUR ACTIONS LACK NUANCE FROM THIS ASSOCIATION.

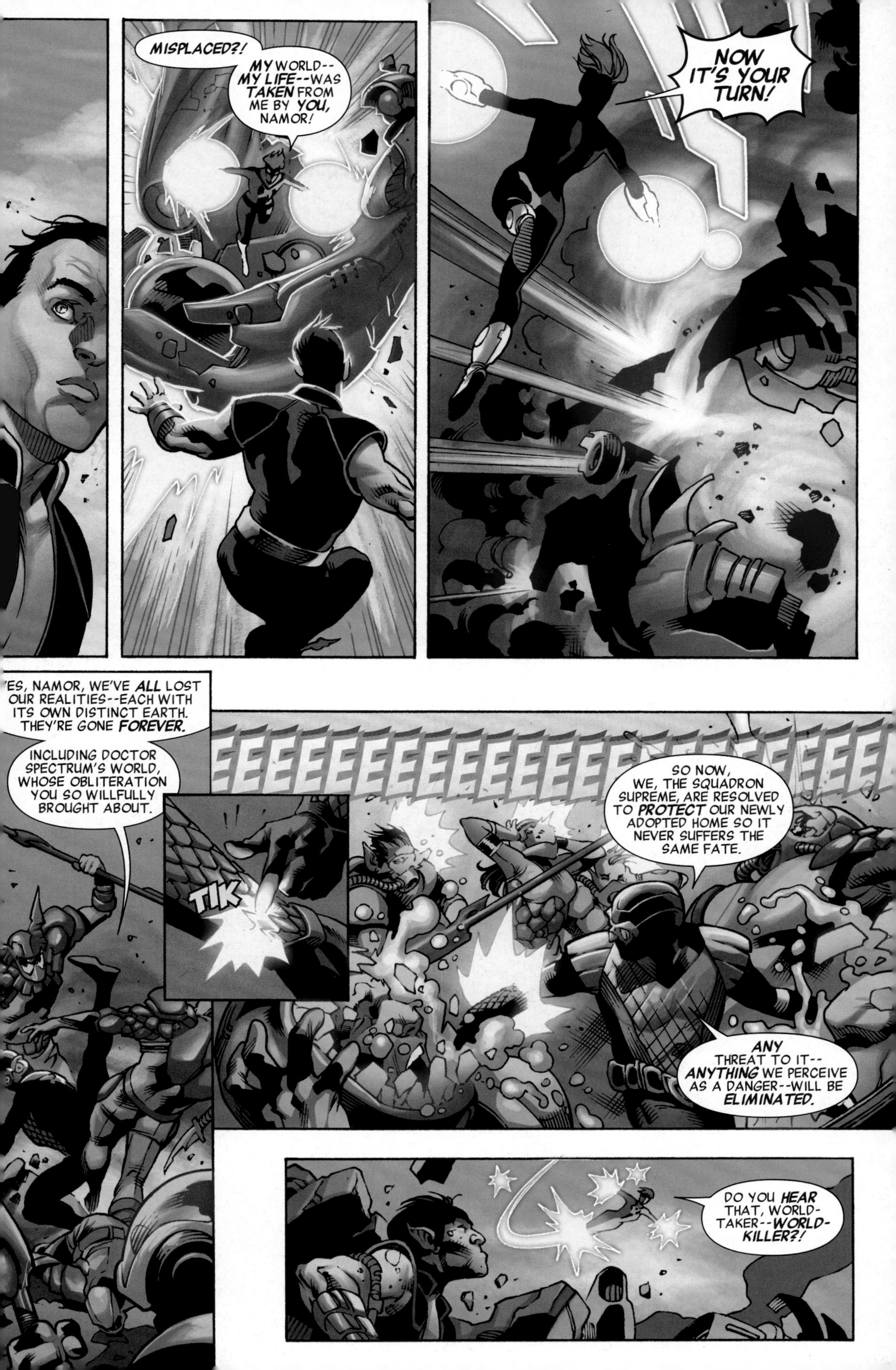

MISPLACED?!
MY WORLD-- MY LIFE--WAS TAKEN FROM ME BY YOU, NAMOR!
NOW IT'S YOUR TURN!
YES, NAMOR, WE'VE ALL LOST OUR REALITIES--EACH WITH ITS OWN DISTINCT EARTH. THEY'RE GONE FOREVER.
INCLUDING DOCTOR SPECTRUM'S WORLD, WHOSE OBLITERATION YOU SO WILLFULLY BROUGHT ABOUT.
EEEEEEEEEEEEEEEEEEEEEEEEEEEE
TIK
SO NOW, WE, THE SQUADRON SUPREME, ARE RESOLVED TO PROTECT OUR NEWLY ADOPTED HOME SO IT NEVER SUFFERS THE SAME FATE.
ANY THREAT TO IT--ANYTHING WE PERCEIVE AS A DANGER--WILL BE ELIMINATED.
DO YOU HEAR THAT, WORLD-TAKER--WORLD-KILLER?!

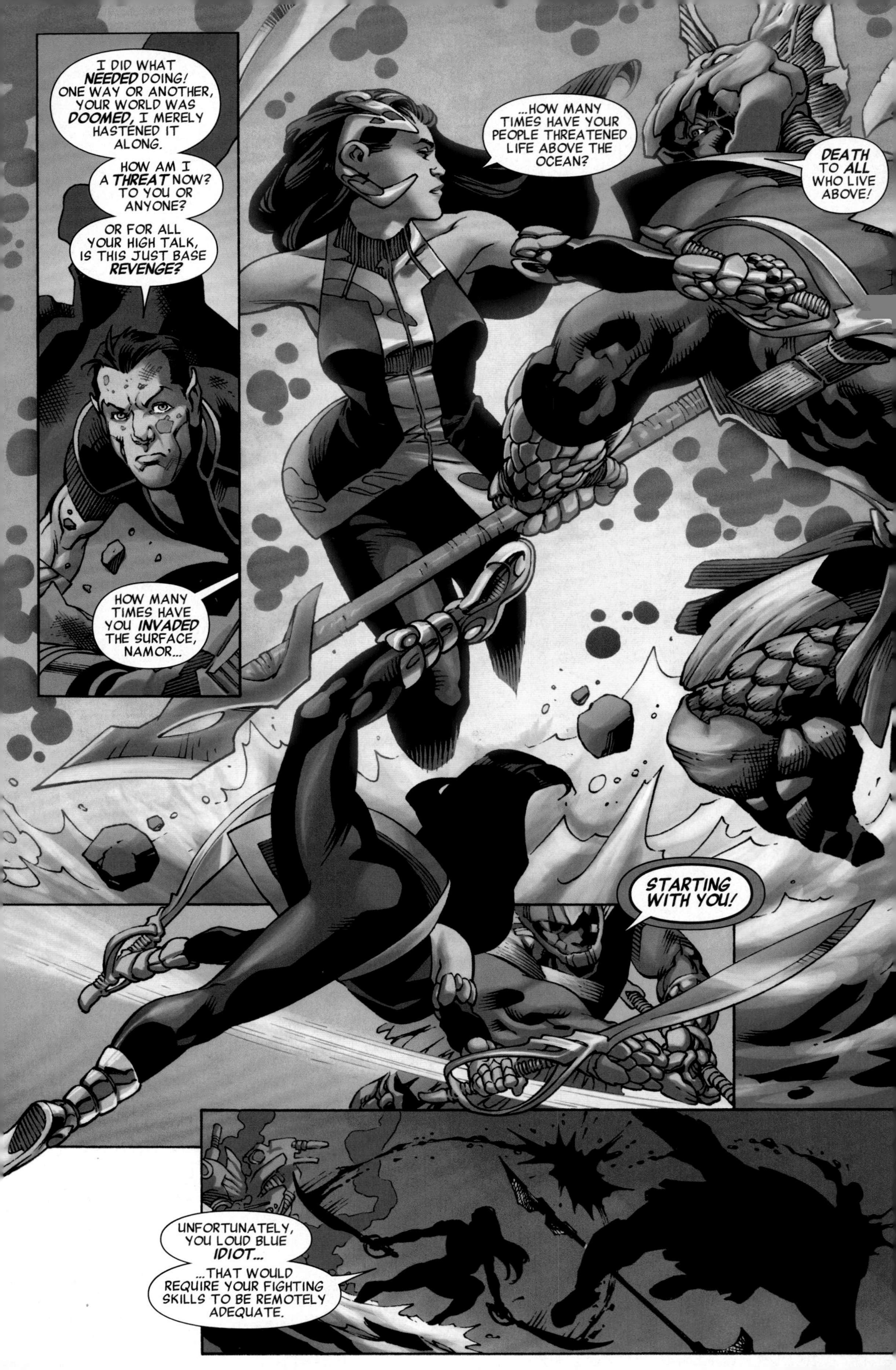
I DID WHAT NEEDED DOING! ONE WAY OR ANOTHER, YOUR WORLD WAS DOOMED, I MERELY HASTENED IT ALONG.
HOW AM I A THREAT NOW? TO YOU OR ANYONE?
OR FOR ALL YOUR HIGH TALK, IS THIS JUST BASE REVENGE?
HOW MANY TIMES HAVE YOU INVADED THE SURFACE, NAMOR...
...HOW MANY TIMES HAVE YOUR PEOPLE THREATENED LIFE ABOVE THE OCEAN?
DEATH TO ALL WHO LIVE ABOVE!
STARTING WITH YOU!
UNFORTUNATELY, YOU LOUD BLUE IDIOT...
...THAT WOULD REQUIRE YOUR FIGHTING SKILLS TO BE REMOTELY ADEQUATE.

NO, LISTEN... ...HOW MANY TIMES HAS THE SURFACE WORLD THREATENED *MINE?*

I ATTACK TO DEFEND.

AND

SO

DO

WE!

MAYBE IT'S ATLANTIS' PRESENCE IN THE WORLD THAT'S THE PROBLEM--ITS VERY EXISTENCE.

LET'S SEE, SHALL WE? LET'S SEE WHAT HAPPENS...

...IF WE *REMOVE* IT FROM THE TABLE.

HYPERION. WHENEVER YOU'RE READY.

RRRMRRRRRMMM

BUBBUB UBUBBUB

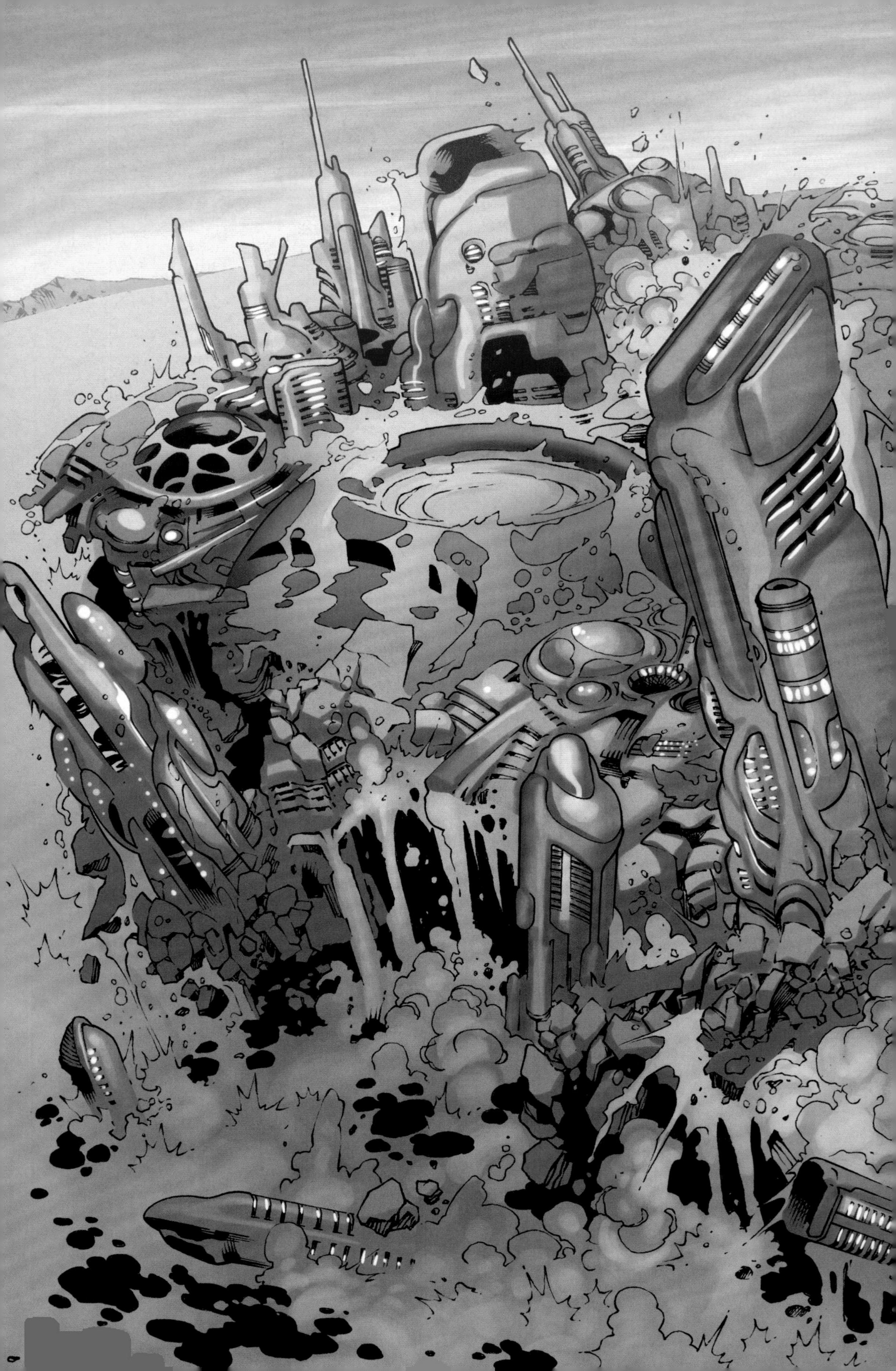

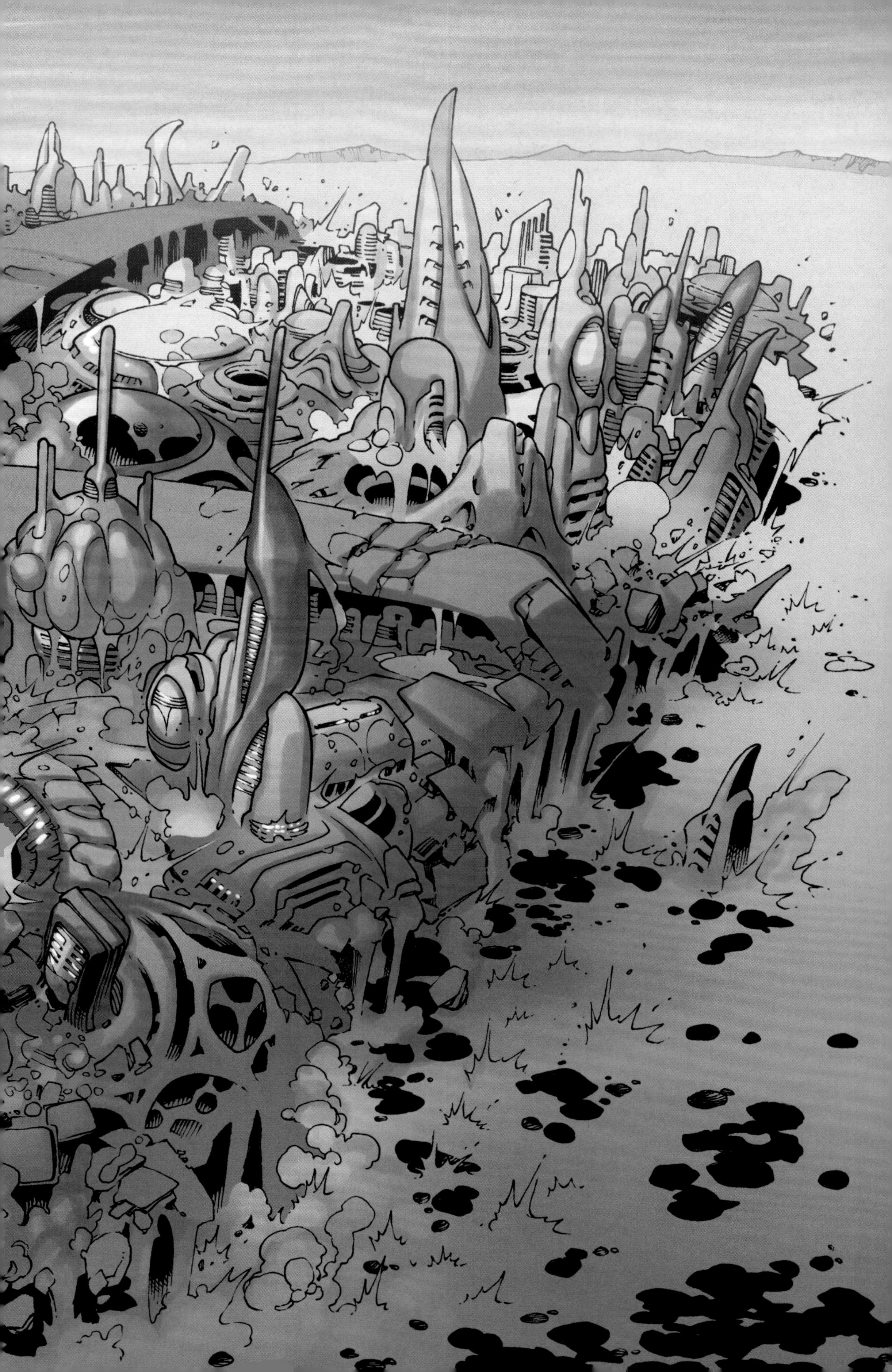

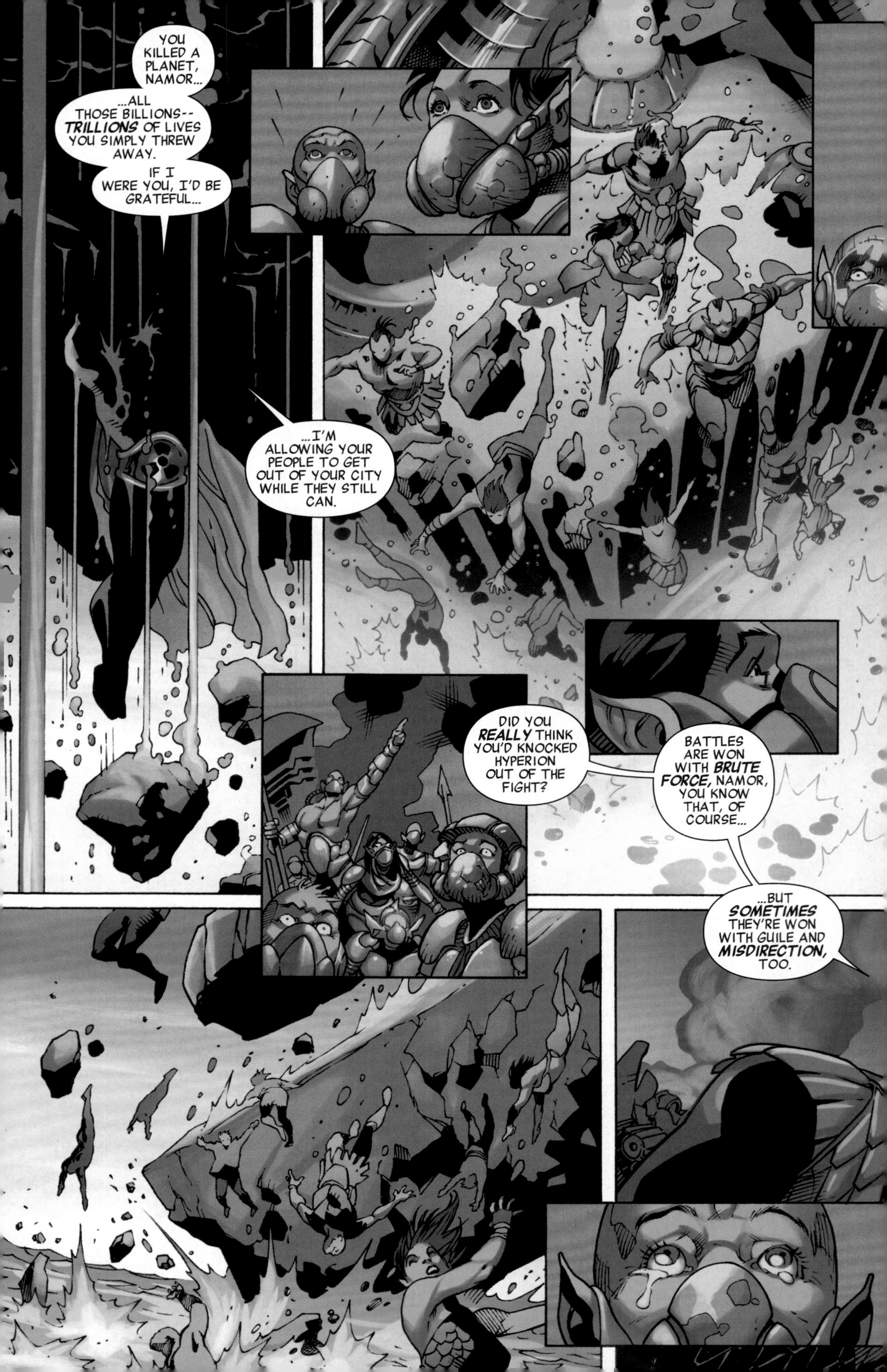
YOU KILLED A PLANET, NAMOR...
...ALL THOSE BILLIONS-- TRILLIONS OF LIVES YOU SIMPLY THREW AWAY.
IF I WERE YOU, I'D BE GRATEFUL...
...I'M ALLOWING YOUR PEOPLE TO GET OUT OF YOUR CITY WHILE THEY STILL CAN.
DID YOU REALLY THINK YOU'D KNOCKED HYPERION OUT OF THE FIGHT?
BATTLES ARE WON WITH BRUTE FORCE, NAMOR, YOU KNOW THAT, OF COURSE...
...BUT SOMETIMES THEY'RE WON WITH GUILE AND MISDIRECTION, TOO.

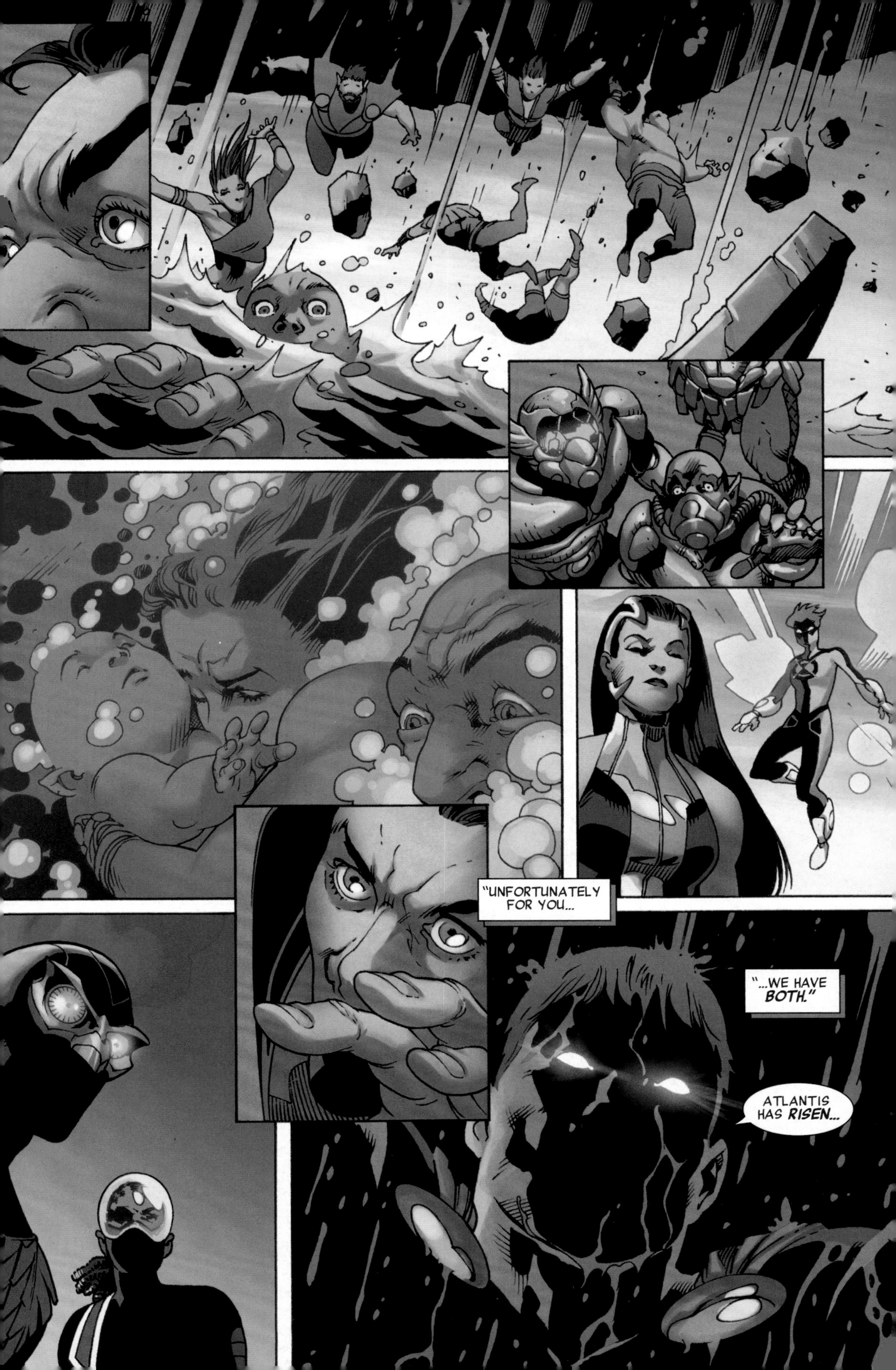
"UNFORTUNATELY FOR YOU...
"...WE HAVE BOTH."
ATLANTIS HAS RISEN...

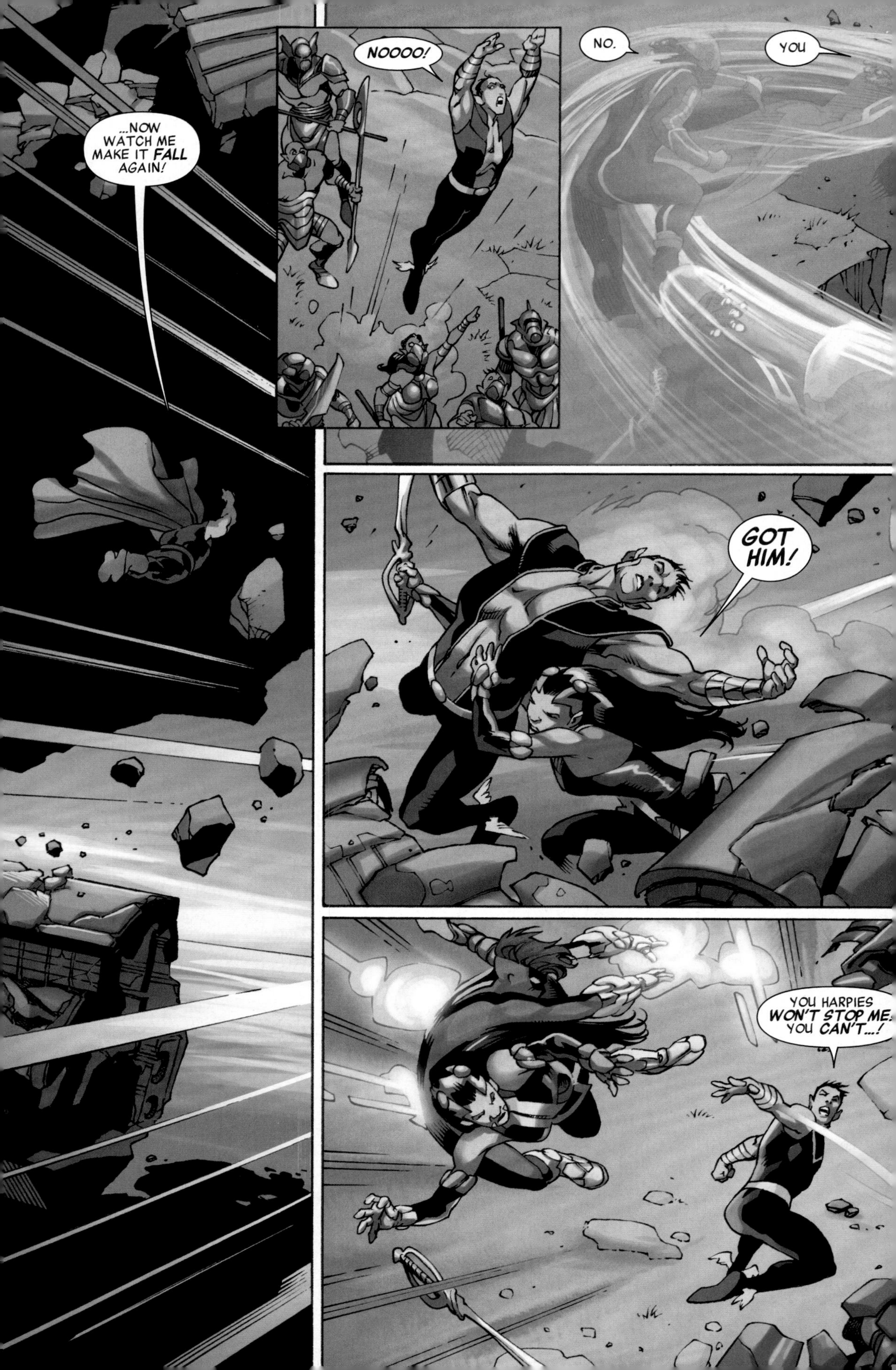
...NOW WATCH ME MAKE IT FALL AGAIN!
NOOOO!
NO.
YOU
GOT HIM!
YOU HARPIES WON'T STOP ME. YOU CAN'T...!

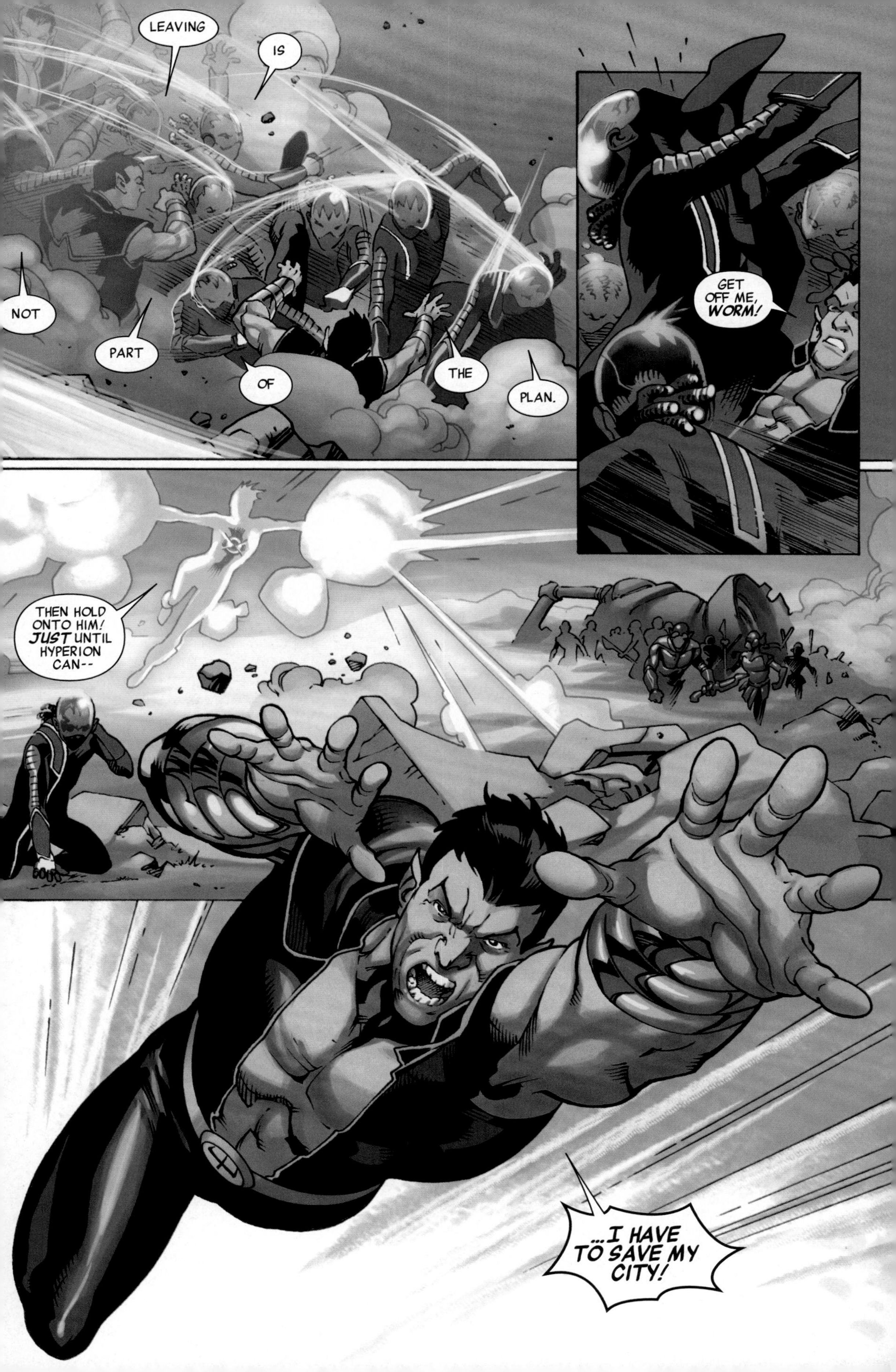
LEAVING
IS
NOT
PART
OF
THE
PLAN.
GET OFF ME, WORM!
THEN HOLD ONTO HIM! JUST UNTIL HYPERION CAN--
...I HAVE TO SAVE MY CITY!

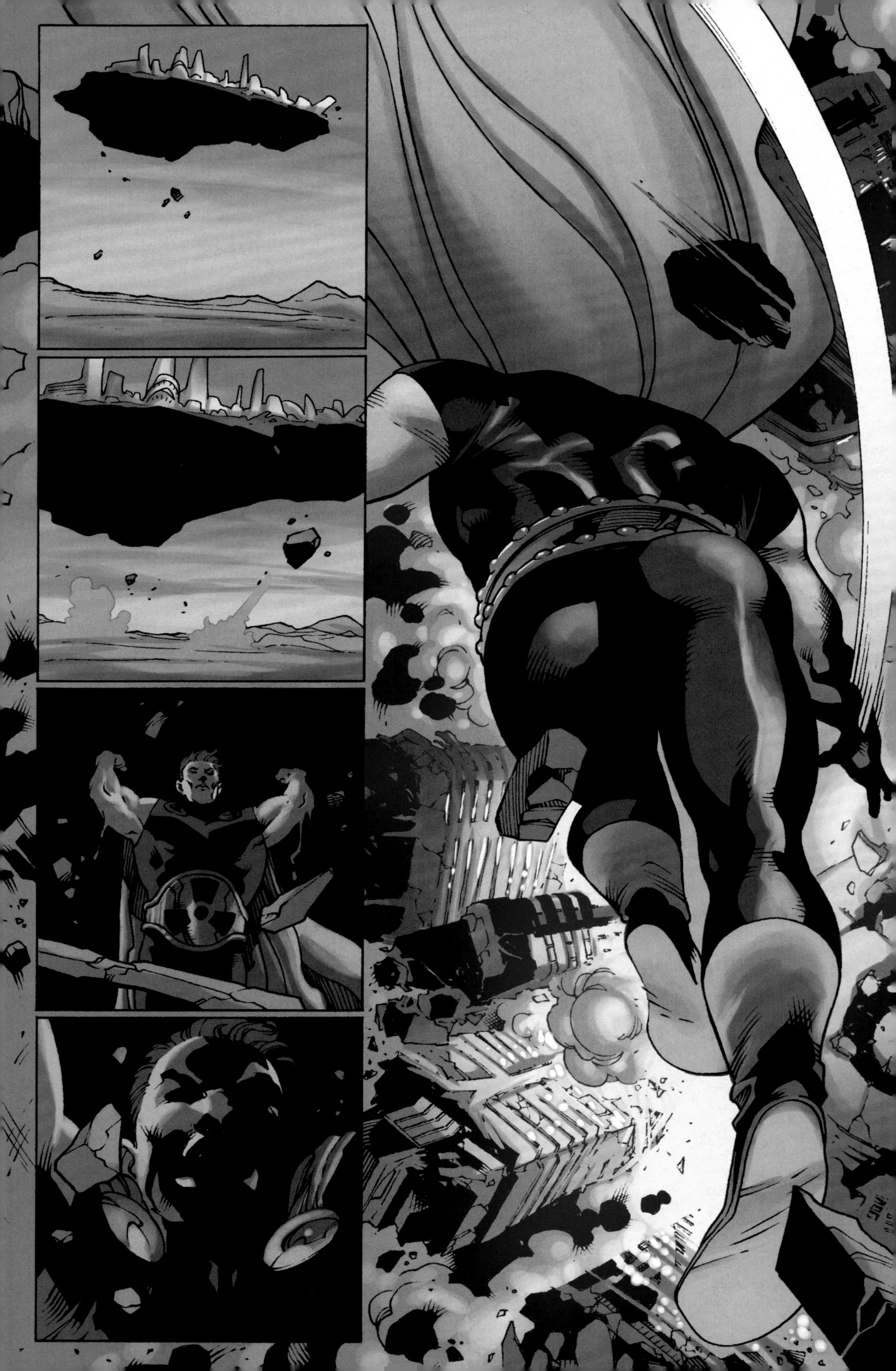

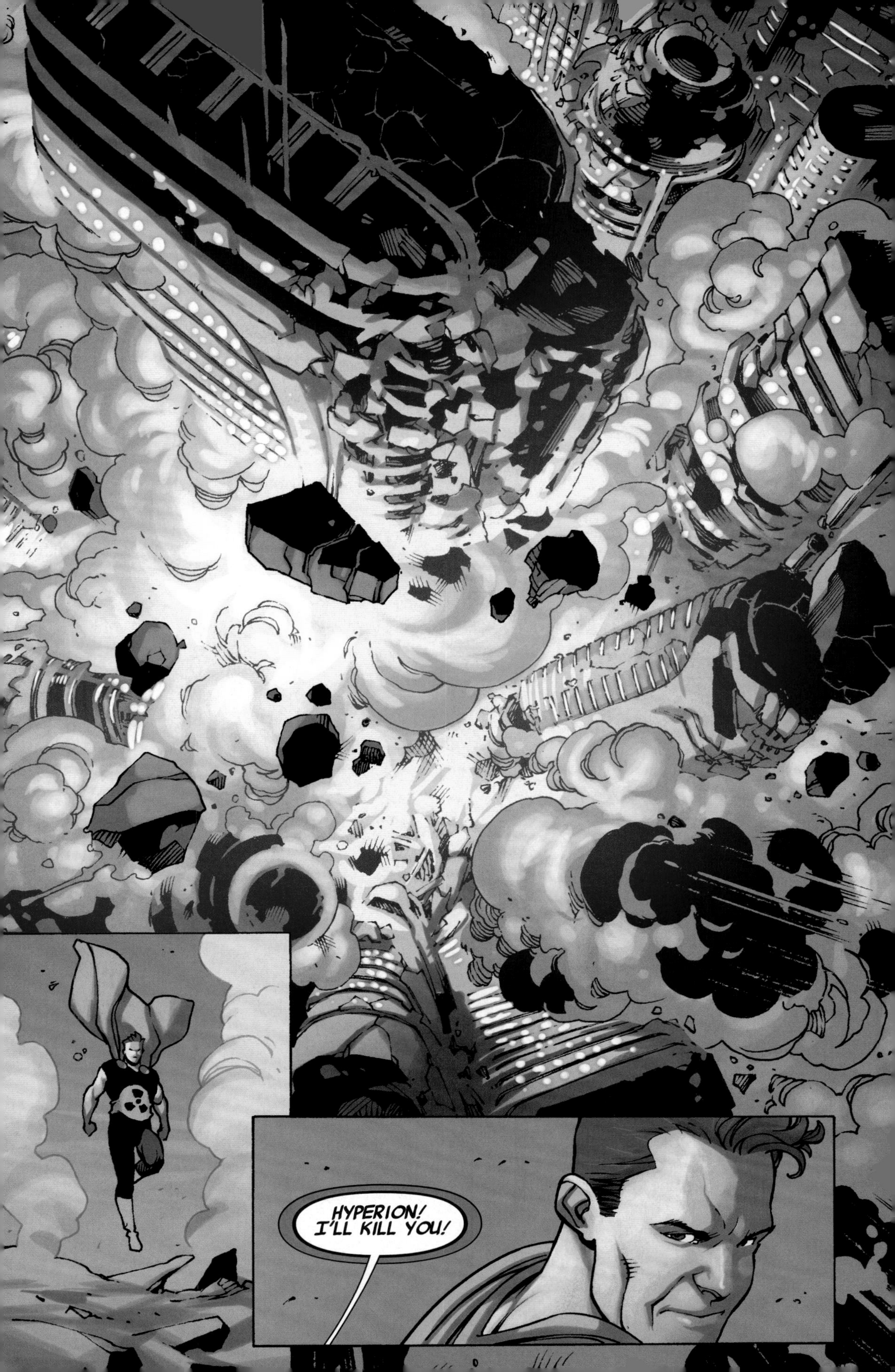
HYPERION! I'LL KILL YOU!

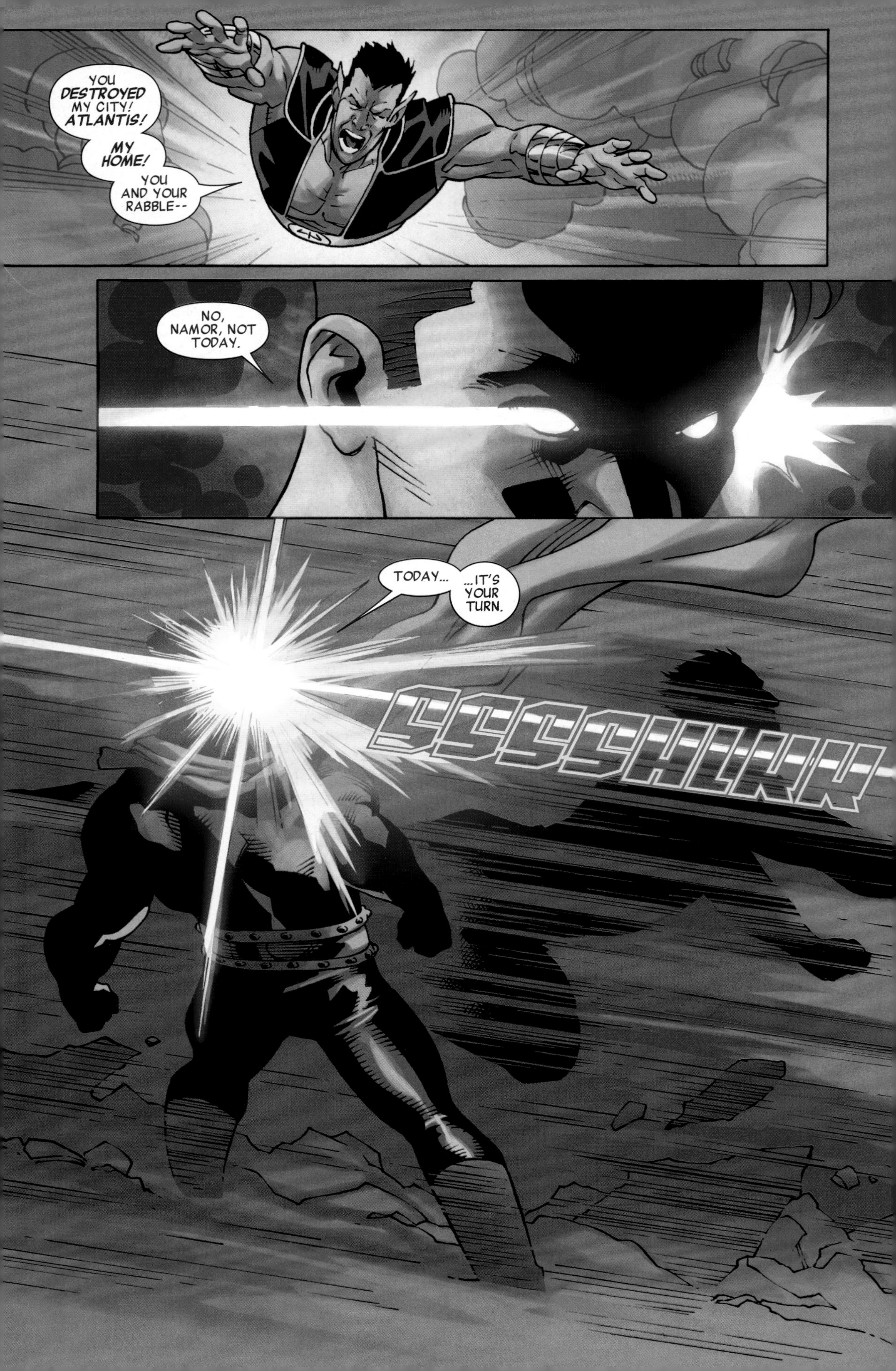

YOU DESTROYED MY CITY! ATLANTIS!
MY HOME!
YOU AND YOUR RABBLE--
NO, NAMOR, NOT TODAY.
TODAY...
...IT'S YOUR TURN.
SSSSCHLKK

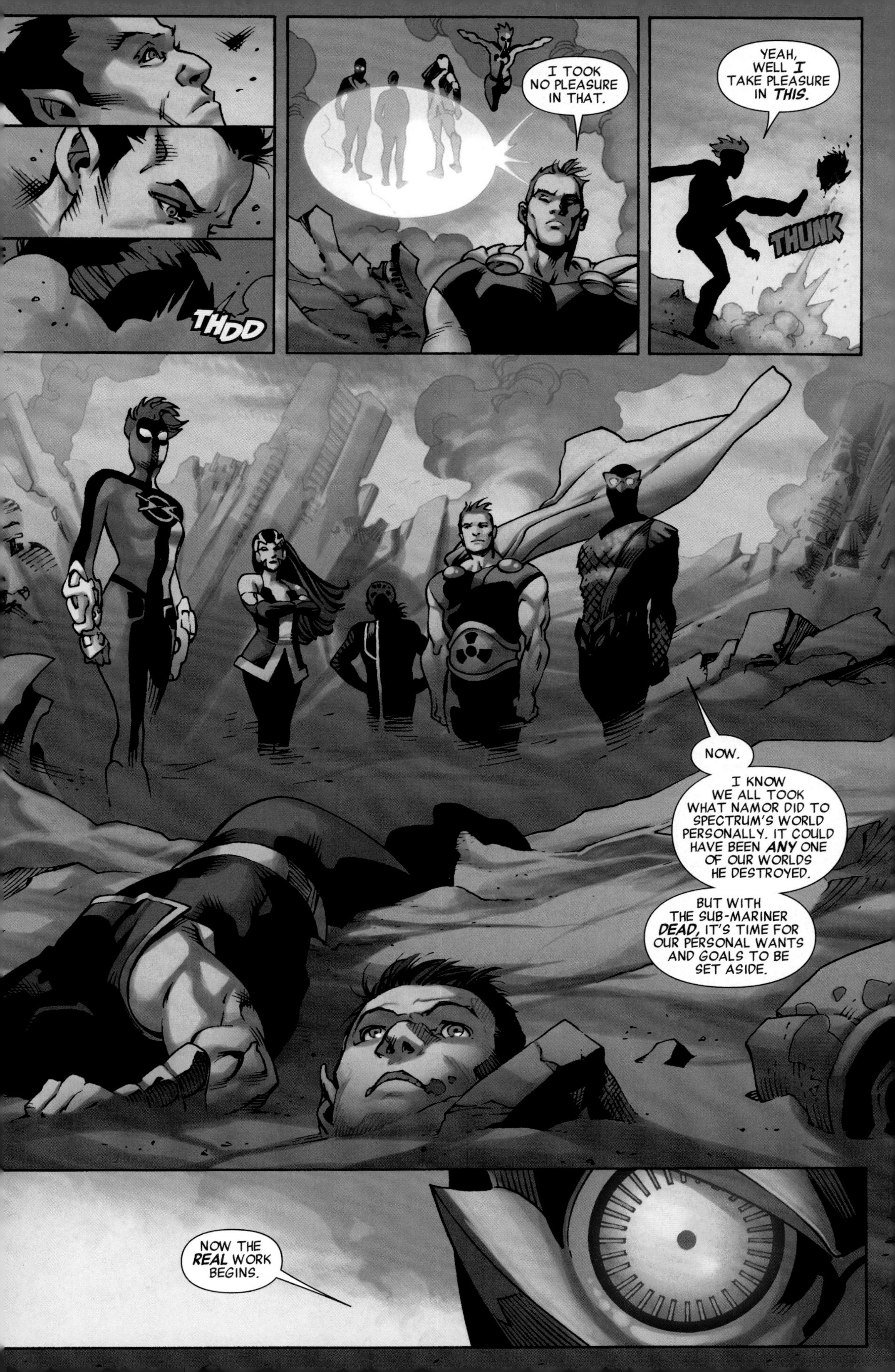
THDD
I TOOK NO PLEASURE IN THAT.
YEAH, WELL I TAKE PLEASURE IN THIS.
THUNK
NOW.
I KNOW WE ALL TOOK WHAT NAMOR DID TO SPECTRUM'S WORLD PERSONALLY. IT COULD HAVE BEEN ANY ONE OF OUR WORLDS HE DESTROYED.
BUT WITH THE SUB-MARINER DEAD, IT'S TIME FOR OUR PERSONAL WANTS AND GOALS TO BE SET ASIDE.
NOW THE REAL WORK BEGINS.

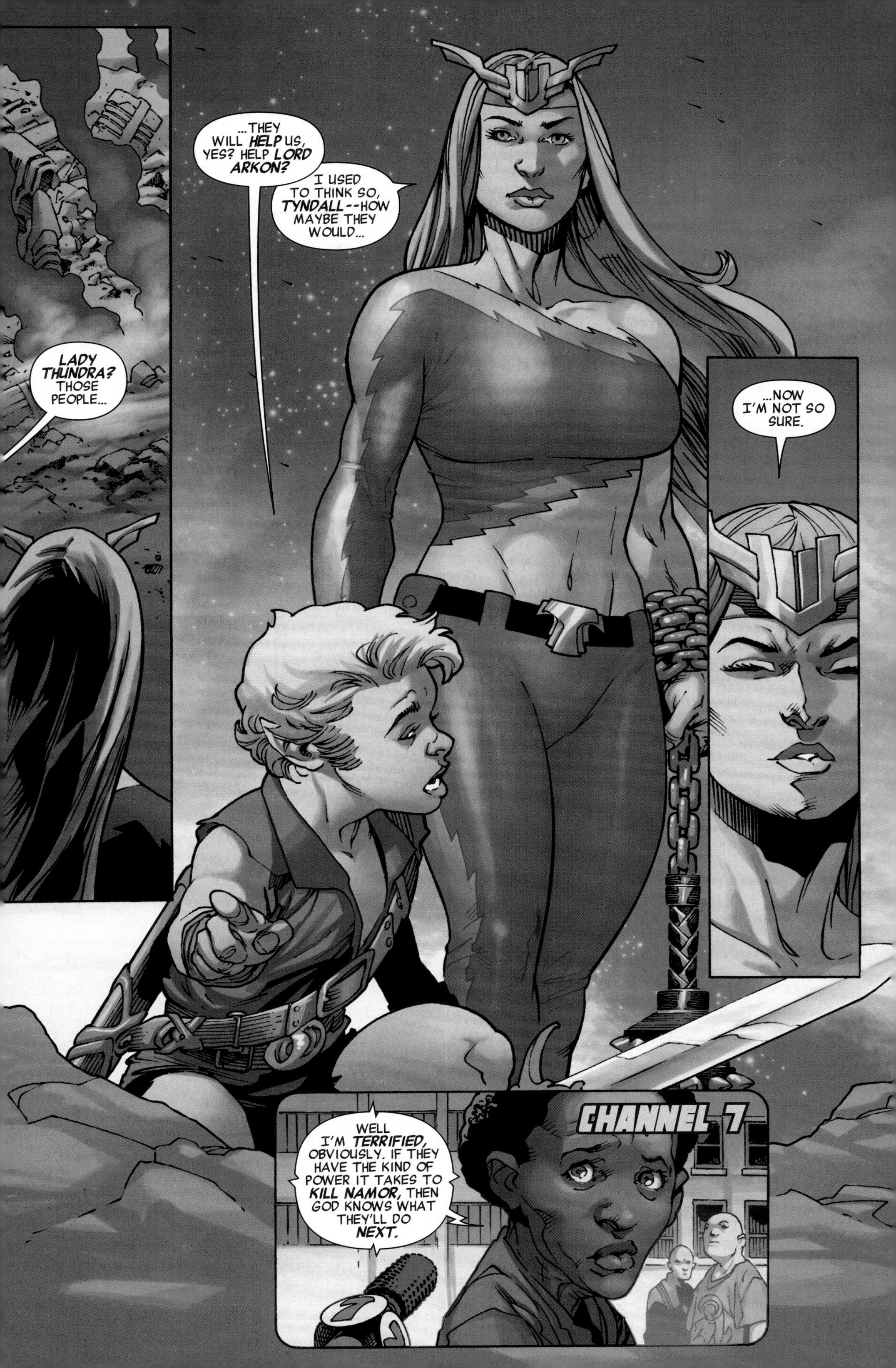
LADY THUNDRA? THOSE PEOPLE...
...THEY WILL HELP US, YES? HELP LORD ARKON?
I USED TO THINK SO, TYNDALL--HOW MAYBE THEY WOULD...
...NOW I'M NOT SO SURE.
CHANNEL 7
WELL I'M TERRIFIED, OBVIOUSLY. IF THEY HAVE THE KIND OF POWER IT TAKES TO KILL NAMOR, THEN GOD KNOWS WHAT THEY'LL DO NEXT.

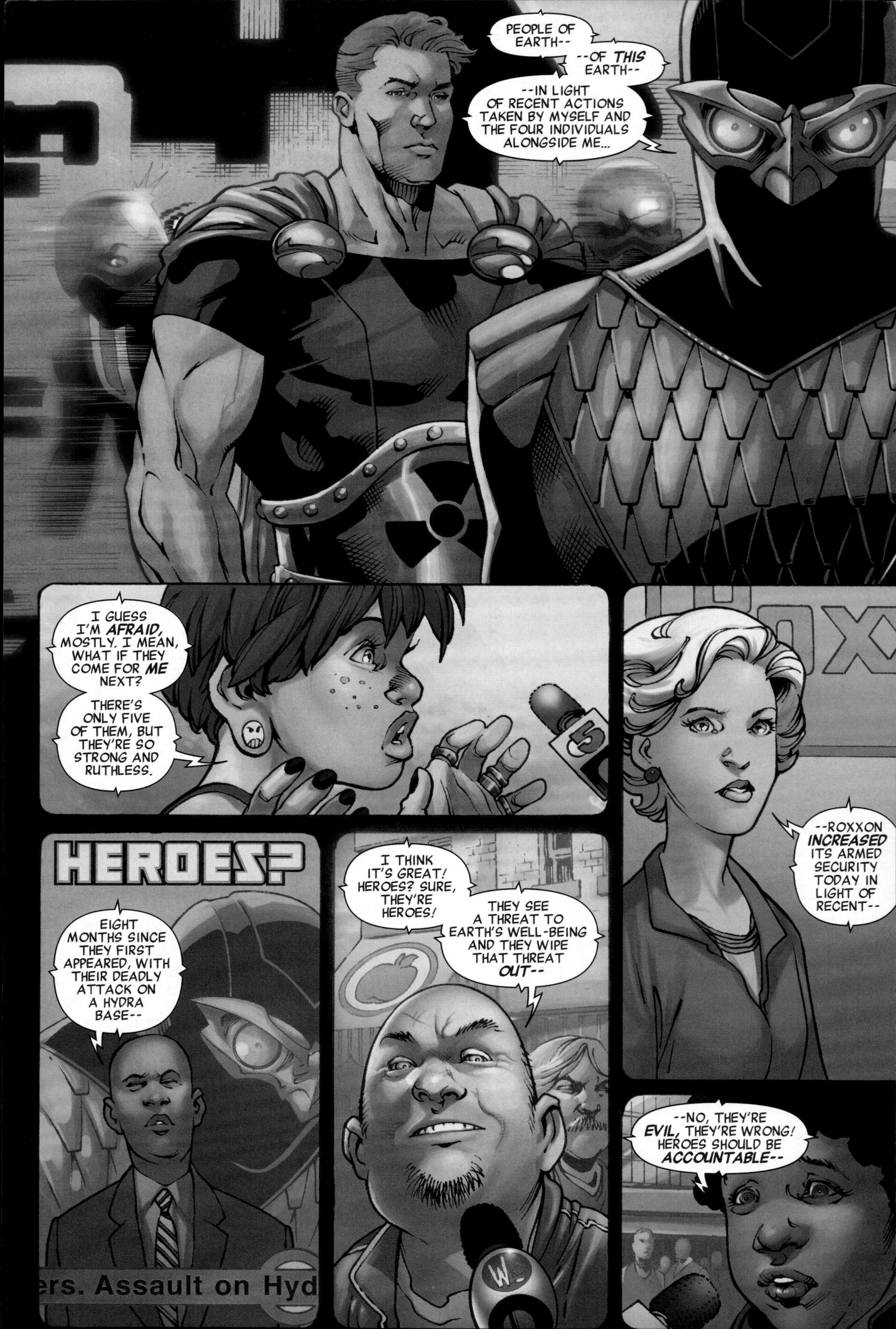
PEOPLE OF EARTH--
--OF THIS EARTH--
--IN LIGHT OF RECENT ACTIONS TAKEN BY MYSELF AND THE FOUR INDIVIDUALS ALONGSIDE ME...
I GUESS I'M AFRAID, MOSTLY. I MEAN, WHAT IF THEY COME FOR ME NEXT?
THERE'S ONLY FIVE OF THEM, BUT THEY'RE SO STRONG AND RUTHLESS.
--ROXXON INCREASED ITS ARMED SECURITY TODAY IN LIGHT OF RECENT--
HEROES?
EIGHT MONTHS SINCE THEY FIRST APPEARED, WITH THEIR DEADLY ATTACK ON A HYDRA BASE--
ers. Assault on Hyd
I THINK IT'S GREAT! HEROES? SURE, THEY'RE HEROES!
THEY SEE A THREAT TO EARTH'S WELL-BEING AND THEY WIPE THAT THREAT OUT--
--NO, THEY'RE EVIL, THEY'RE WRONG! HEROES SHOULD BE ACCOUNTABLE--

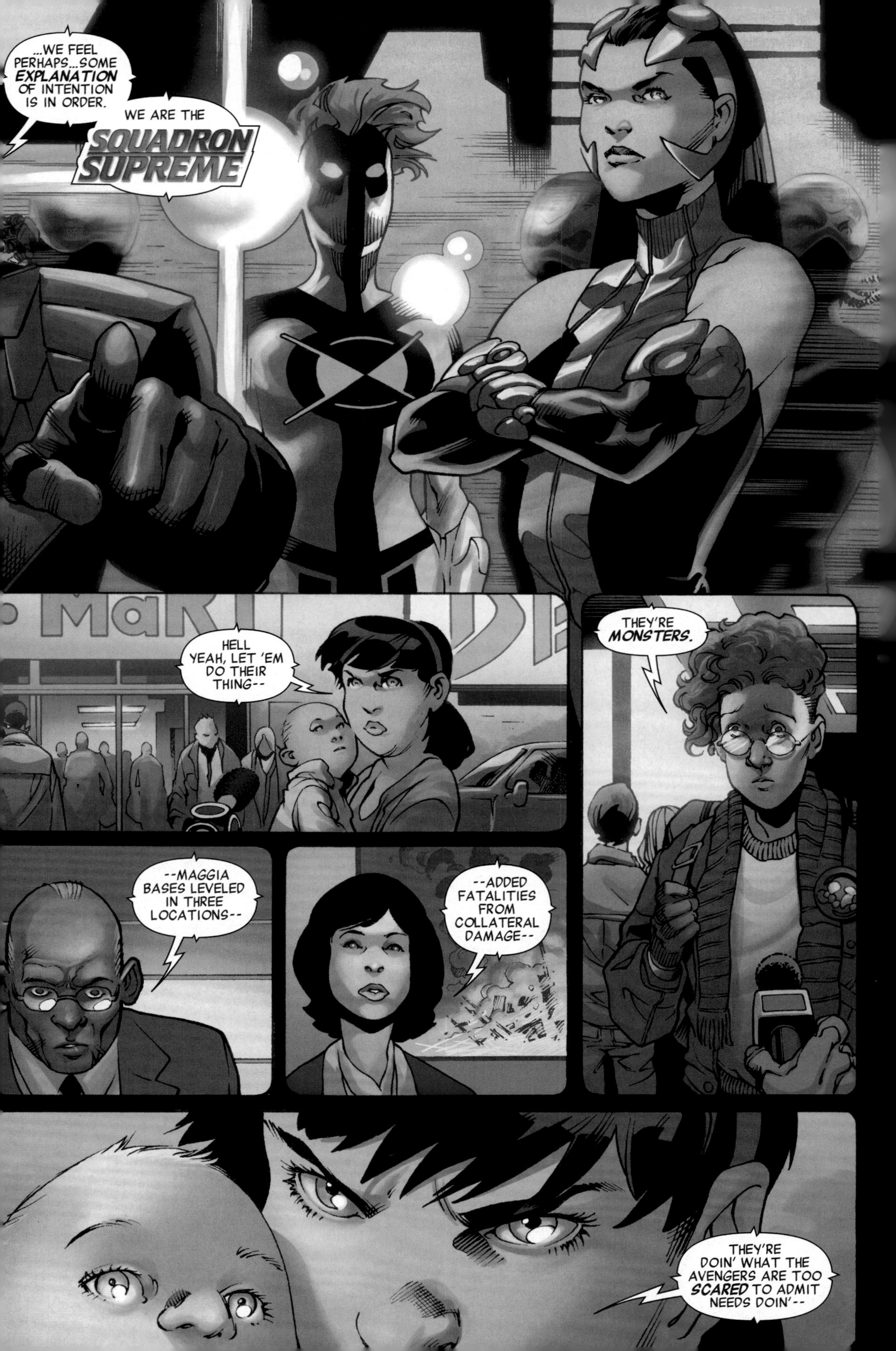
...WE FEEL PERHAPS...SOME EXPLANATION OF INTENTION IS IN ORDER.
WE ARE THE SQUADRON SUPREME
HELL YEAH, LET 'EM DO THEIR THING--
THEY'RE MONSTERS.
--MAGGIA BASES LEVELED IN THREE LOCATIONS--
--ADDED FATALITIES FROM COLLATERAL DAMAGE--
THEY'RE DOIN' WHAT THE AVENGERS ARE TOO SCARED TO ADMIT NEEDS DOIN'--

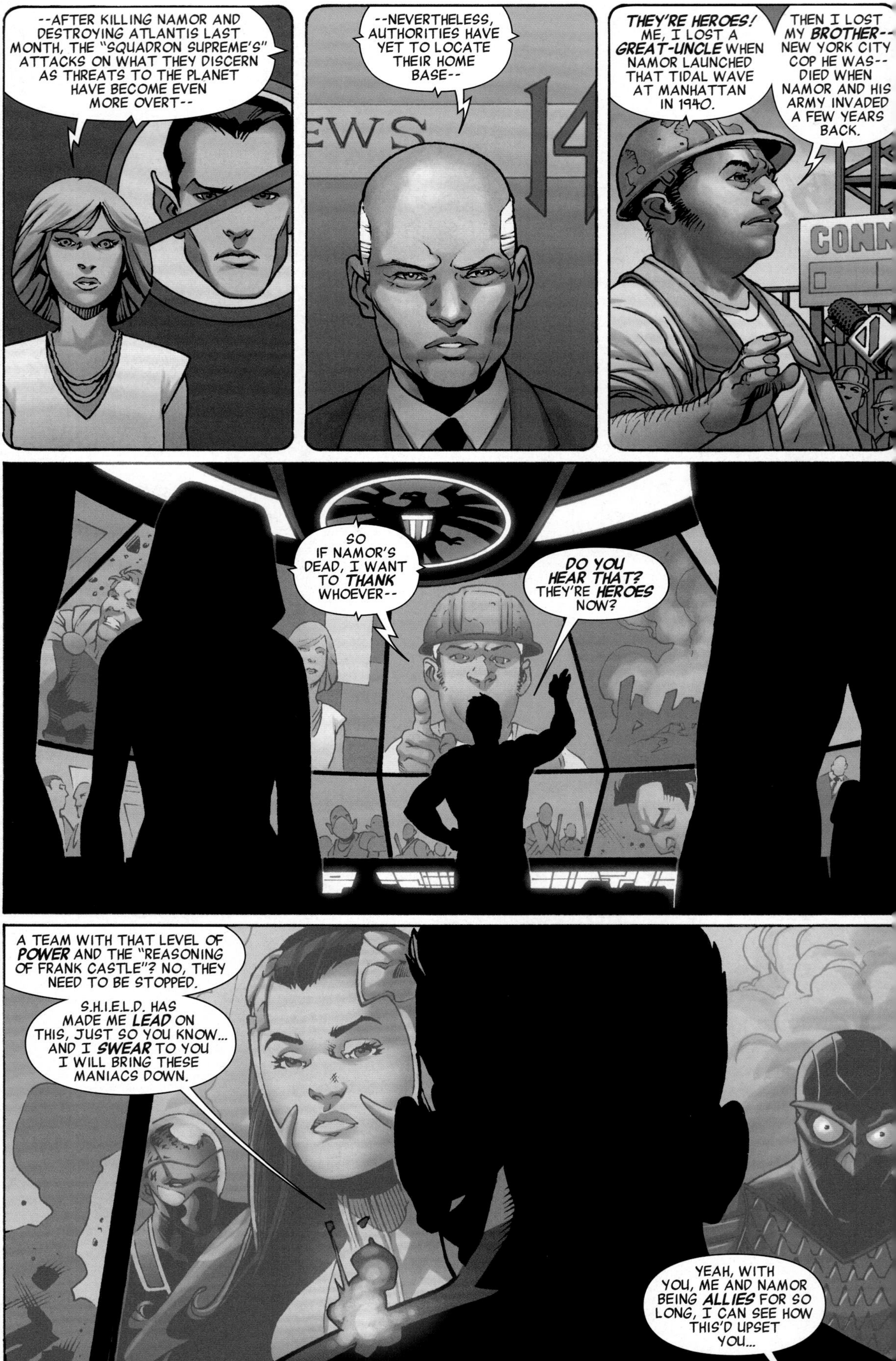
--AFTER KILLING NAMOR AND DESTROYING ATLANTIS LAST MONTH, THE "SQUADRON SUPREME'S" ATTACKS ON WHAT THEY DISCERN AS THREATS TO THE PLANET HAVE BECOME EVEN MORE OVERT--
--NEVERTHELESS, AUTHORITIES HAVE YET TO LOCATE THEIR HOME BASE--
EWS
THEY'RE HEROES! ME, I LOST A GREAT-UNCLE WHEN NAMOR LAUNCHED THAT TIDAL WAVE AT MANHATTAN IN 1940.
THEN I LOST MY BROTHER--NEW YORK CITY COP HE WAS--DIED WHEN NAMOR AND HIS ARMY INVADED A FEW YEARS BACK.
CONN
SO IF NAMOR'S DEAD, I WANT TO THANK WHOEVER--
DO YOU HEAR THAT? THEY'RE HEROES NOW?
A TEAM WITH THAT LEVEL OF POWER AND THE "REASONING OF FRANK CASTLE"? NO, THEY NEED TO BE STOPPED.
S.H.I.E.L.D. HAS MADE ME LEAD ON THIS, JUST SO YOU KNOW... AND I SWEAR TO YOU I WILL BRING THESE MANIACS DOWN.
YEAH, WITH YOU, ME AND NAMOR BEING ALLIES FOR SO LONG, I CAN SEE HOW THIS'D UPSET YOU...

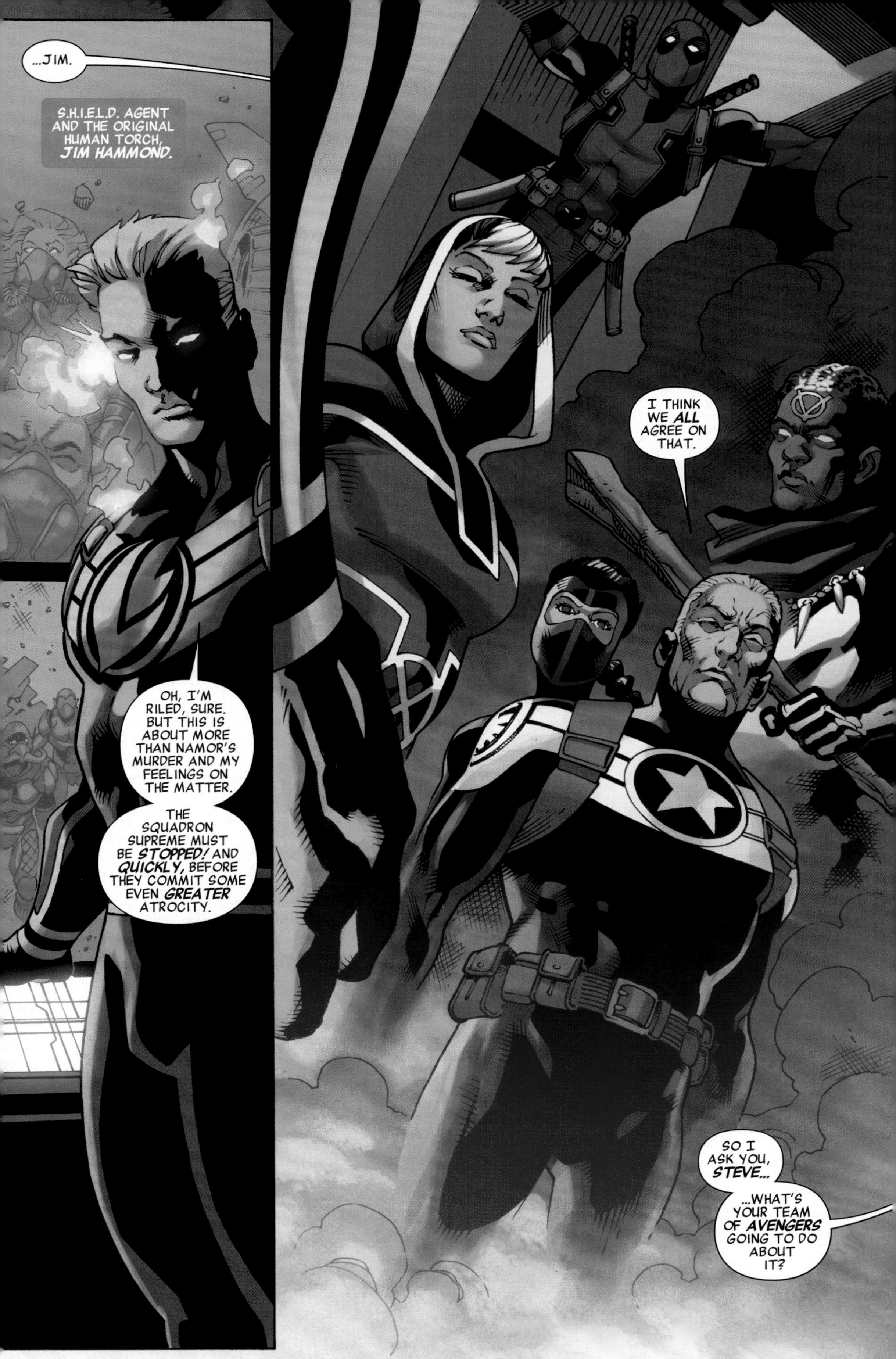
...JIM.
S.H.I.E.L.D. AGENT AND THE ORIGINAL HUMAN TORCH, JIM HAMMOND.
OH, I'M RILED, SURE. BUT THIS IS ABOUT MORE THAN NAMOR'S MURDER AND MY FEELINGS ON THE MATTER.
THE SQUADRON SUPREME MUST BE STOPPED! AND QUICKLY, BEFORE THEY COMMIT SOME EVEN GREATER ATROCITY.
I THINK WE ALL AGREE ON THAT.
SO I ASK YOU, STEVE...
...WHAT'S YOUR TEAM OF AVENGERS GOING TO DO ABOUT IT?

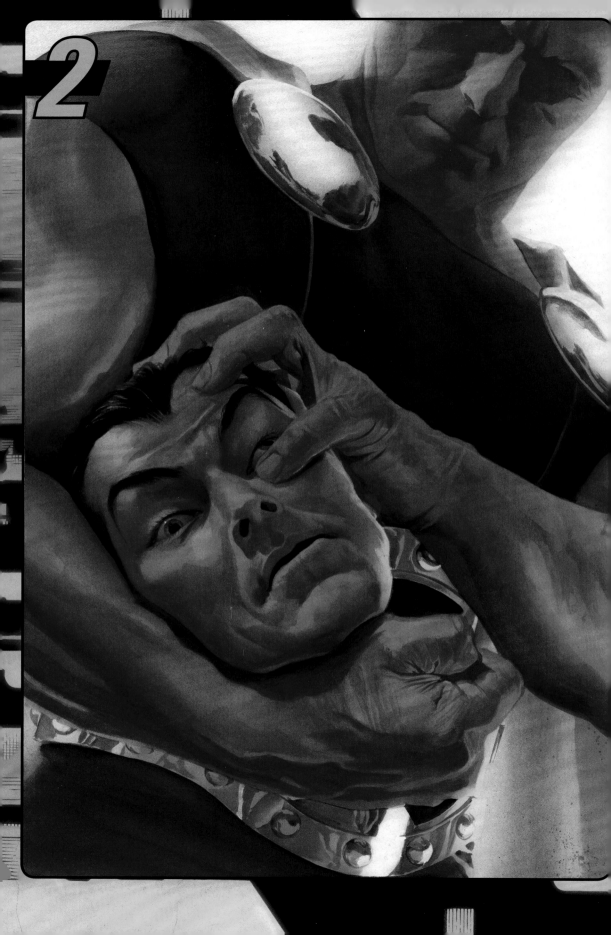

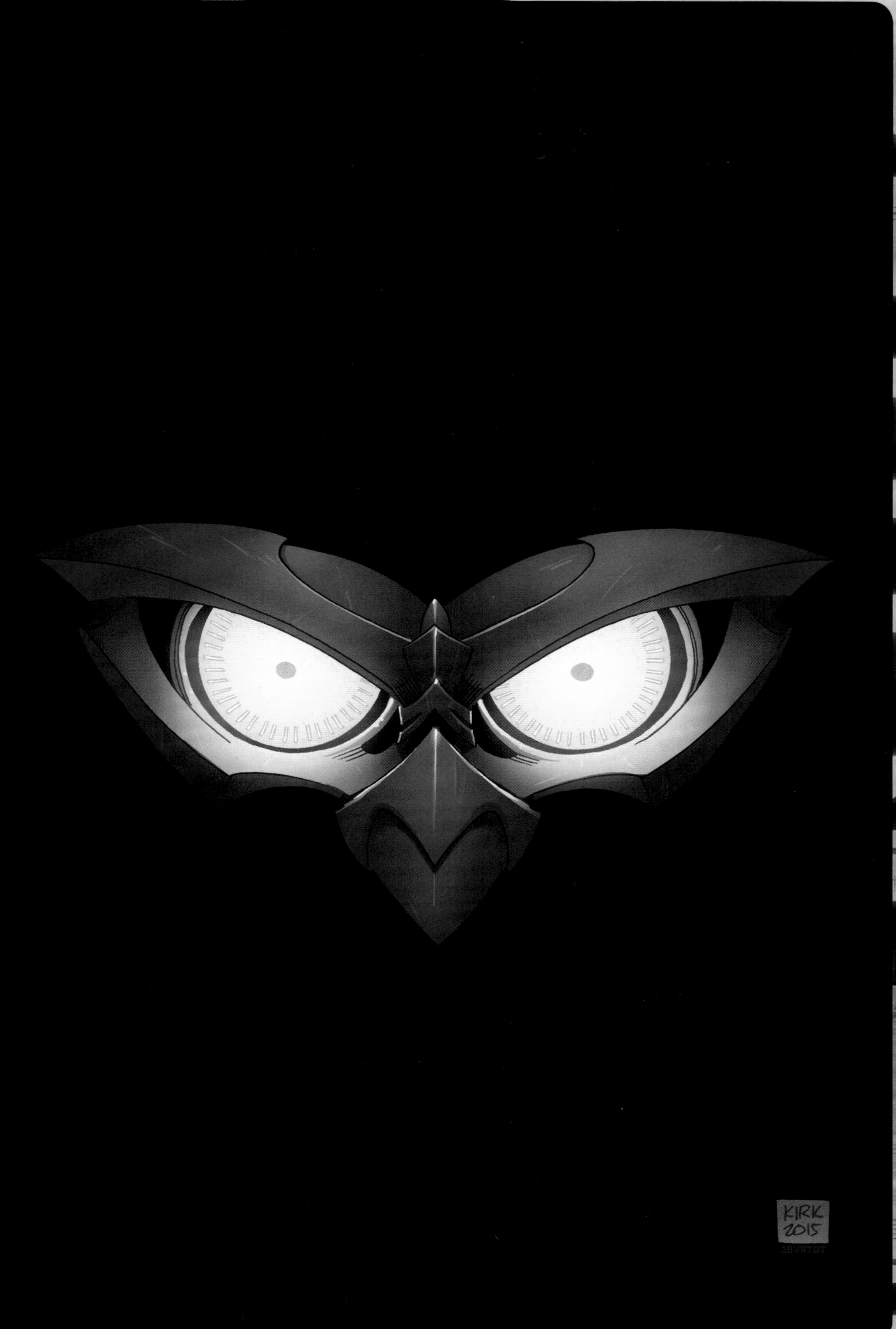
KIRK
2015
ABURTOV

#2 VARIANT BY **LEONARD KIRK & JESUS ABURTOV**

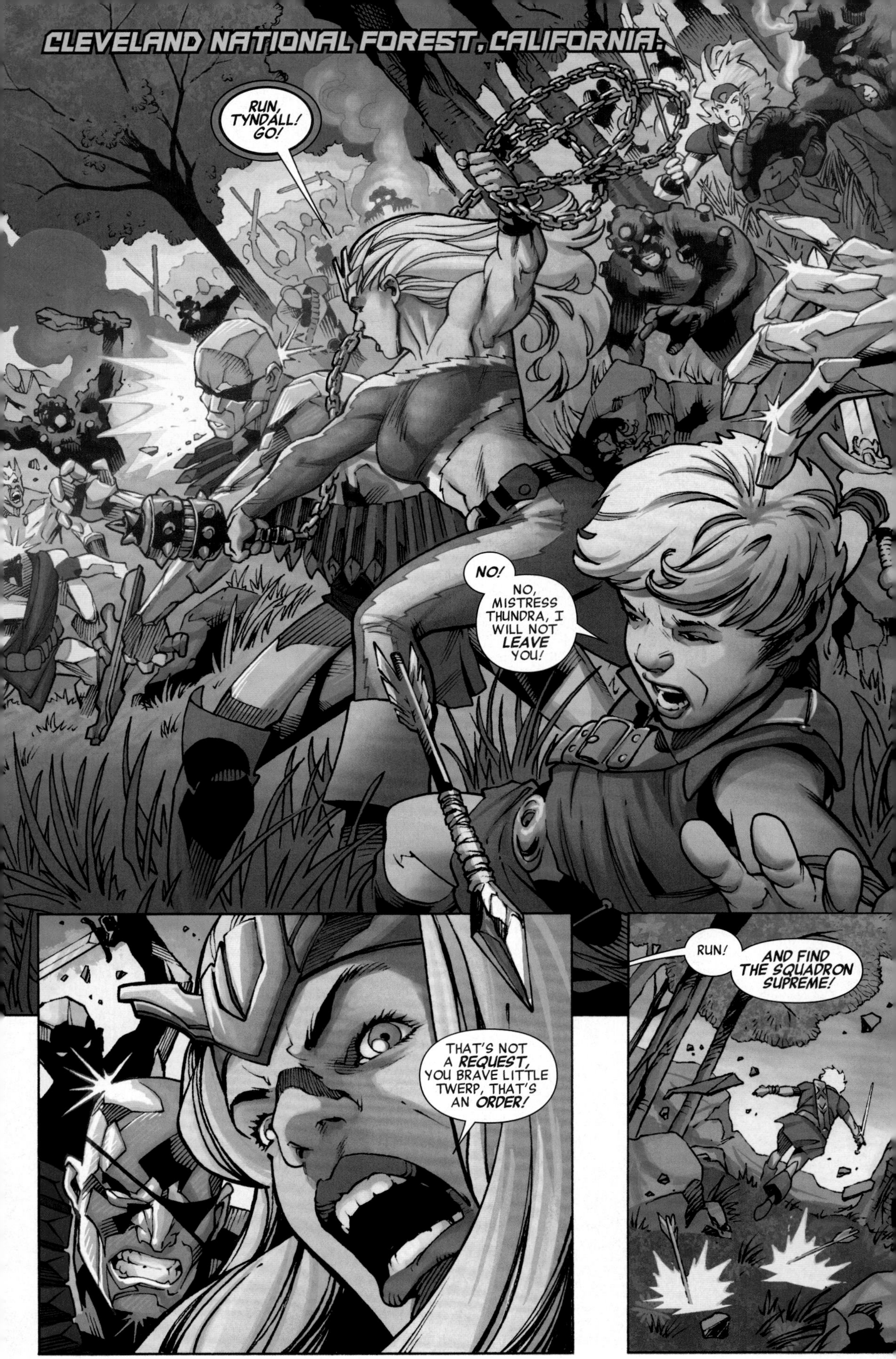
CLEVELAND NATIONAL FOREST, CALIFORNIA:
RUN, TYNDALL! GO!
NO! NO, MISTRESS THUNDRA, I WILL NOT LEAVE YOU!
THAT'S NOT A REQUEST, YOU BRAVE LITTLE TWERP, THAT'S AN ORDER!
RUN!
AND FIND THE SQUADRON SUPREME!

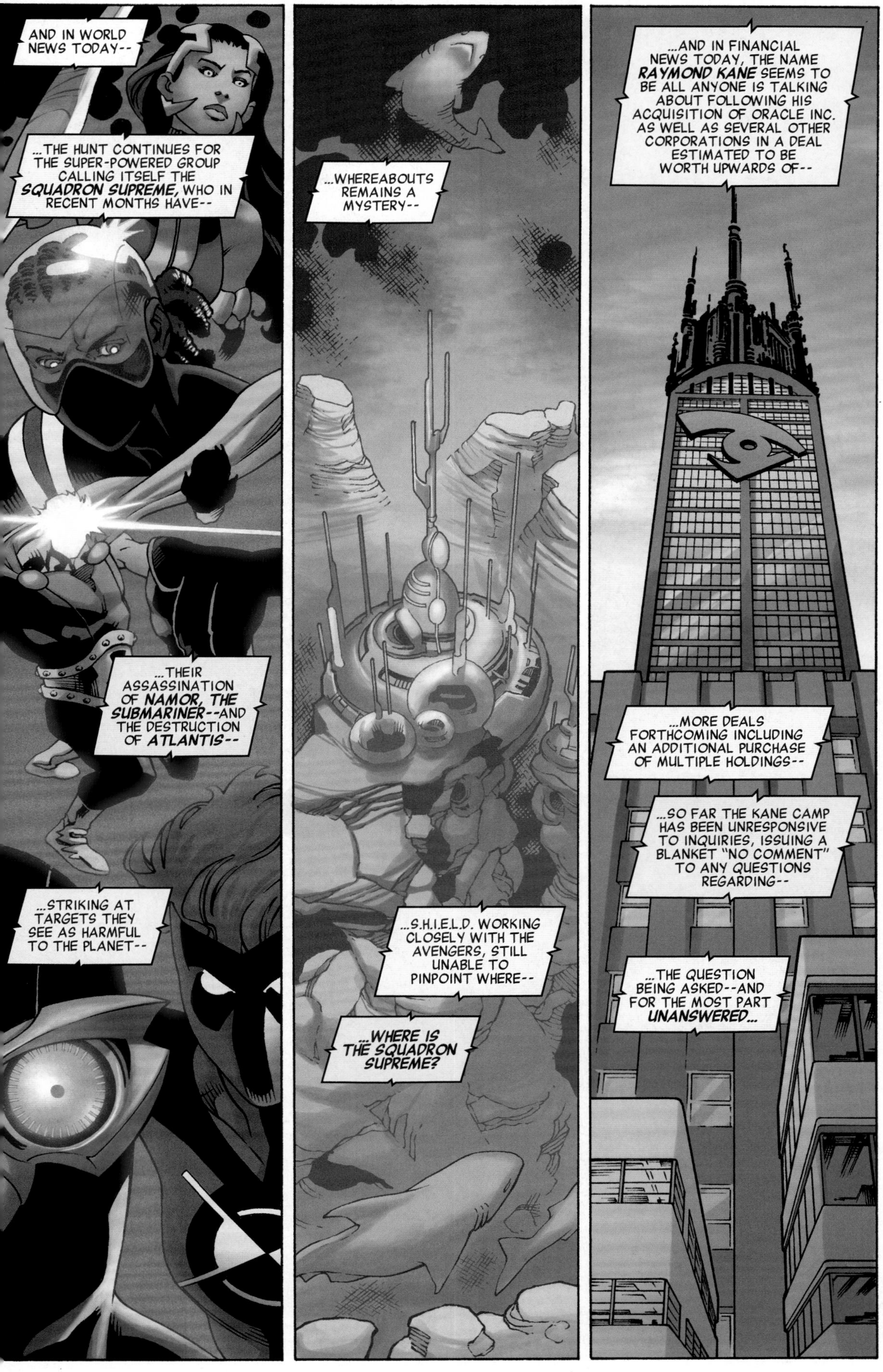
AND IN WORLD NEWS TODAY--
...THE HUNT CONTINUES FOR THE SUPER-POWERED GROUP CALLING ITSELF THE SQUADRON SUPREME, WHO IN RECENT MONTHS HAVE--
...THEIR ASSASSINATION OF NAMOR, THE SUBMARINER--AND THE DESTRUCTION OF ATLANTIS--
...STRIKING AT TARGETS THEY SEE AS HARMFUL TO THE PLANET--
...WHEREABOUTS REMAINS A MYSTERY--
...S.H.I.E.L.D. WORKING CLOSELY WITH THE AVENGERS, STILL UNABLE TO PINPOINT WHERE--
...WHERE IS THE SQUADRON SUPREME?
...AND IN FINANCIAL NEWS TODAY, THE NAME RAYMOND KANE SEEMS TO BE ALL ANYONE IS TALKING ABOUT FOLLOWING HIS ACQUISITION OF ORACLE INC. AS WELL AS SEVERAL OTHER CORPORATIONS IN A DEAL ESTIMATED TO BE WORTH UPWARDS OF--
...MORE DEALS FORTHCOMING INCLUDING AN ADDITIONAL PURCHASE OF MULTIPLE HOLDINGS--
...SO FAR THE KANE CAMP HAS BEEN UNRESPONSIVE TO INQUIRIES, ISSUING A BLANKET "NO COMMENT" TO ANY QUESTIONS REGARDING--
...THE QUESTION BEING ASKED--AND FOR THE MOST PART UNANSWERED...

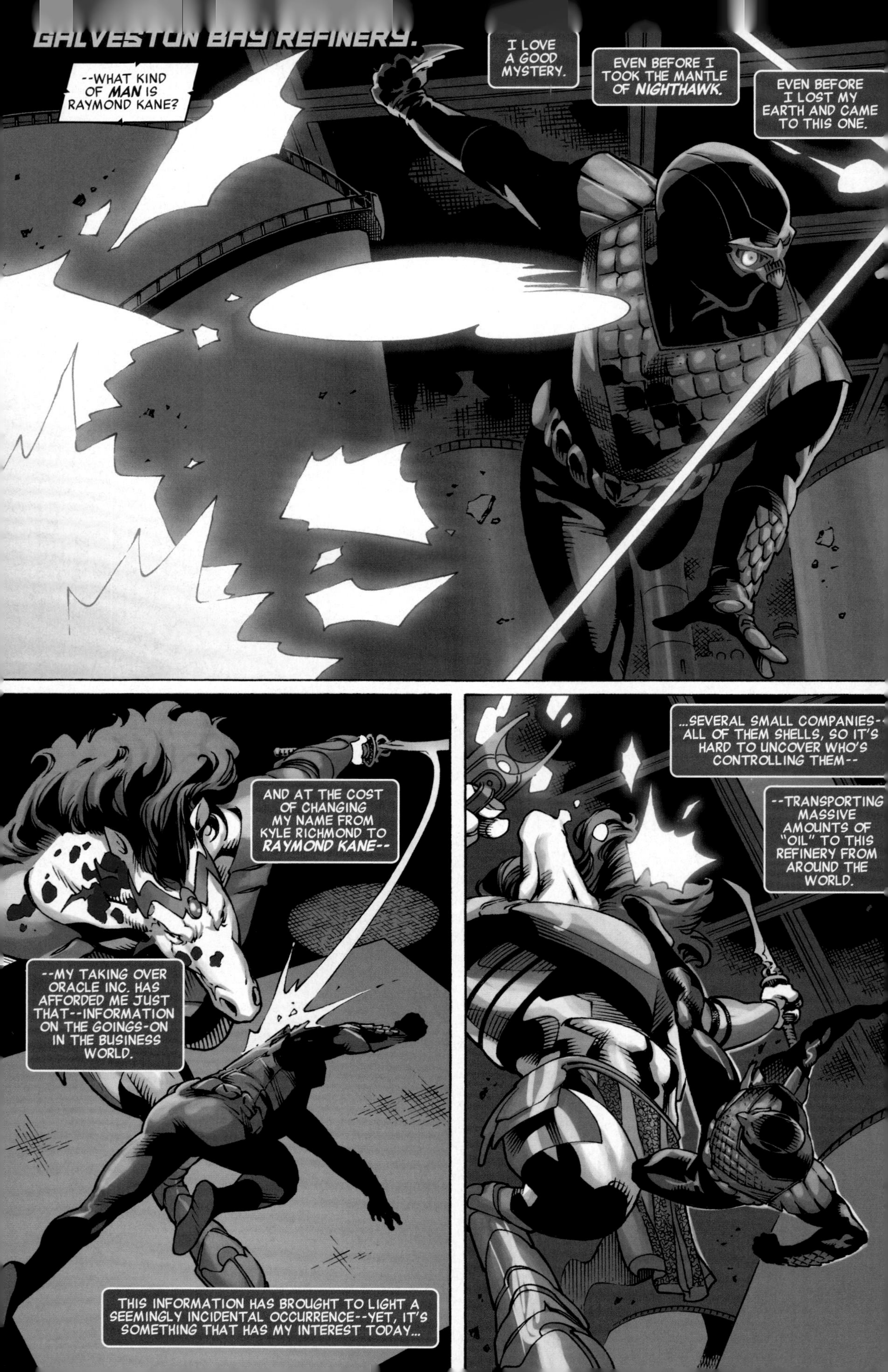
GALVESTON BAY REFINERY.
--WHAT KIND OF MAN IS RAYMOND KANE?
I LOVE A GOOD MYSTERY.
EVEN BEFORE I TOOK THE MANTLE OF NIGHTHAWK.
EVEN BEFORE I LOST MY EARTH AND CAME TO THIS ONE.
AND AT THE COST OF CHANGING MY NAME FROM KYLE RICHMOND TO RAYMOND KANE--
--MY TAKING OVER ORACLE INC. HAS AFFORDED ME JUST THAT--INFORMATION ON THE GOINGS-ON IN THE BUSINESS WORLD.
THIS INFORMATION HAS BROUGHT TO LIGHT A SEEMINGLY INCIDENTAL OCCURRENCE--YET, IT'S SOMETHING THAT HAS MY INTEREST TODAY...
...SEVERAL SMALL COMPANIES--ALL OF THEM SHELLS, SO IT'S HARD TO UNCOVER WHO'S CONTROLLING THEM--
--TRANSPORTING MASSIVE AMOUNTS OF "OIL" TO THIS REFINERY FROM AROUND THE WORLD.

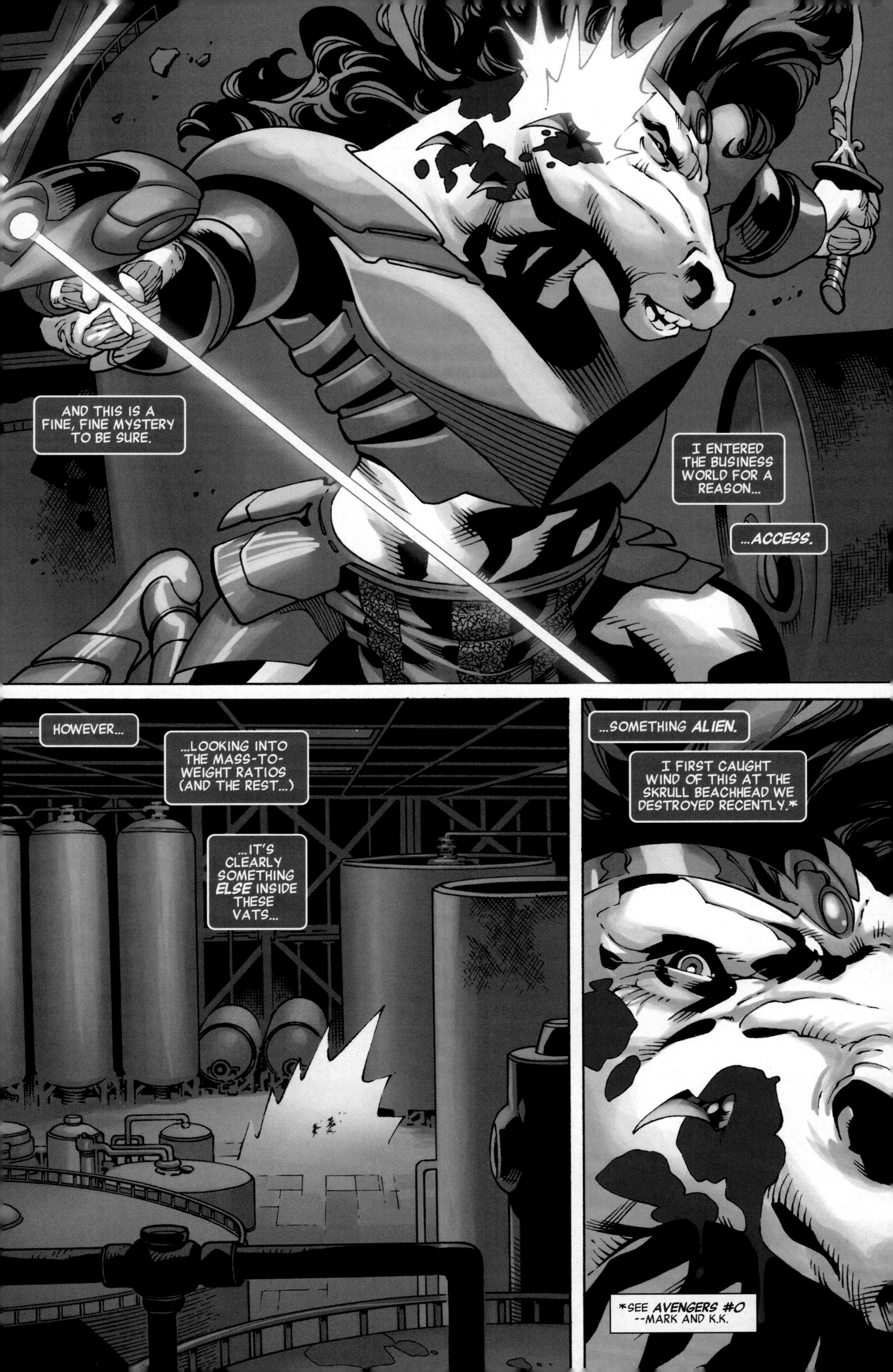
AND THIS IS A FINE, FINE MYSTERY TO BE SURE.
I ENTERED THE BUSINESS WORLD FOR A REASON...
...ACCESS.
HOWEVER...
...LOOKING INTO THE MASS-TO-WEIGHT RATIOS (AND THE REST...)
...IT'S CLEARLY SOMETHING ELSE INSIDE THESE VATS...
...SOMETHING ALIEN.
I FIRST CAUGHT WIND OF THIS AT THE SKRULL BEACHHEAD WE DESTROYED RECENTLY.*
*SEE AVENGERS #0 --MARK AND K.K.

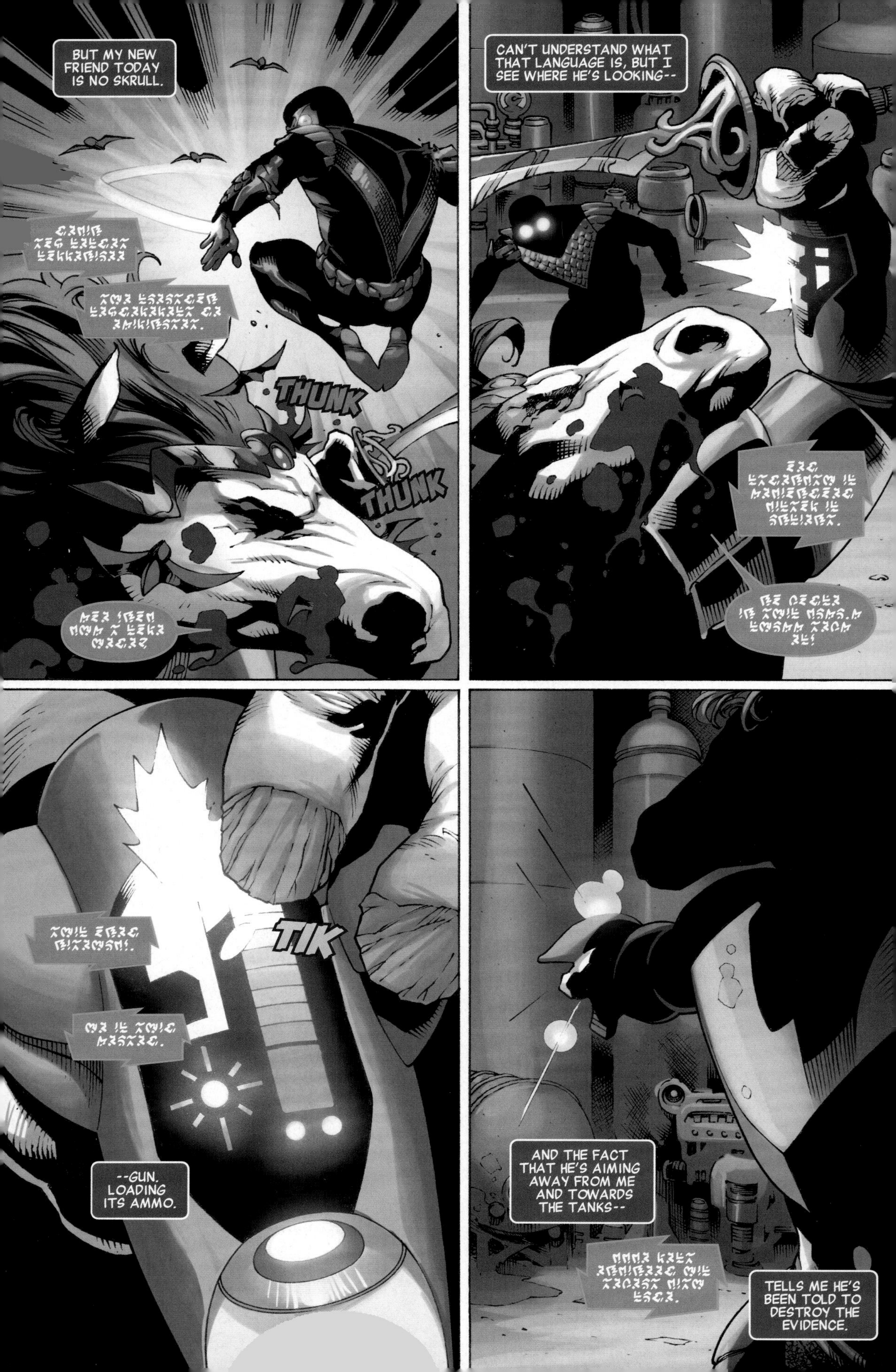

BUT MY NEW FRIEND TODAY IS NO SKRULL.
THUNK
THUNK
CAN'T UNDERSTAND WHAT THAT LANGUAGE IS, BUT I SEE WHERE HE'S LOOKING--
TIK
--GUN. LOADING ITS AMMO.
AND THE FACT THAT HE'S AIMING AWAY FROM ME AND TOWARDS THE TANKS--
TELLS ME HE'S BEEN TOLD TO DESTROY THE EVIDENCE.

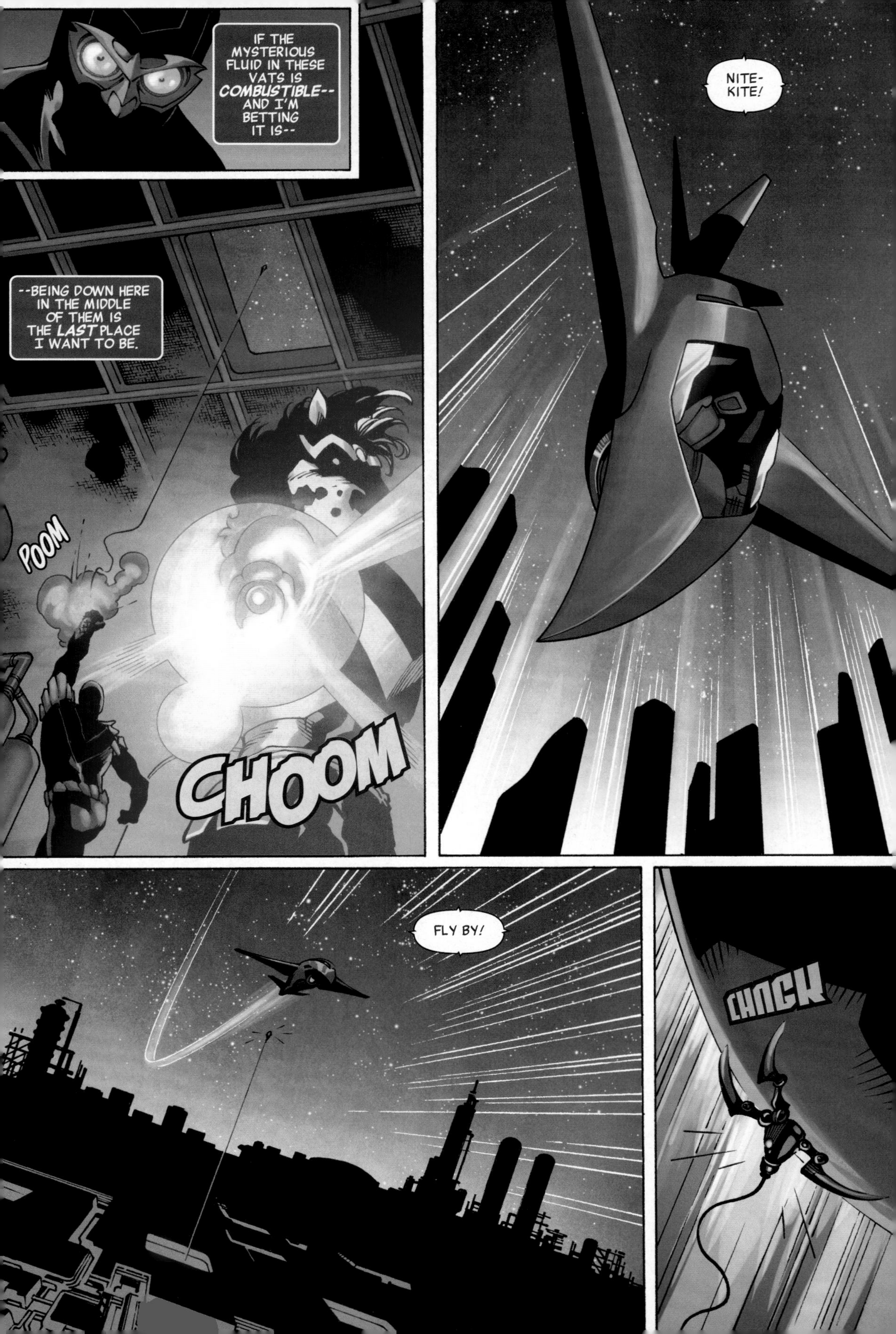
IF THE MYSTERIOUS FLUID IN THESE VATS IS COMBUSTIBLE-- AND I'M BETTING IT IS--
--BEING DOWN HERE IN THE MIDDLE OF THEM IS THE LAST PLACE I WANT TO BE.
POOM
CHOOM
NITE-KITE!
FLY BY!
CHNCK

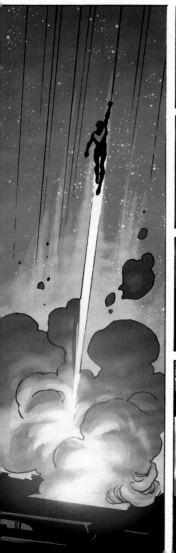

NITE-KITE IS RETROFITTED FROM A STATE-OF-THE-ART ATLANTEAN MISTICO...

...THE FIRST OF MANY NEW TOYS.

THE EXPLOSION WILL DRAW ATTENTION--AUTHORITIES-- HEROES--

--NOT WHAT I WANT RIGHT NOW.

I SHOULD NOTIFY THE OTHERS OF MY FINDINGS.

I'M ESPECIALLY CURIOUS WHAT *HYPERION* WILL MAKE OF ALL THIS...

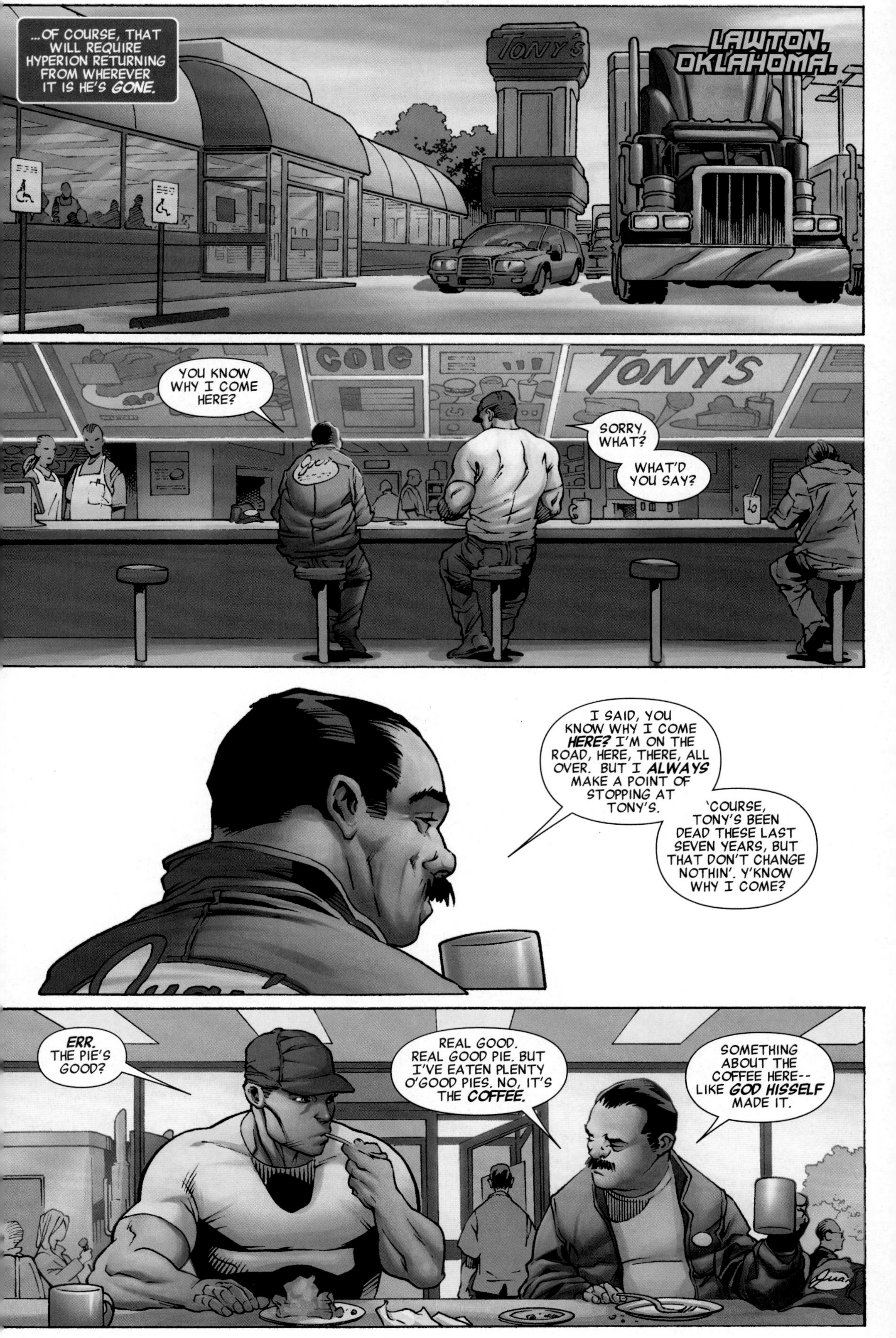

...OF COURSE, THAT WILL REQUIRE HYPERION RETURNING FROM WHEREVER IT IS HE'S GONE.
LAWTON, OKLAHOMA.
TONY'S
YOU KNOW WHY I COME HERE?
SORRY, WHAT?
WHAT'D YOU SAY?
I SAID, YOU KNOW WHY I COME HERE? I'M ON THE ROAD, HERE, THERE, ALL OVER. BUT I ALWAYS MAKE A POINT OF STOPPING AT TONY'S.
'COURSE, TONY'S BEEN DEAD THESE LAST SEVEN YEARS, BUT THAT DON'T CHANGE NOTHIN'. Y'KNOW WHY I COME?
ERR. THE PIE'S GOOD?
REAL GOOD. REAL GOOD PIE. BUT I'VE EATEN PLENTY O'GOOD PIES. NO, IT'S THE COFFEE.
SOMETHING ABOUT THE COFFEE HERE-- LIKE GOD HISSELF MADE IT.

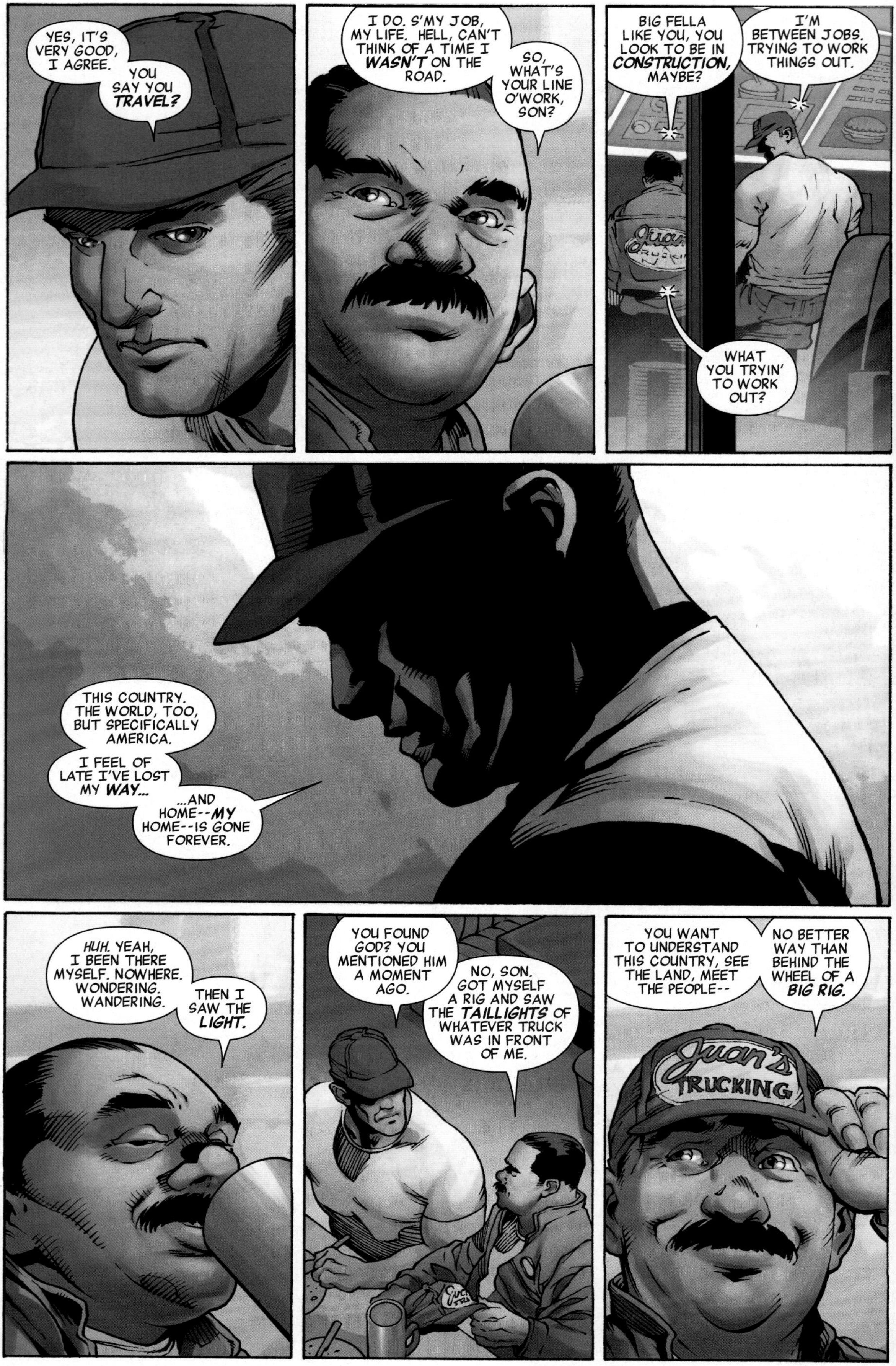
YES, IT'S VERY GOOD, I AGREE.
YOU SAY YOU TRAVEL?
I DO. S'MY JOB, MY LIFE. HELL, CAN'T THINK OF A TIME I WASN'T ON THE ROAD.
SO, WHAT'S YOUR LINE O'WORK, SON?
BIG FELLA LIKE YOU, YOU LOOK TO BE IN CONSTRUCTION, MAYBE?
I'M BETWEEN JOBS. TRYING TO WORK THINGS OUT.
WHAT YOU TRYIN' TO WORK OUT?
THIS COUNTRY. THE WORLD, TOO, BUT SPECIFICALLY AMERICA.
I FEEL OF LATE I'VE LOST MY WAY...
...AND HOME--MY HOME--IS GONE FOREVER.
HUH. YEAH, I BEEN THERE MYSELF. NOWHERE. WONDERING. WANDERING.
THEN I SAW THE LIGHT.
YOU FOUND GOD? YOU MENTIONED HIM A MOMENT AGO.
NO, SON. GOT MYSELF A RIG AND SAW THE TAILLIGHTS OF WHATEVER TRUCK WAS IN FRONT OF ME.
YOU WANT TO UNDERSTAND THIS COUNTRY, SEE THE LAND, MEET THE PEOPLE--
NO BETTER WAY THAN BEHIND THE WHEEL OF A BIG RIG.
Juan's TRUCKING

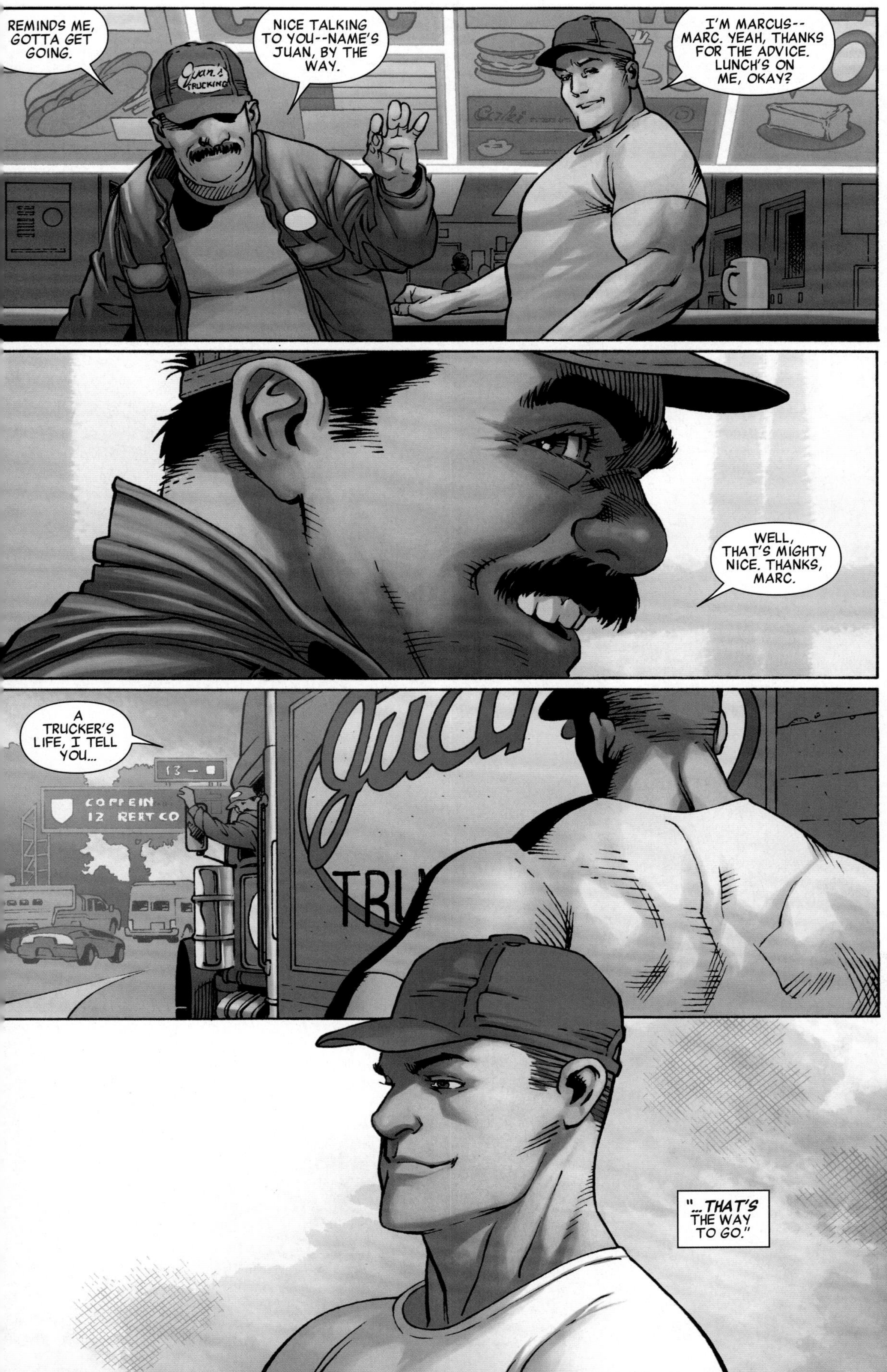
REMINDS ME, GOTTA GET GOING.
NICE TALKING TO YOU--NAME'S JUAN, BY THE WAY.
Juan's TRUCKING
I'M MARCUS--MARC. YEAH, THANKS FOR THE ADVICE. LUNCH'S ON ME, OKAY?
WELL, THAT'S MIGHTY NICE. THANKS, MARC.
A TRUCKER'S LIFE, I TELL YOU...
"...THAT'S THE WAY TO GO."

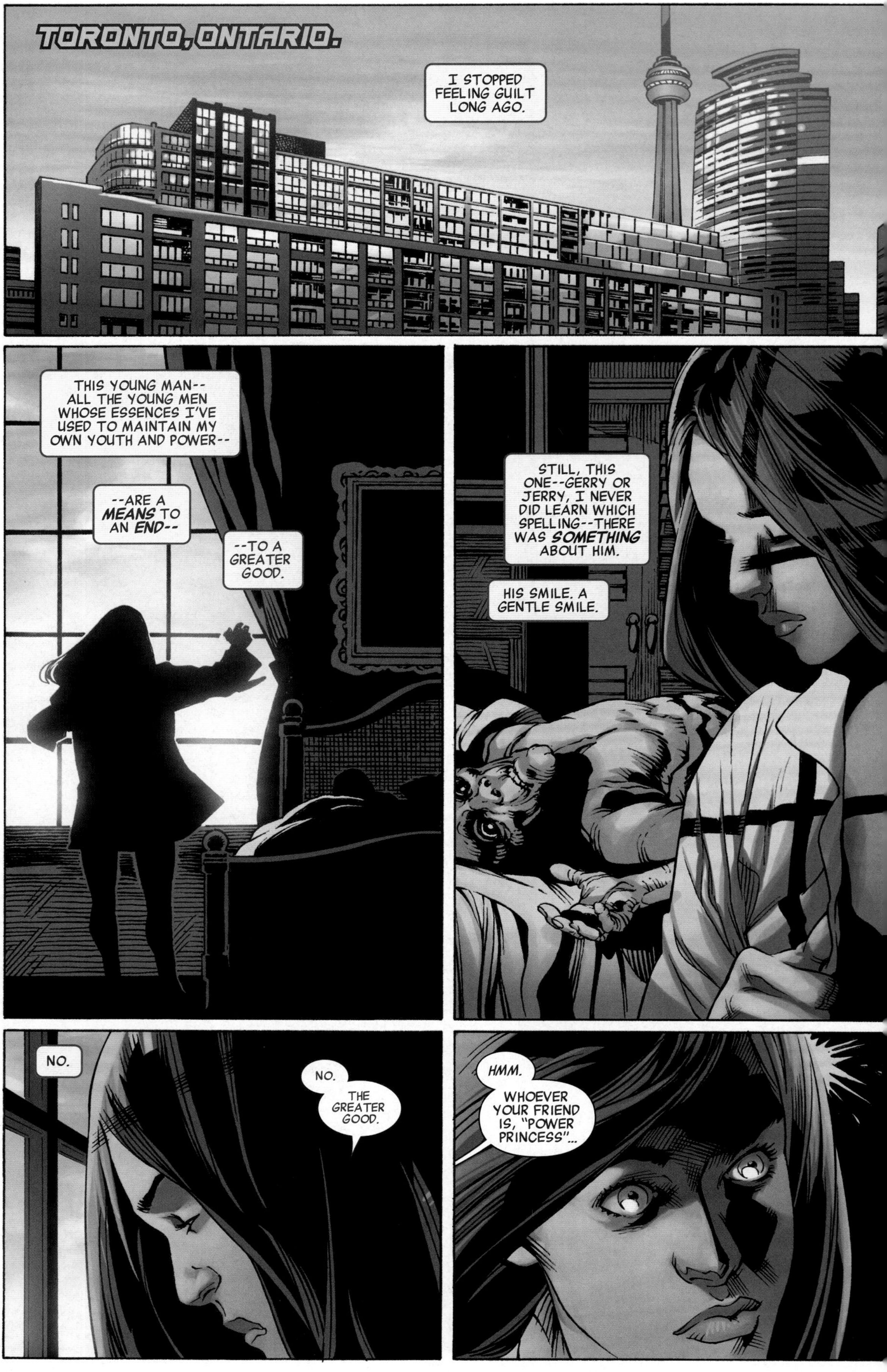
TORONTO, ONTARIO.
I STOPPED FEELING GUILT LONG AGO.
THIS YOUNG MAN--ALL THE YOUNG MEN WHOSE ESSENCES I'VE USED TO MAINTAIN MY OWN YOUTH AND POWER--
--ARE A MEANS TO AN END--
--TO A GREATER GOOD.
STILL, THIS ONE--GERRY OR JERRY, I NEVER DID LEARN WHICH SPELLING--THERE WAS SOMETHING ABOUT HIM.
HIS SMILE. A GENTLE SMILE.
NO.
NO.
THE GREATER GOOD.
HMM.
WHOEVER YOUR FRIEND IS, "POWER PRINCESS"...

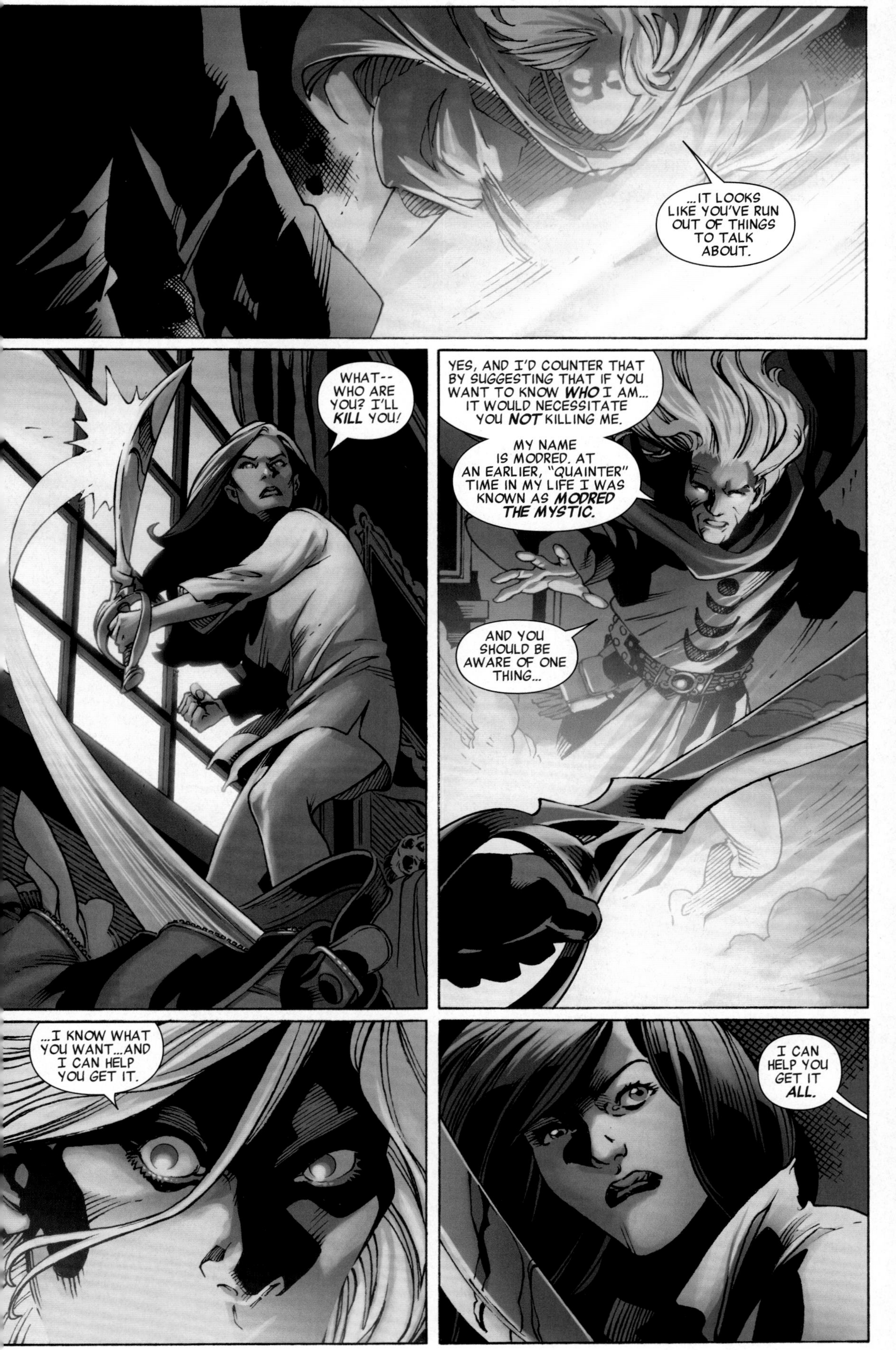
...IT LOOKS LIKE YOU'VE RUN OUT OF THINGS TO TALK ABOUT.
WHAT-- WHO ARE YOU? I'LL **KILL** YOU!
YES, AND I'D COUNTER THAT BY SUGGESTING THAT IF YOU WANT TO KNOW **WHO** I AM... IT WOULD NECESSITATE YOU **NOT** KILLING ME.
MY NAME IS MODRED. AT AN EARLIER, "QUAINTER" TIME IN MY LIFE I WAS KNOWN AS **MODRED THE MYSTIC.**
AND YOU SHOULD BE AWARE OF ONE THING...
...I KNOW WHAT YOU WANT...AND I CAN HELP YOU GET IT.
I CAN HELP YOU GET IT **ALL.**

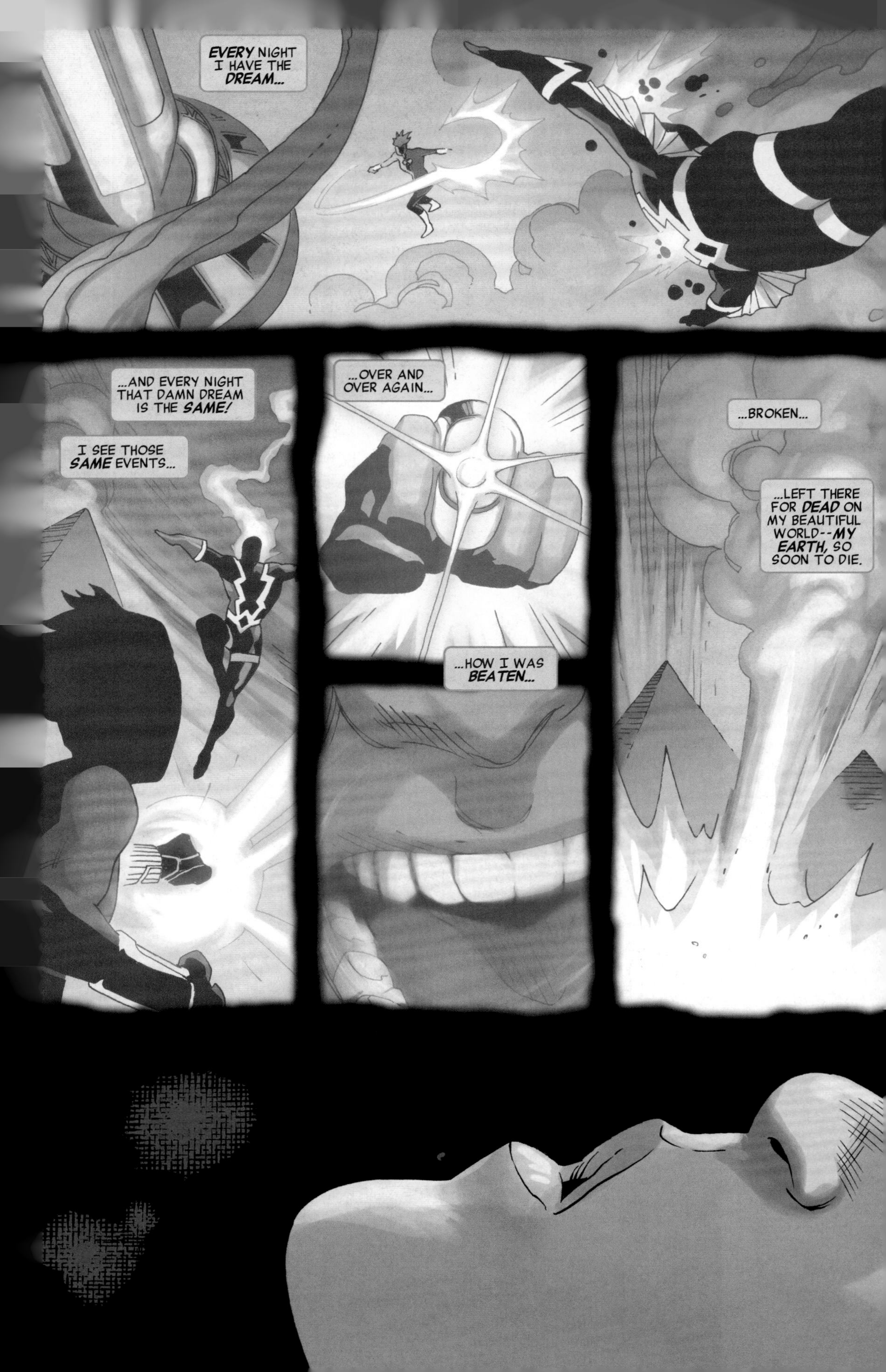
EVERY NIGHT I HAVE THE DREAM...
...AND EVERY NIGHT THAT DAMN DREAM IS THE SAME!
I SEE THOSE SAME EVENTS...
...OVER AND OVER AGAIN...
...HOW I WAS BEATEN...
...BROKEN...
...LEFT THERE FOR DEAD ON MY BEAUTIFUL WORLD--MY EARTH, SO SOON TO DIE.

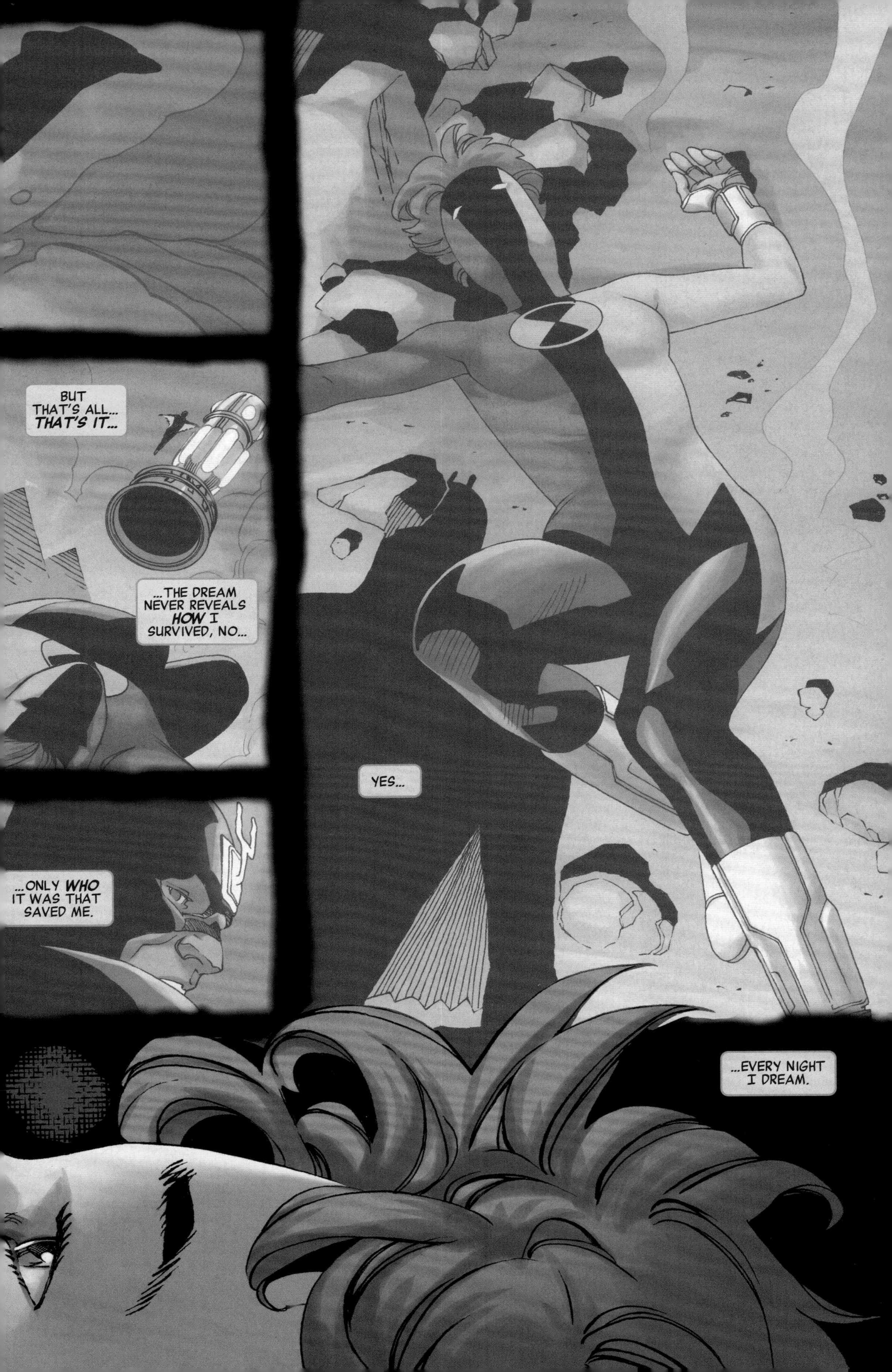
BUT THAT'S ALL... THAT'S IT...
...THE DREAM NEVER REVEALS HOW I SURVIVED, NO...
...ONLY WHO IT WAS THAT SAVED ME.
YES...
...EVERY NIGHT I DREAM.

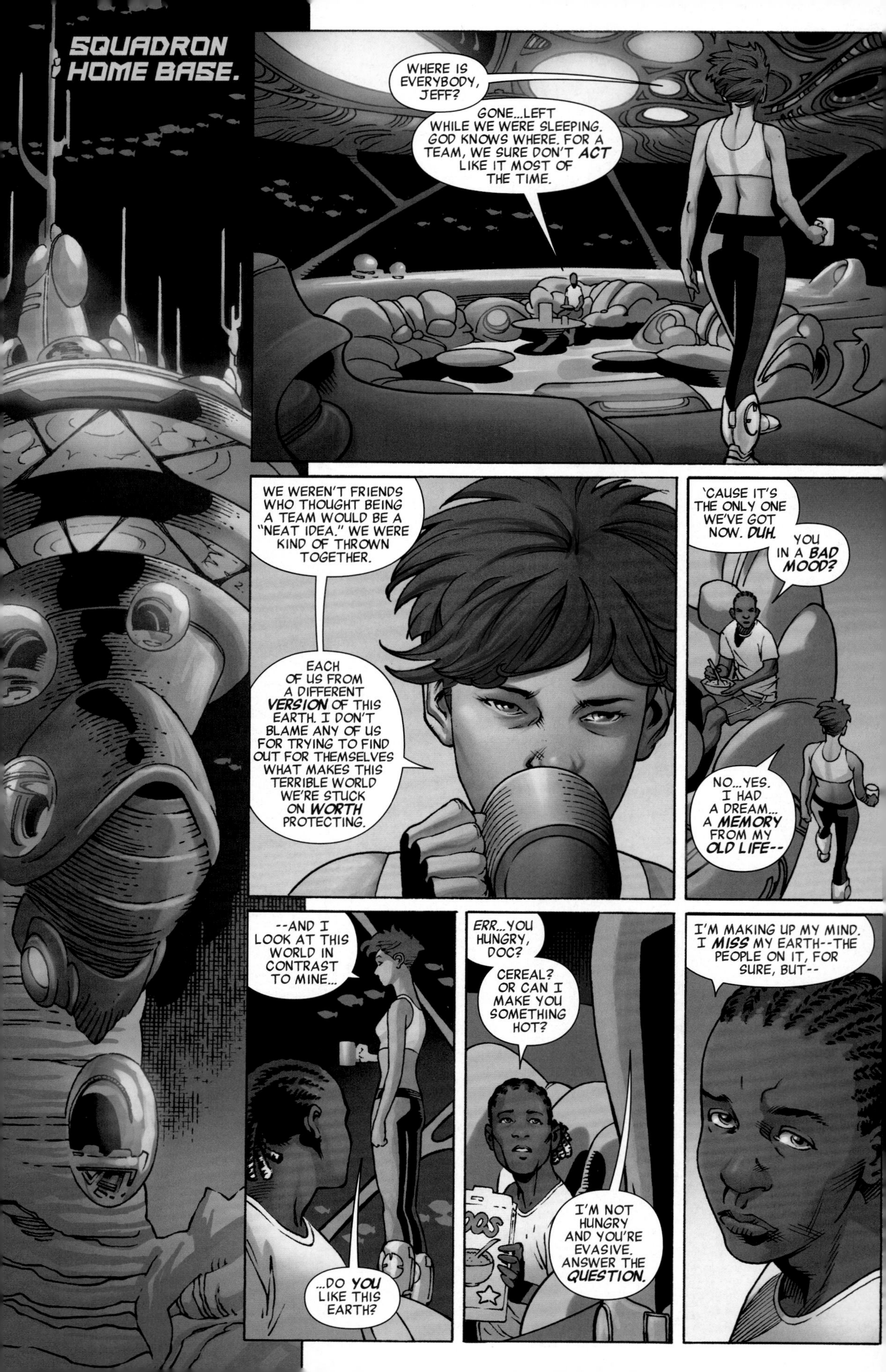

SQUADRON HOME BASE.
WHERE IS EVERYBODY, JEFF?
GONE...LEFT WHILE WE WERE SLEEPING. GOD KNOWS WHERE. FOR A TEAM, WE SURE DON'T ACT LIKE IT MOST OF THE TIME.
WE WEREN'T FRIENDS WHO THOUGHT BEING A TEAM WOULD BE A "NEAT IDEA." WE WERE KIND OF THROWN TOGETHER.
EACH OF US FROM A DIFFERENT VERSION OF THIS EARTH. I DON'T BLAME ANY OF US FOR TRYING TO FIND OUT FOR THEMSELVES WHAT MAKES THIS TERRIBLE WORLD WE'RE STUCK ON WORTH PROTECTING.
'CAUSE IT'S THE ONLY ONE WE'VE GOT NOW. DUH.
YOU IN A BAD MOOD?
NO...YES. I HAD A DREAM... A MEMORY FROM MY OLD LIFE--
--AND I LOOK AT THIS WORLD IN CONTRAST TO MINE...
...DO YOU LIKE THIS EARTH?
ERR...YOU HUNGRY, DOC?
CEREAL? OR CAN I MAKE YOU SOMETHING HOT?
I'M NOT HUNGRY AND YOU'RE EVASIVE. ANSWER THE QUESTION.
I'M MAKING UP MY MIND. I MISS MY EARTH--THE PEOPLE ON IT, FOR SURE, BUT--

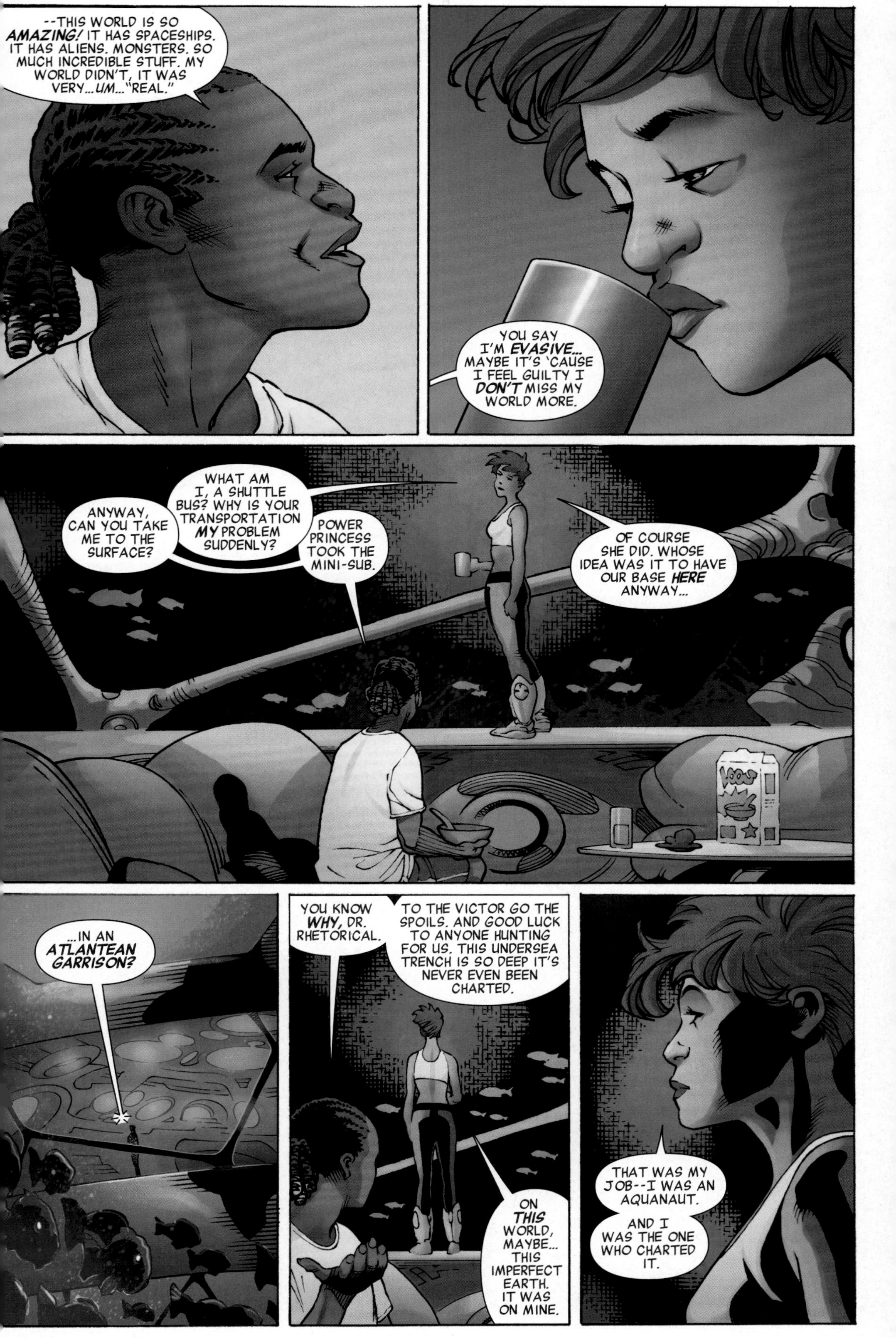
--THIS WORLD IS SO AMAZING! IT HAS SPACESHIPS. IT HAS ALIENS. MONSTERS. SO MUCH INCREDIBLE STUFF. MY WORLD DIDN'T, IT WAS VERY...UM..."REAL."
YOU SAY I'M EVASIVE... MAYBE IT'S 'CAUSE I FEEL GUILTY I DON'T MISS MY WORLD MORE.
ANYWAY, CAN YOU TAKE ME TO THE SURFACE?
WHAT AM I, A SHUTTLE BUS? WHY IS YOUR TRANSPORTATION MY PROBLEM SUDDENLY?
POWER PRINCESS TOOK THE MINI-SUB.
OF COURSE SHE DID. WHOSE IDEA WAS IT TO HAVE OUR BASE HERE ANYWAY...
...IN AN ATLANTEAN GARRISON?
YOU KNOW WHY, DR. RHETORICAL.
TO THE VICTOR GO THE SPOILS. AND GOOD LUCK TO ANYONE HUNTING FOR US. THIS UNDERSEA TRENCH IS SO DEEP IT'S NEVER EVEN BEEN CHARTED.
ON THIS WORLD, MAYBE... THIS IMPERFECT EARTH. IT WAS ON MINE.
THAT WAS MY JOB--I WAS AN AQUANAUT.
AND I WAS THE ONE WHO CHARTED IT.

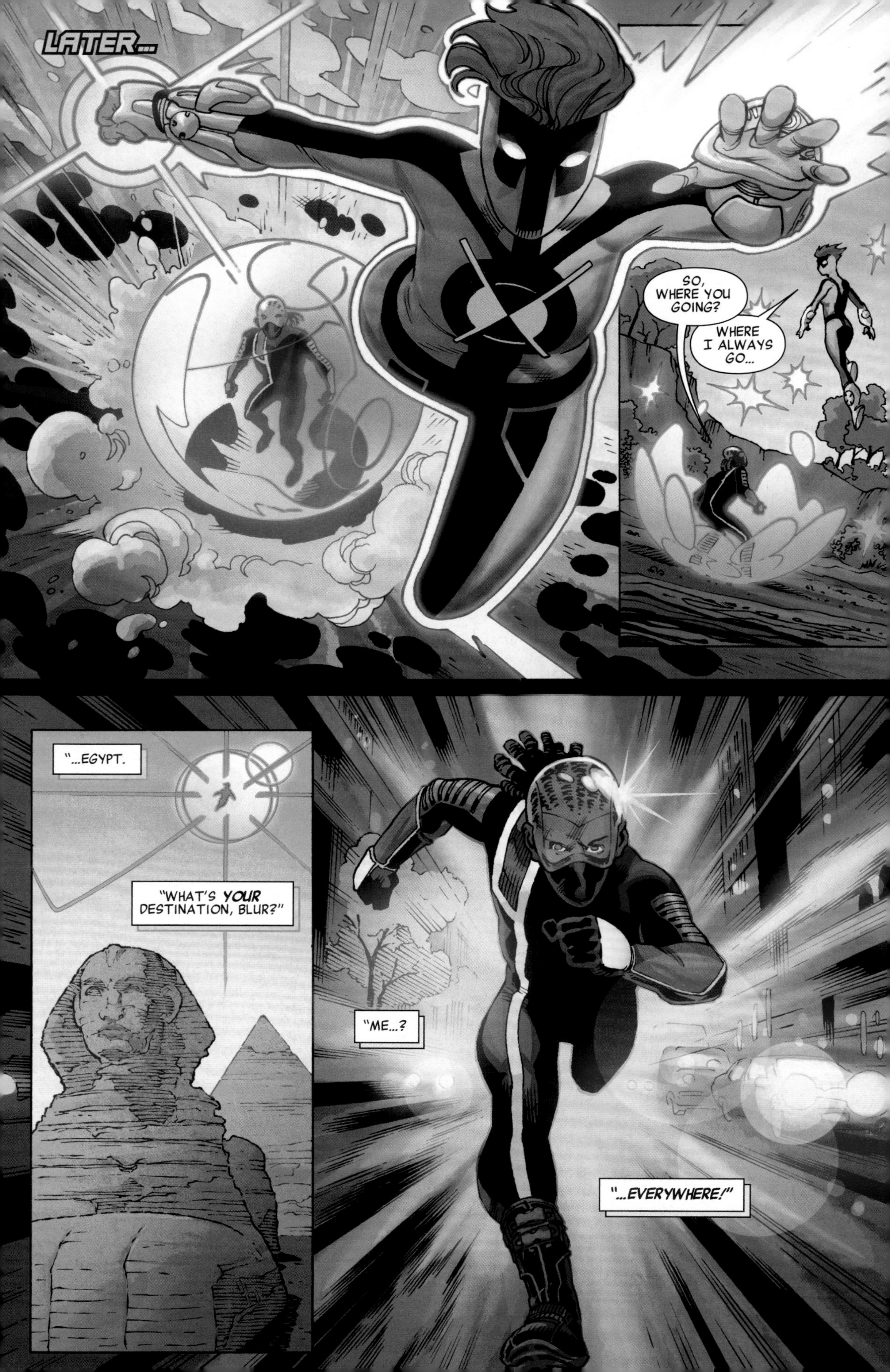
LATER...
SO, WHERE YOU GOING?
WHERE I ALWAYS GO...
"...EGYPT.
"WHAT'S YOUR DESTINATION, BLUR?"
"ME...?
"...EVERYWHERE!"

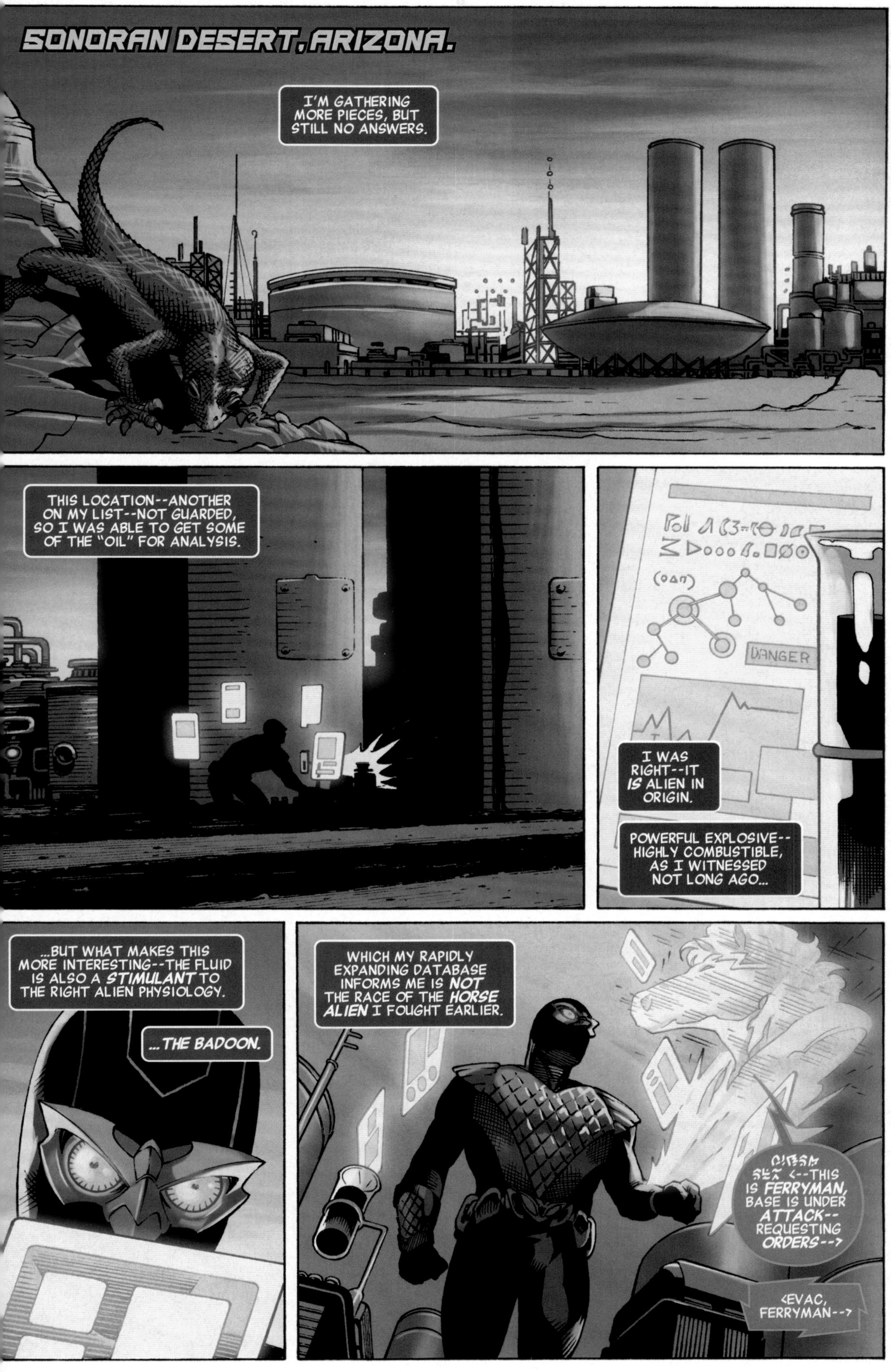
SONORAN DESERT, ARIZONA.
I'M GATHERING MORE PIECES, BUT STILL NO ANSWERS.
THIS LOCATION--ANOTHER ON MY LIST--NOT GUARDED, SO I WAS ABLE TO GET SOME OF THE "OIL" FOR ANALYSIS.
DANGER
I WAS RIGHT--IT IS ALIEN IN ORIGIN.
POWERFUL EXPLOSIVE--HIGHLY COMBUSTIBLE, AS I WITNESSED NOT LONG AGO...
...BUT WHAT MAKES THIS MORE INTERESTING--THE FLUID IS ALSO A STIMULANT TO THE RIGHT ALIEN PHYSIOLOGY.
...THE BADOON.
WHICH MY RAPIDLY EXPANDING DATABASE INFORMS ME IS NOT THE RACE OF THE HORSE ALIEN I FOUGHT EARLIER.
<--THIS IS FERRYMAN, BASE IS UNDER ATTACK--REQUESTING ORDERS-->
<EVAC, FERRYMAN-->

HE IS A **KYMELLIAN**...

<DESTROY THE PLANT AND EVAC!>

<NIGHTHAWK HAS THREATENED THIS LOCATION-- IT IS NO LONGER SAFE.>

<GET OUT OF THERE!>

BUT WHEN I IDENTIFIED THE LANGUAGE SPOKEN TO THIS "FERRYMAN" FOR TRANSLATION... I DISCOVERED IT WAS **KREE.**

SKRULL, KREE, BADOON, KYMELLIAN.

A LOT OF ALIEN RACES WHO'VE WARRED AND HATED EACH OTHER... NOW WORKING **TOGETHER?**

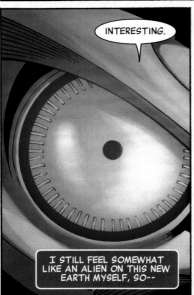

INTERESTING.

I STILL FEEL SOMEWHAT LIKE AN ALIEN ON THIS NEW EARTH MYSELF, SO--

NO MOVES, MISTER!

YOU SO MUCH AS **TWITCH,** YOU'RE GOING DOWN!

HMM.

ABOUT **TIME,** I SUPPOSE.

I'M IMPRESSED YOU **FOUND** ME.

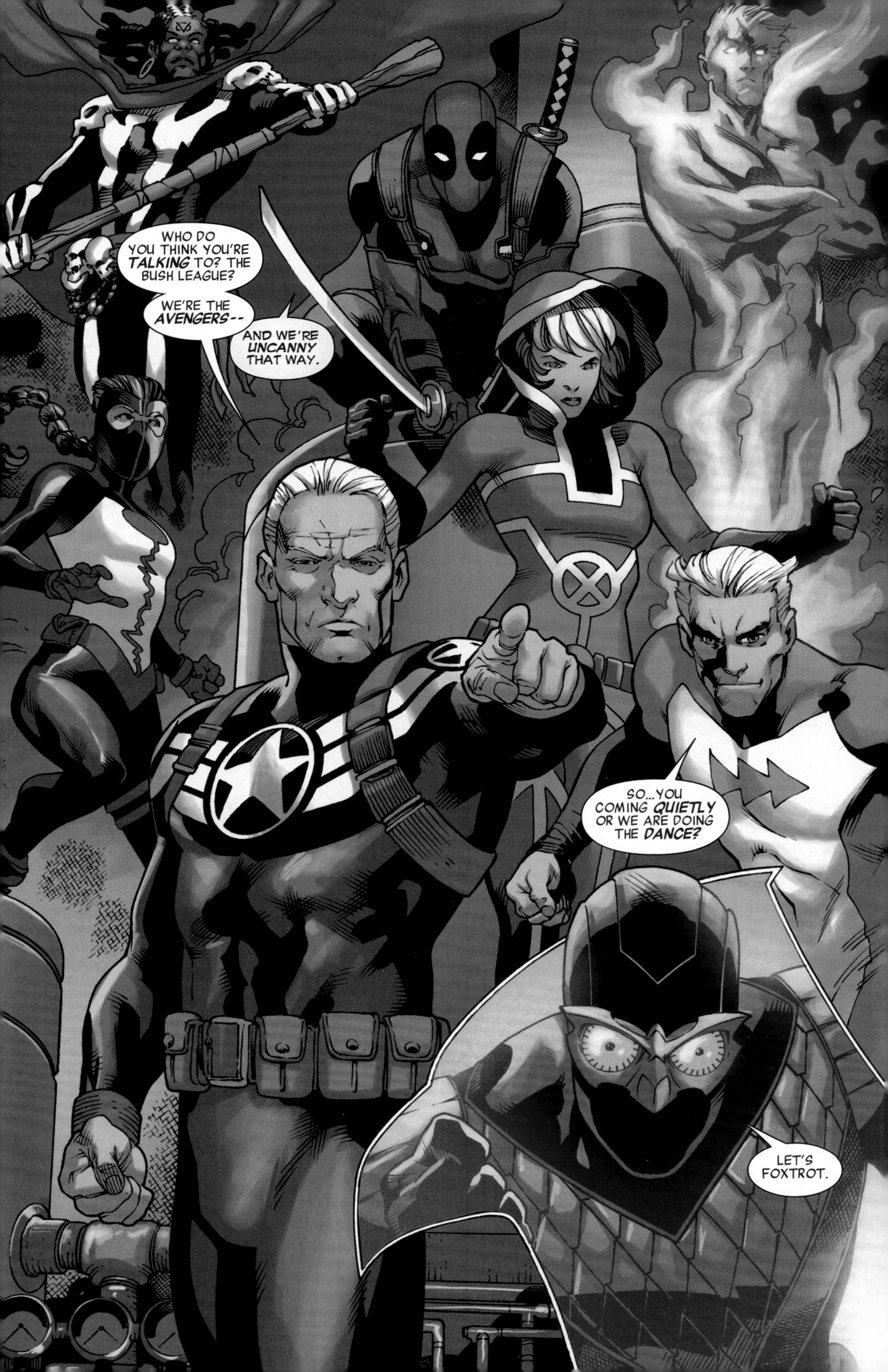
WHO DO YOU THINK YOU'RE TALKING TO? THE BUSH LEAGUE?
WE'RE THE AVENGERS--
AND WE'RE UNCANNY THAT WAY.
SO...YOU COMING QUIETLY OR WE ARE DOING THE DANCE?
LET'S FOXTROT.

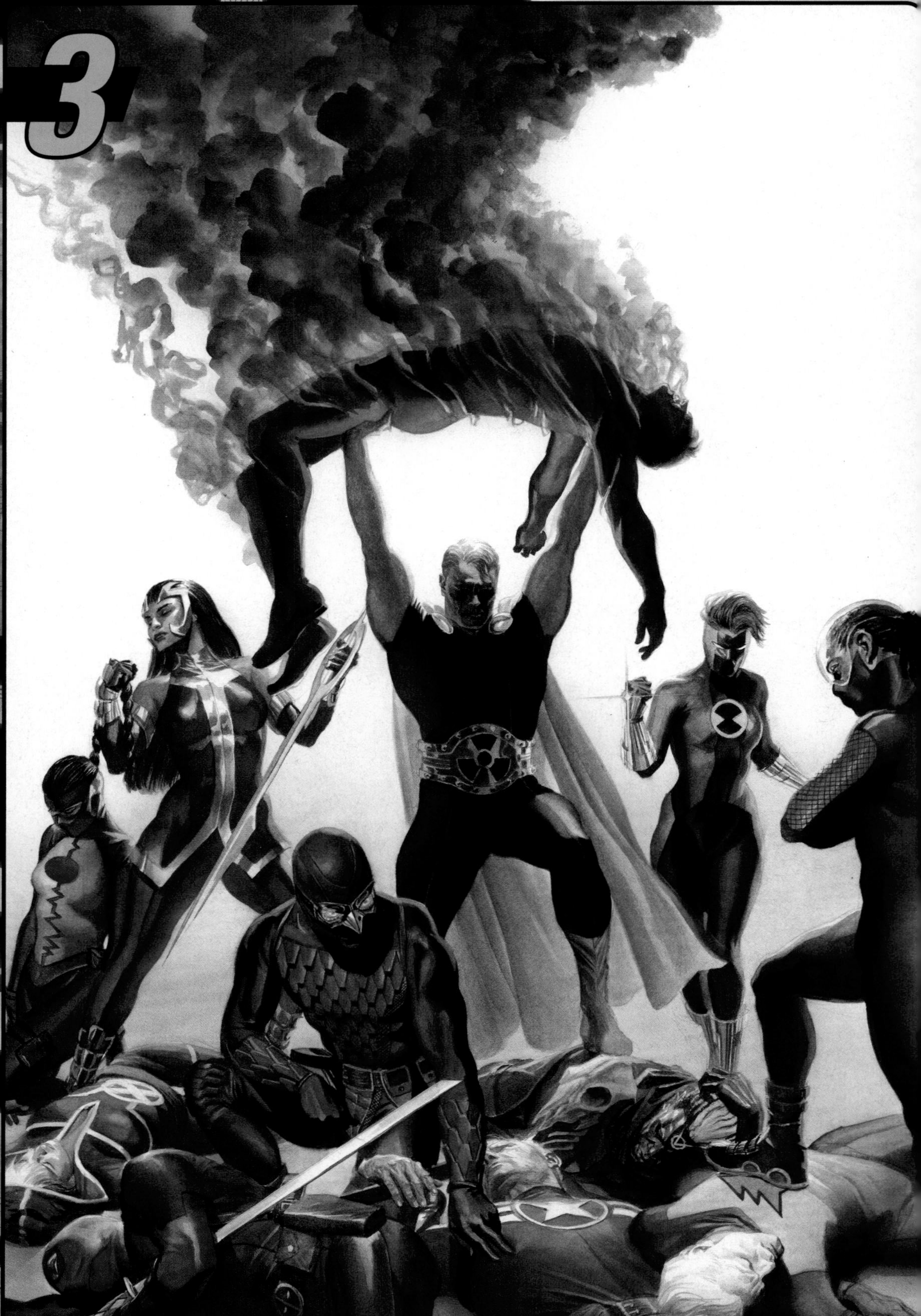
3

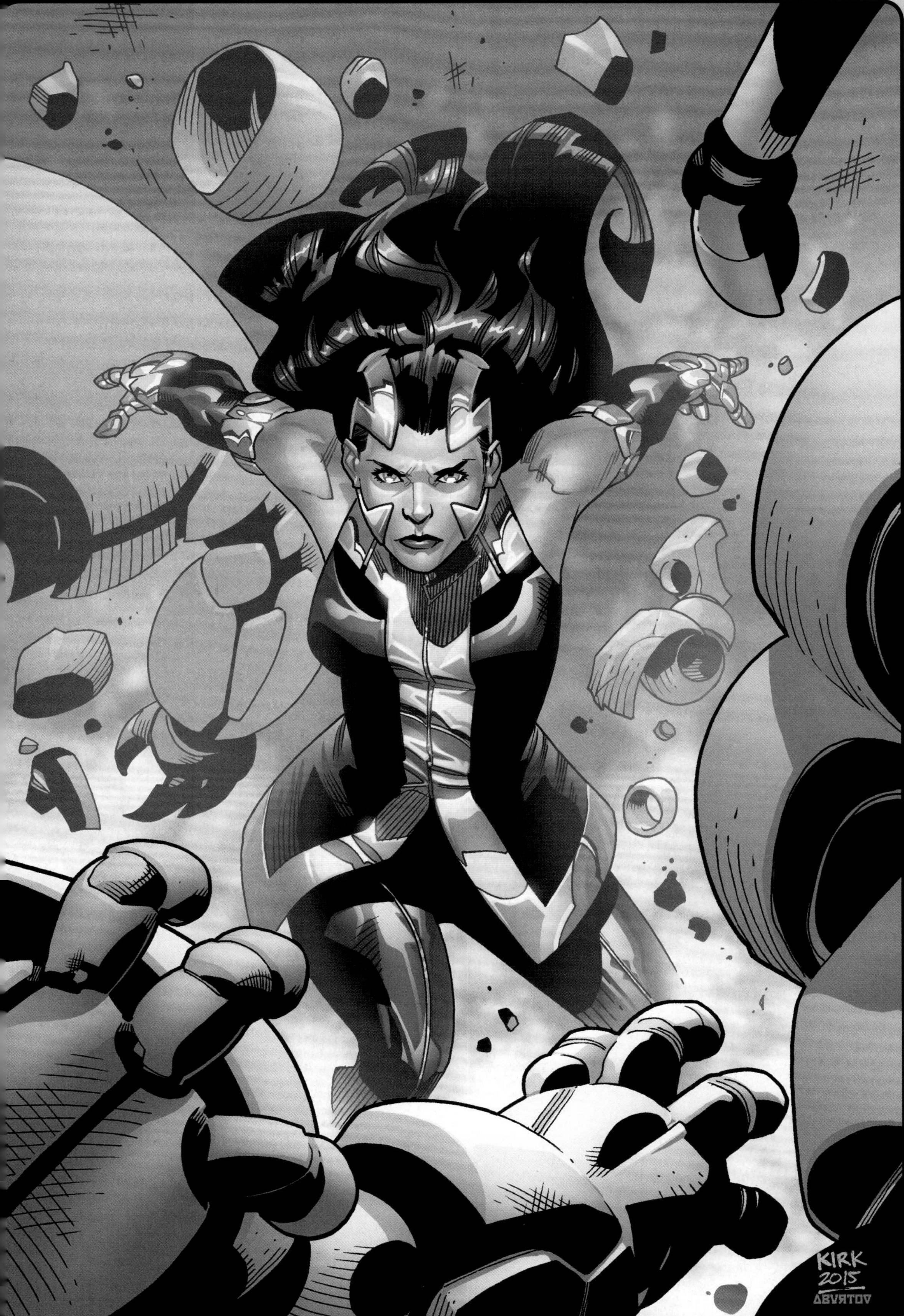
KIRK
2015
ABURTOV

#3 VARIANT BY **LEONARD KIRK** & **JESUS ABURTOV**

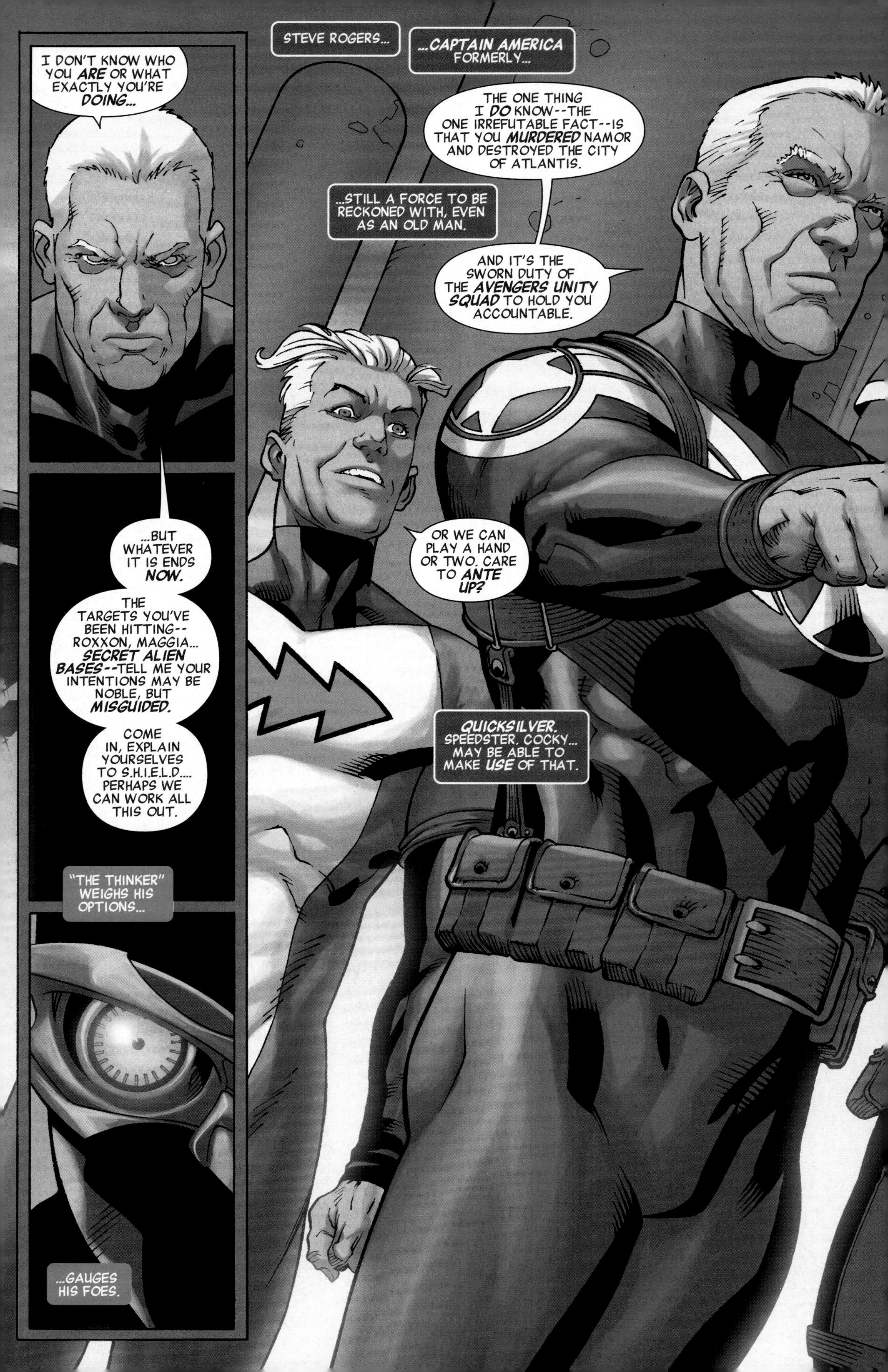

STEVE ROGERS...
...CAPTAIN AMERICA FORMERLY...
I DON'T KNOW WHO YOU ARE OR WHAT EXACTLY YOU'RE DOING...
THE ONE THING I DO KNOW--THE ONE IRREFUTABLE FACT--IS THAT YOU MURDERED NAMOR AND DESTROYED THE CITY OF ATLANTIS.
...STILL A FORCE TO BE RECKONED WITH, EVEN AS AN OLD MAN.
AND IT'S THE SWORN DUTY OF THE AVENGERS UNITY SQUAD TO HOLD YOU ACCOUNTABLE.
...BUT WHATEVER IT IS ENDS NOW.
THE TARGETS YOU'VE BEEN HITTING--ROXXON, MAGGIA... SECRET ALIEN BASES--TELL ME YOUR INTENTIONS MAY BE NOBLE, BUT MISGUIDED.
COME IN, EXPLAIN YOURSELVES TO S.H.I.E.L.D.... PERHAPS WE CAN WORK ALL THIS OUT.
OR WE CAN PLAY A HAND OR TWO. CARE TO ANTE UP?
QUICKSILVER. SPEEDSTER. COCKY... MAY BE ABLE TO MAKE USE OF THAT.
"THE THINKER" WEIGHS HIS OPTIONS...
...GAUGES HIS FOES.

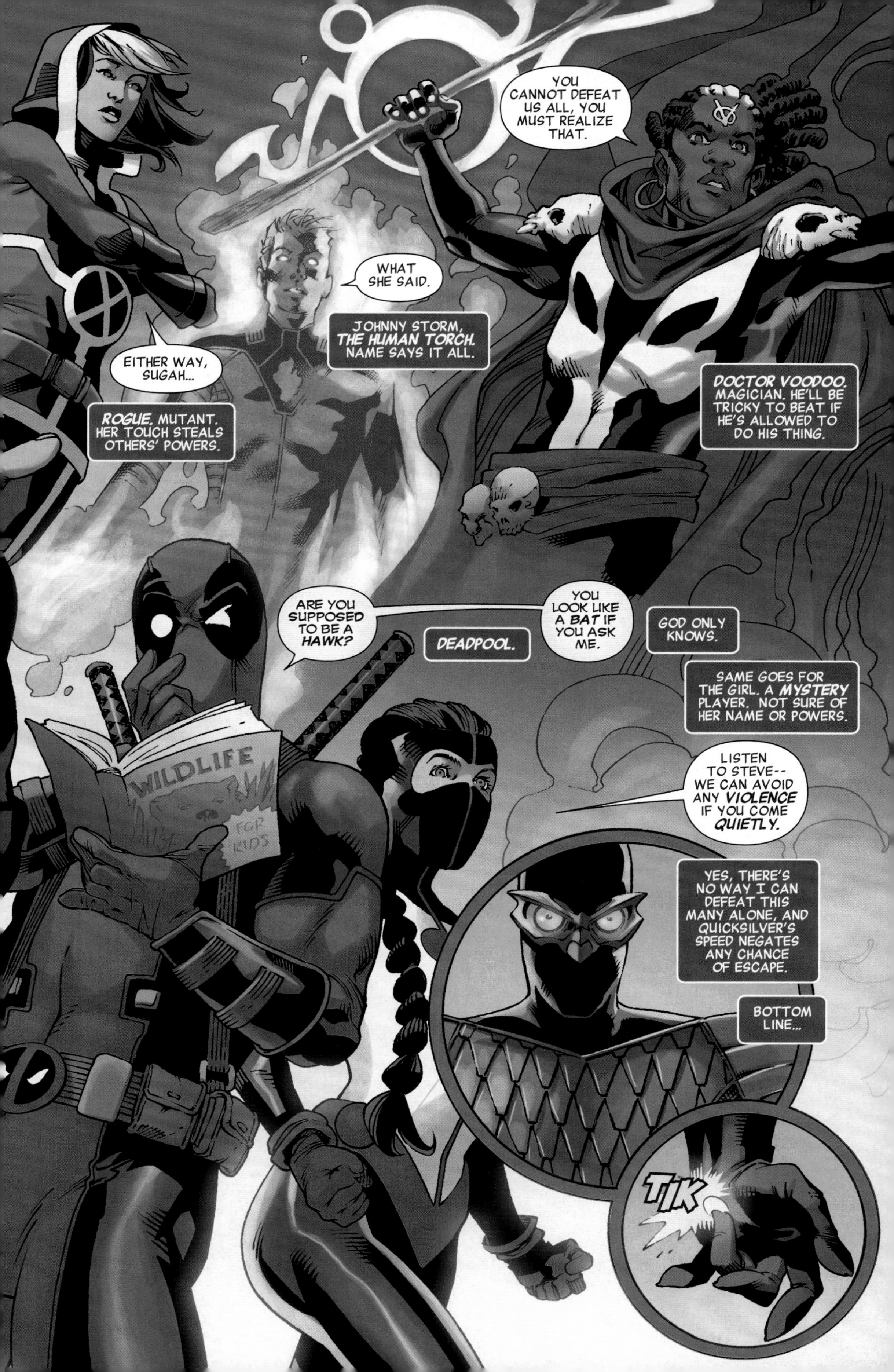
YOU CANNOT DEFEAT US ALL, YOU MUST REALIZE THAT.
WHAT SHE SAID.
JOHNNY STORM, THE HUMAN TORCH. NAME SAYS IT ALL.
EITHER WAY, SUGAH...
ROGUE. MUTANT. HER TOUCH STEALS OTHERS' POWERS.
DOCTOR VOODOO. MAGICIAN. HE'LL BE TRICKY TO BEAT IF HE'S ALLOWED TO DO HIS THING.
ARE YOU SUPPOSED TO BE A HAWK?
YOU LOOK LIKE A BAT IF YOU ASK ME.
DEADPOOL.
GOD ONLY KNOWS.
SAME GOES FOR THE GIRL. A MYSTERY PLAYER. NOT SURE OF HER NAME OR POWERS.
WILDLIFE
FOR KIDS
LISTEN TO STEVE-- WE CAN AVOID ANY VIOLENCE IF YOU COME QUIETLY.
YES, THERE'S NO WAY I CAN DEFEAT THIS MANY ALONE, AND QUICKSILVER'S SPEED NEGATES ANY CHANCE OF ESCAPE.
BOTTOM LINE...
TIK

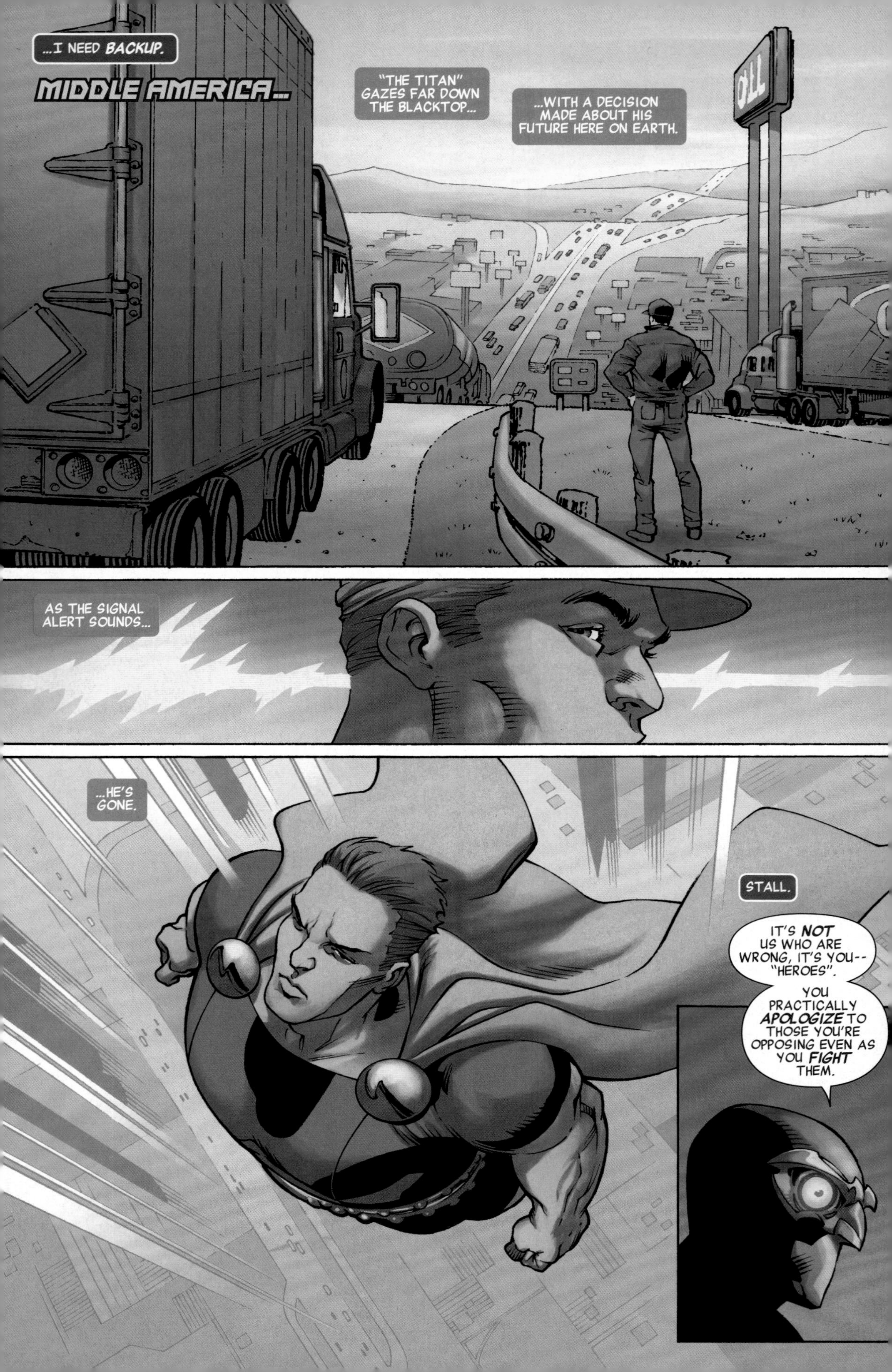
...I NEED BACKUP.
MIDDLE AMERICA...
"THE TITAN" GAZES FAR DOWN THE BLACKTOP...
...WITH A DECISION MADE ABOUT HIS FUTURE HERE ON EARTH.
AS THE SIGNAL ALERT SOUNDS...
...HE'S GONE.
STALL.
IT'S NOT US WHO ARE WRONG, IT'S YOU-- "HEROES". YOU PRACTICALLY APOLOGIZE TO THOSE YOU'RE OPPOSING EVEN AS YOU FIGHT THEM.

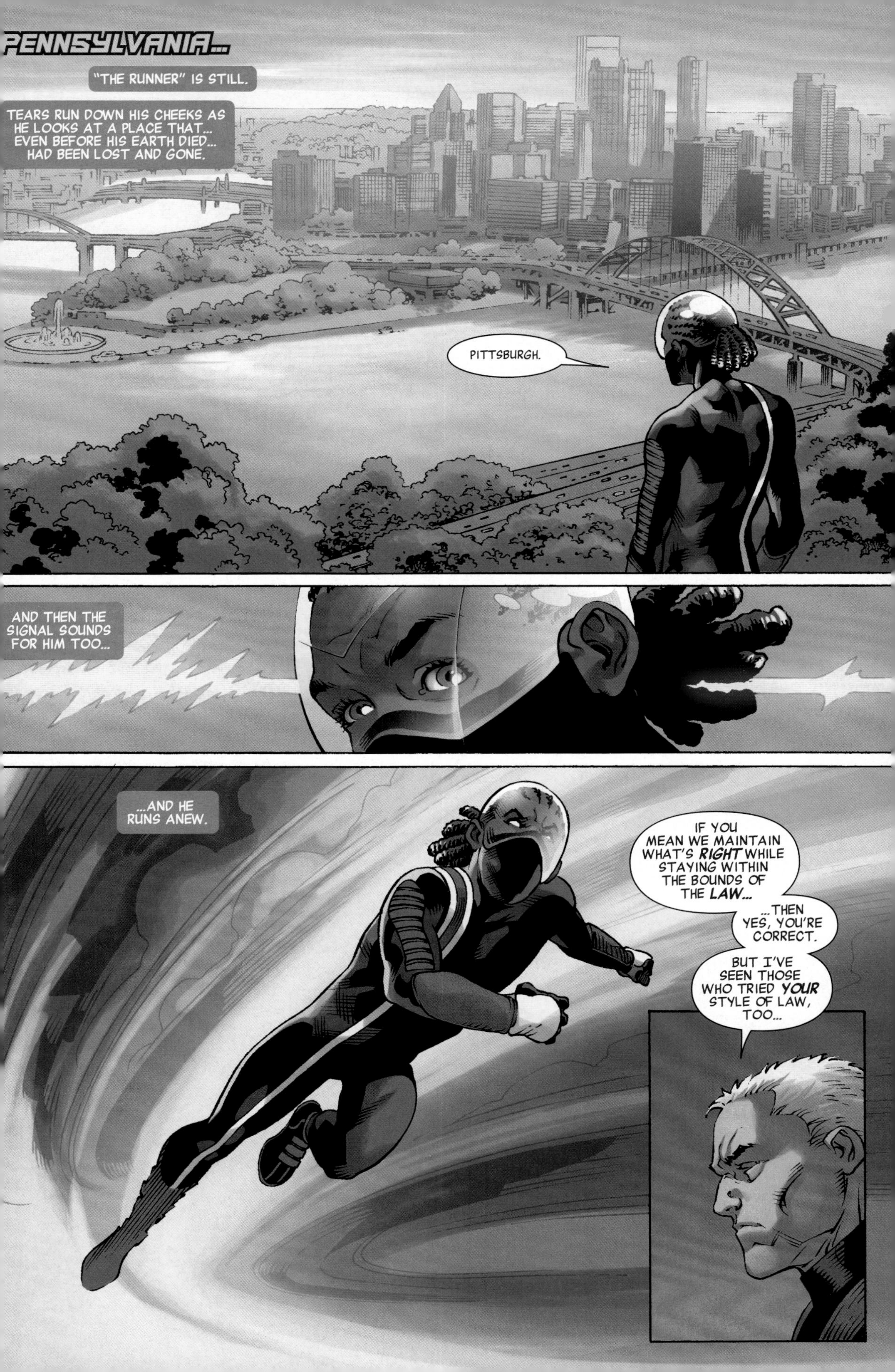
PENNSYLVANIA...
"THE RUNNER" IS STILL.
TEARS RUN DOWN HIS CHEEKS AS HE LOOKS AT A PLACE THAT... EVEN BEFORE HIS EARTH DIED... HAD BEEN LOST AND GONE.
PITTSBURGH.
AND THEN THE SIGNAL SOUNDS FOR HIM TOO...
...AND HE RUNS ANEW.
IF YOU MEAN WE MAINTAIN WHAT'S RIGHT WHILE STAYING WITHIN THE BOUNDS OF THE LAW...
...THEN YES, YOU'RE CORRECT.
BUT I'VE SEEN THOSE WHO TRIED YOUR STYLE OF LAW, TOO...

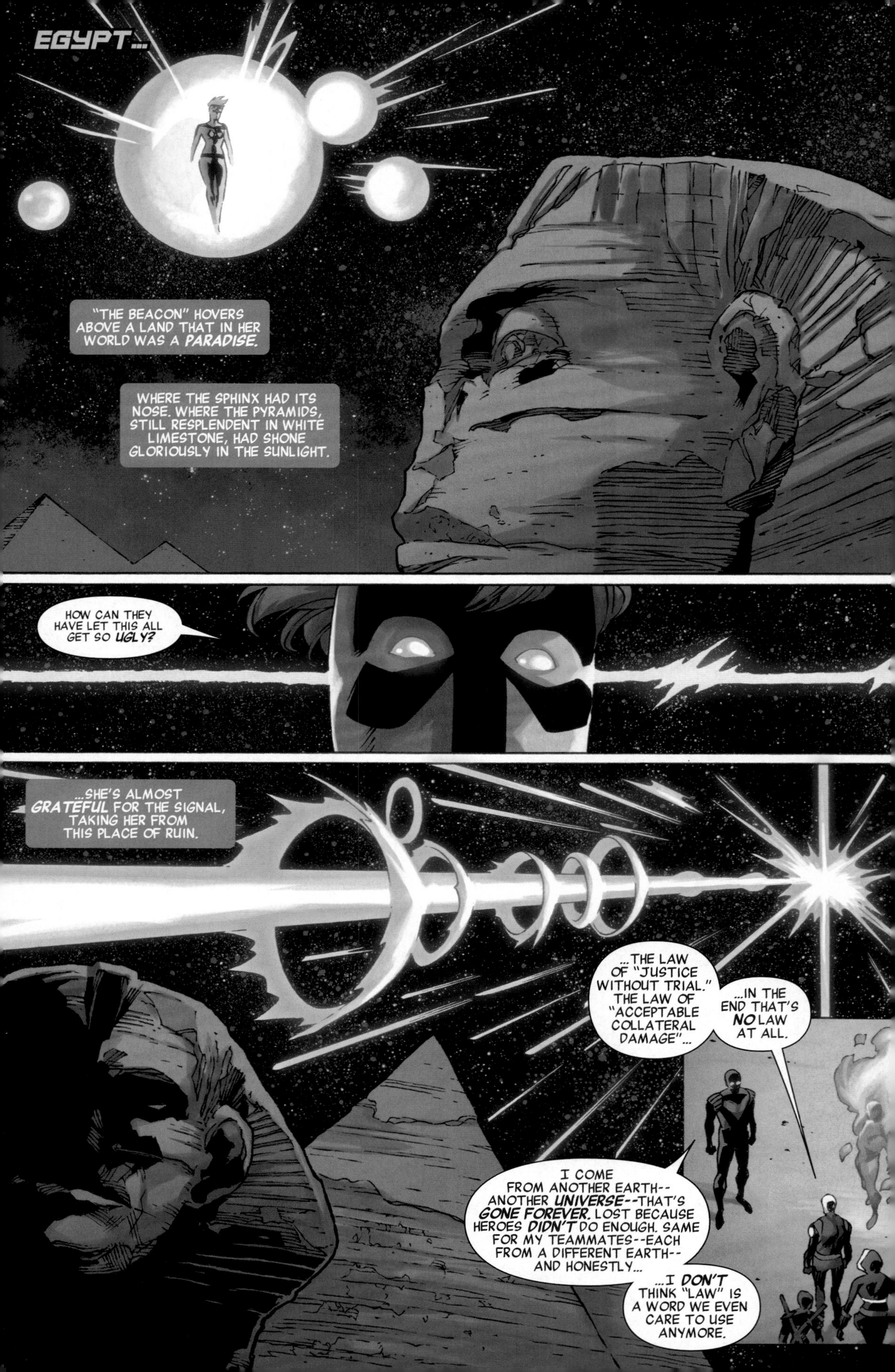
EGYPT...
"THE BEACON" HOVERS ABOVE A LAND THAT IN HER WORLD WAS A PARADISE.
WHERE THE SPHINX HAD ITS NOSE. WHERE THE PYRAMIDS, STILL RESPLENDENT IN WHITE LIMESTONE, HAD SHONE GLORIOUSLY IN THE SUNLIGHT.
HOW CAN THEY HAVE LET THIS ALL GET SO UGLY?
...SHE'S ALMOST GRATEFUL FOR THE SIGNAL, TAKING HER FROM THIS PLACE OF RUIN.
...THE LAW OF "JUSTICE WITHOUT TRIAL." THE LAW OF "ACCEPTABLE COLLATERAL DAMAGE"...
...IN THE END THAT'S NO LAW AT ALL.
I COME FROM ANOTHER EARTH--ANOTHER UNIVERSE--THAT'S GONE FOREVER. LOST BECAUSE HEROES DIDN'T DO ENOUGH. SAME FOR MY TEAMMATES--EACH FROM A DIFFERENT EARTH--AND HONESTLY...
...I DON'T THINK "LAW" IS A WORD WE EVEN CARE TO USE ANYMORE.

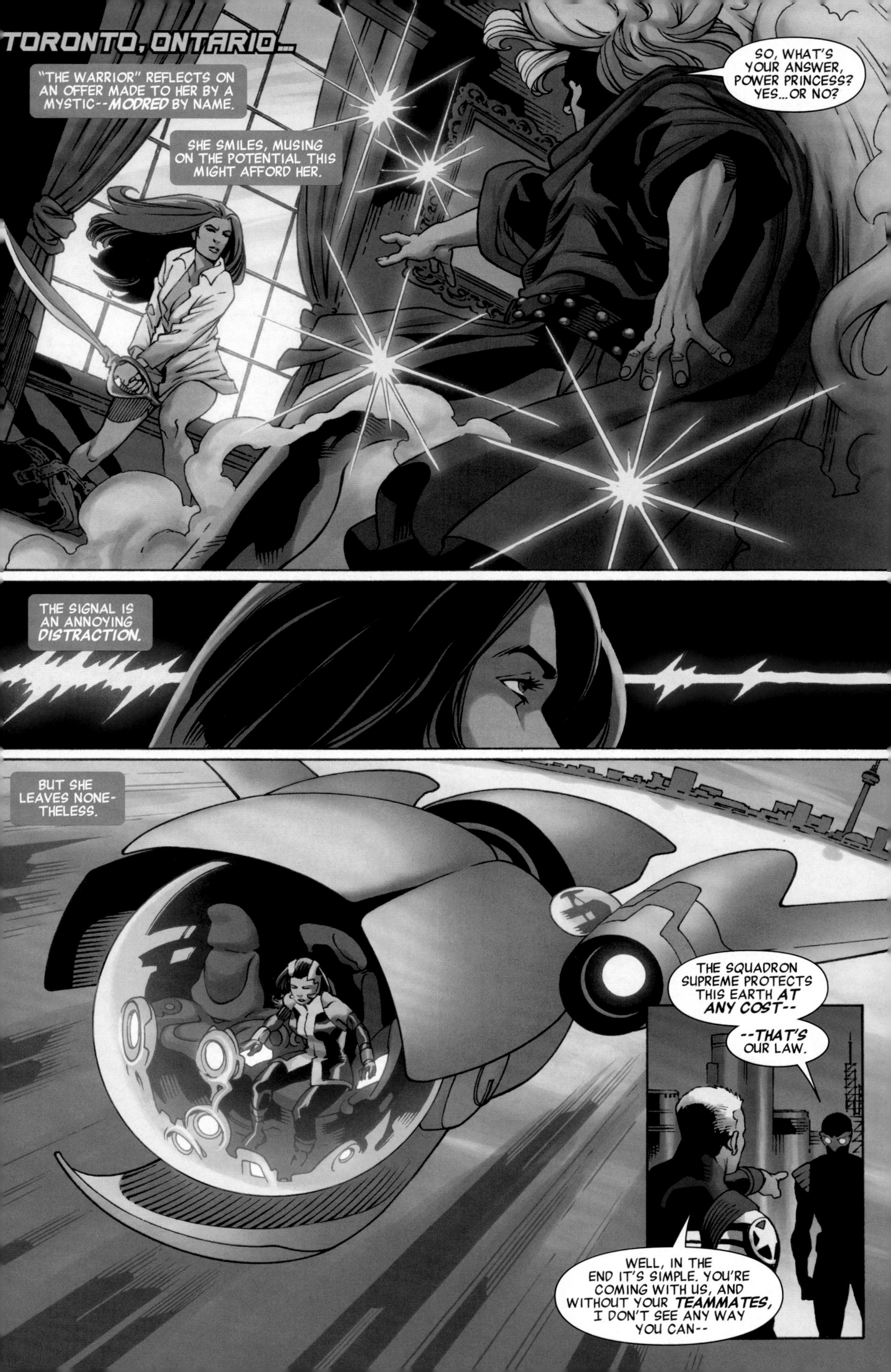
TORONTO, ONTARIO...
"THE WARRIOR" REFLECTS ON AN OFFER MADE TO HER BY A MYSTIC--MODRED BY NAME.
SHE SMILES, MUSING ON THE POTENTIAL THIS MIGHT AFFORD HER.
SO, WHAT'S YOUR ANSWER, POWER PRINCESS? YES...OR NO?
THE SIGNAL IS AN ANNOYING DISTRACTION.
BUT SHE LEAVES NONE-THELESS.
THE SQUADRON SUPREME PROTECTS THIS EARTH AT ANY COST--
--THAT'S OUR LAW.
WELL, IN THE END IT'S SIMPLE. YOU'RE COMING WITH US, AND WITHOUT YOUR TEAMMATES, I DON'T SEE ANY WAY YOU CAN--

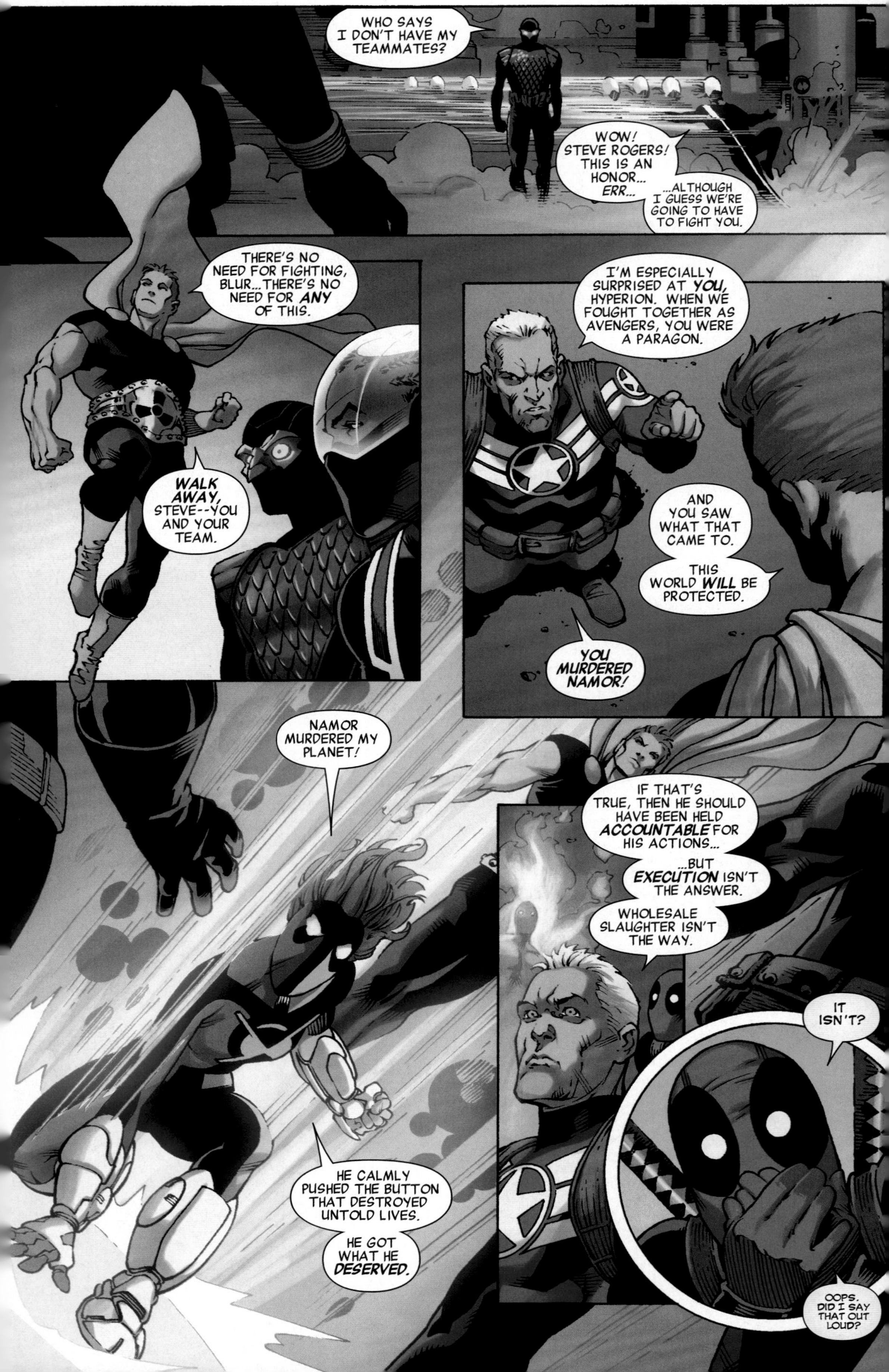
WHO SAYS I DON'T HAVE MY TEAMMATES?
WOW! STEVE ROGERS! THIS IS AN HONOR... ERR...
...ALTHOUGH I GUESS WE'RE GOING TO HAVE TO FIGHT YOU.
THERE'S NO NEED FOR FIGHTING, BLUR...THERE'S NO NEED FOR ANY OF THIS.
WALK AWAY, STEVE--YOU AND YOUR TEAM.
I'M ESPECIALLY SURPRISED AT YOU, HYPERION. WHEN WE FOUGHT TOGETHER AS AVENGERS, YOU WERE A PARAGON.
AND YOU SAW WHAT THAT CAME TO.
THIS WORLD WILL BE PROTECTED.
YOU MURDERED NAMOR!
NAMOR MURDERED MY PLANET!
HE CALMLY PUSHED THE BUTTON THAT DESTROYED UNTOLD LIVES.
HE GOT WHAT HE DESERVED.
IF THAT'S TRUE, THEN HE SHOULD HAVE BEEN HELD ACCOUNTABLE FOR HIS ACTIONS...
...BUT EXECUTION ISN'T THE ANSWER.
WHOLESALE SLAUGHTER ISN'T THE WAY.
IT ISN'T?
OOPS. DID I SAY THAT OUT LOUD?

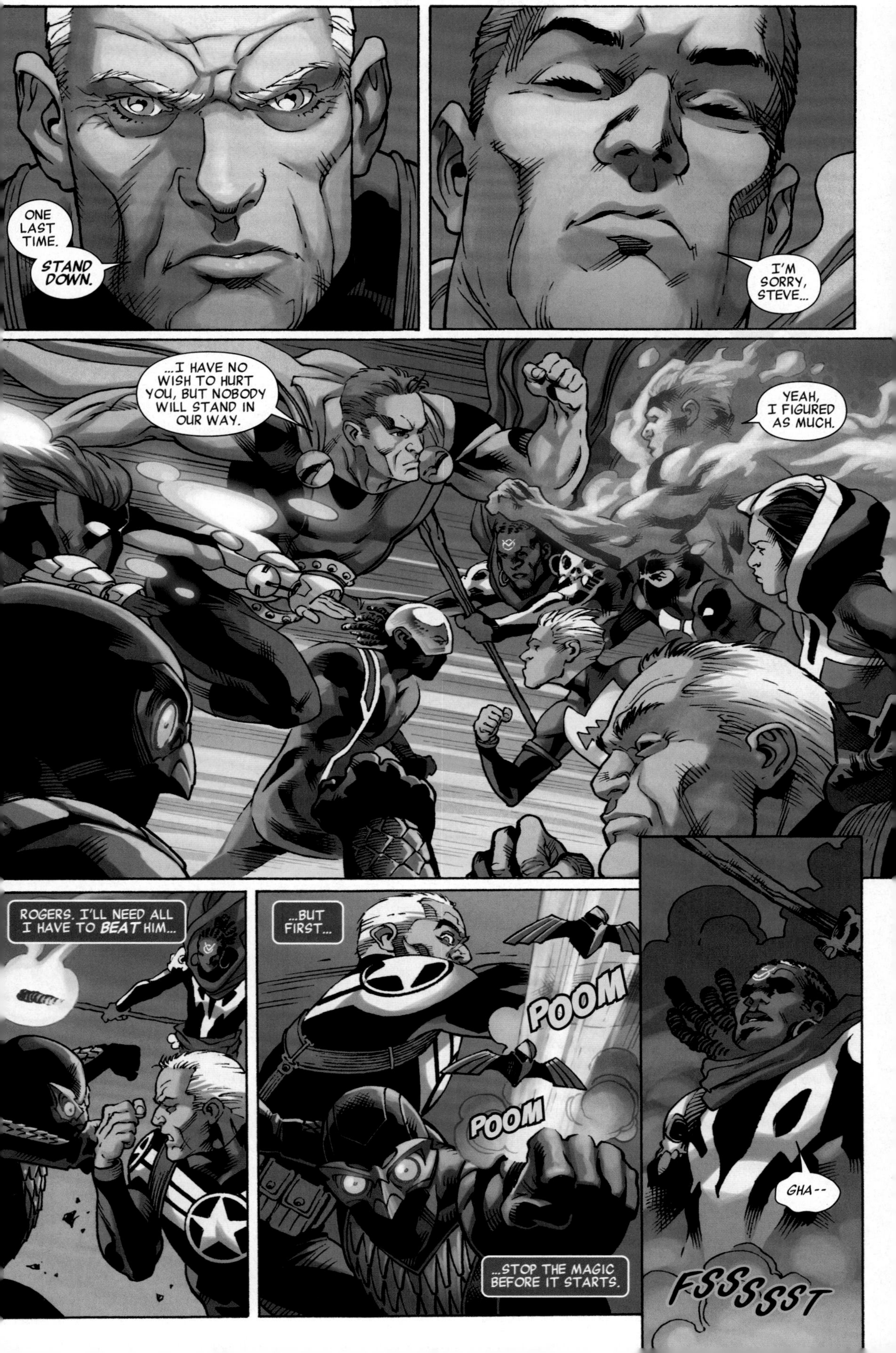
ONE LAST TIME.
STAND DOWN.
I'M SORRY, STEVE...
...I HAVE NO WISH TO HURT YOU, BUT NOBODY WILL STAND IN OUR WAY.
YEAH, I FIGURED AS MUCH.
ROGERS. I'LL NEED ALL I HAVE TO BEAT HIM...
...BUT FIRST...
POOM
POOM
...STOP THE MAGIC BEFORE IT STARTS.
GHA--
FSSSSST

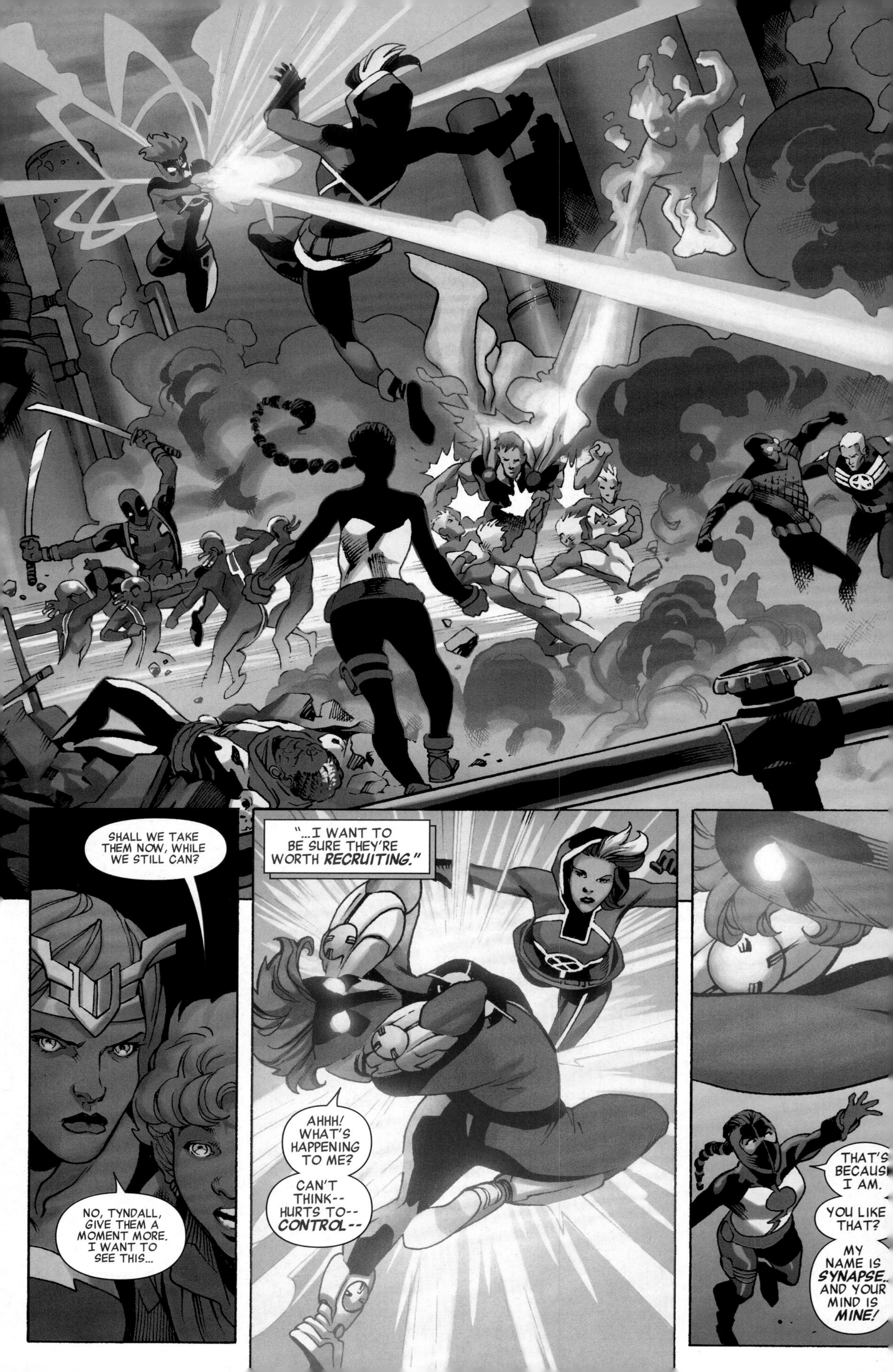
SHALL WE TAKE THEM NOW, WHILE WE STILL CAN?
NO, TYNDALL, GIVE THEM A MOMENT MORE. I WANT TO SEE THIS...
"...I WANT TO BE SURE THEY'RE WORTH RECRUITING."
AHHH! WHAT'S HAPPENING TO ME?
CAN'T THINK-- HURTS TO-- CONTROL--
THAT'S BECAUS I AM.
YOU LIKE THAT?
MY NAME IS SYNAPSE.. AND YOUR MIND IS MINE!

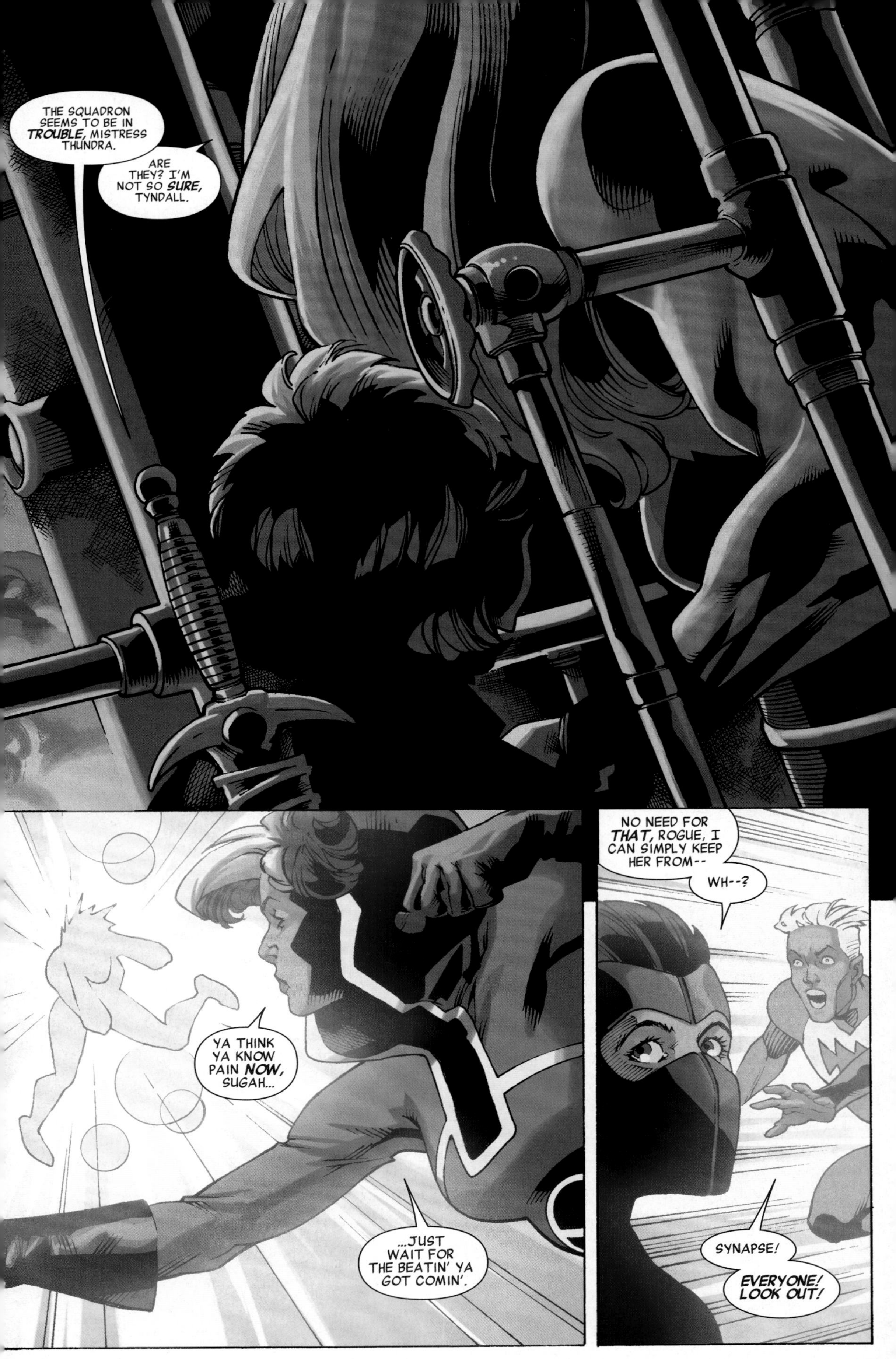
THE SQUADRON SEEMS TO BE IN TROUBLE, MISTRESS THUNDRA.
ARE THEY? I'M NOT SO SURE, TYNDALL.
YA THINK YA KNOW PAIN NOW, SUGAH...
...JUST WAIT FOR THE BEATIN' YA GOT COMIN'.
NO NEED FOR THAT, ROGUE, I CAN SIMPLY KEEP HER FROM--
WH--?
SYNAPSE!
EVERYONE! LOOK OUT!

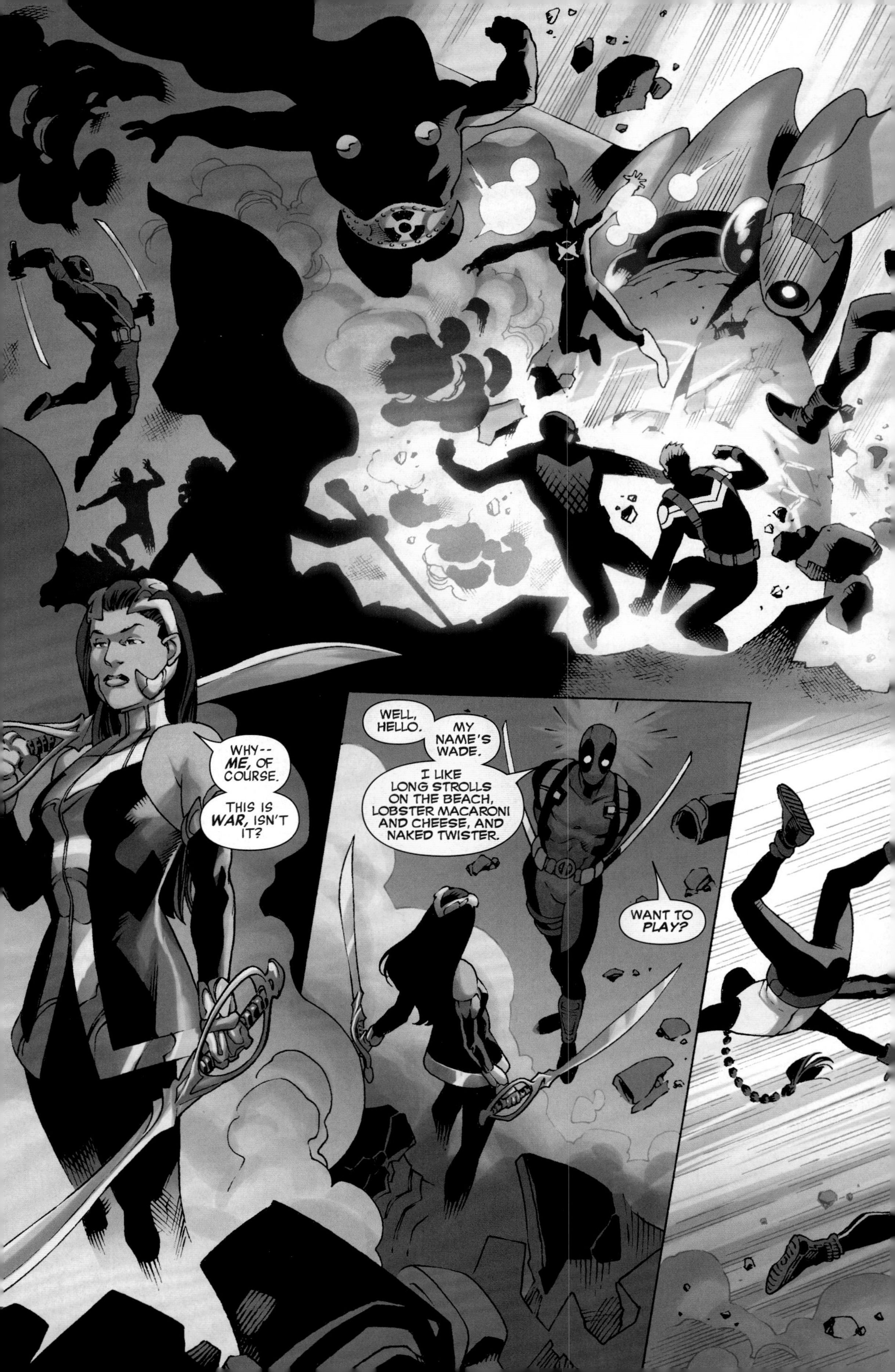
WHY-- ME, OF COURSE.
THIS IS WAR, ISN'T IT?
WELL, HELLO.
MY NAME'S WADE.
I LIKE LONG STROLLS ON THE BEACH, LOBSTER MACARONI AND CHEESE, AND NAKED TWISTER.
WANT TO PLAY?

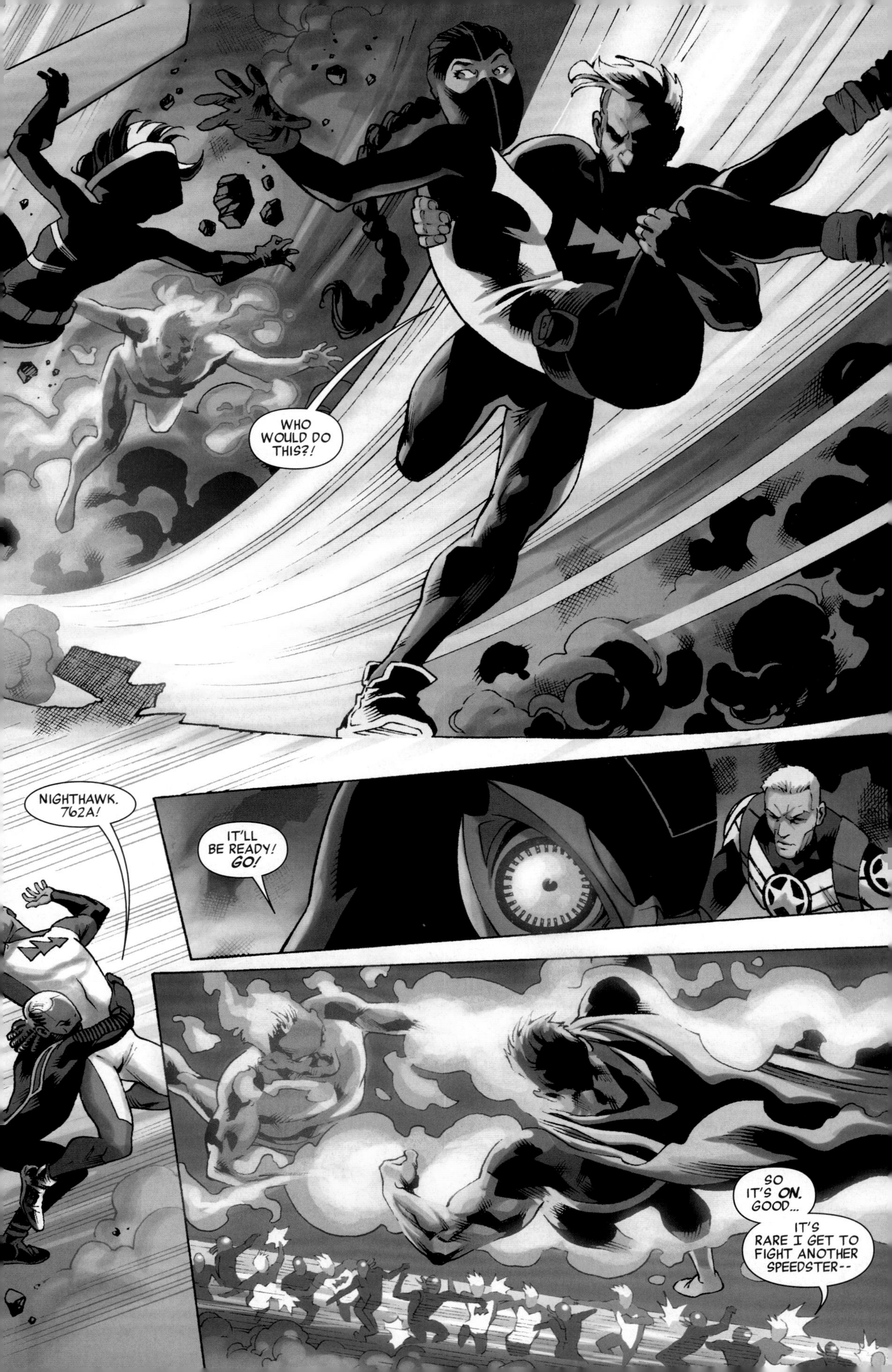
WHO WOULD DO THIS?!
NIGHTHAWK. 762A!
IT'LL BE READY! GO!
SO IT'S ON. GOOD...
IT'S RARE I GET TO FIGHT ANOTHER SPEEDSTER--

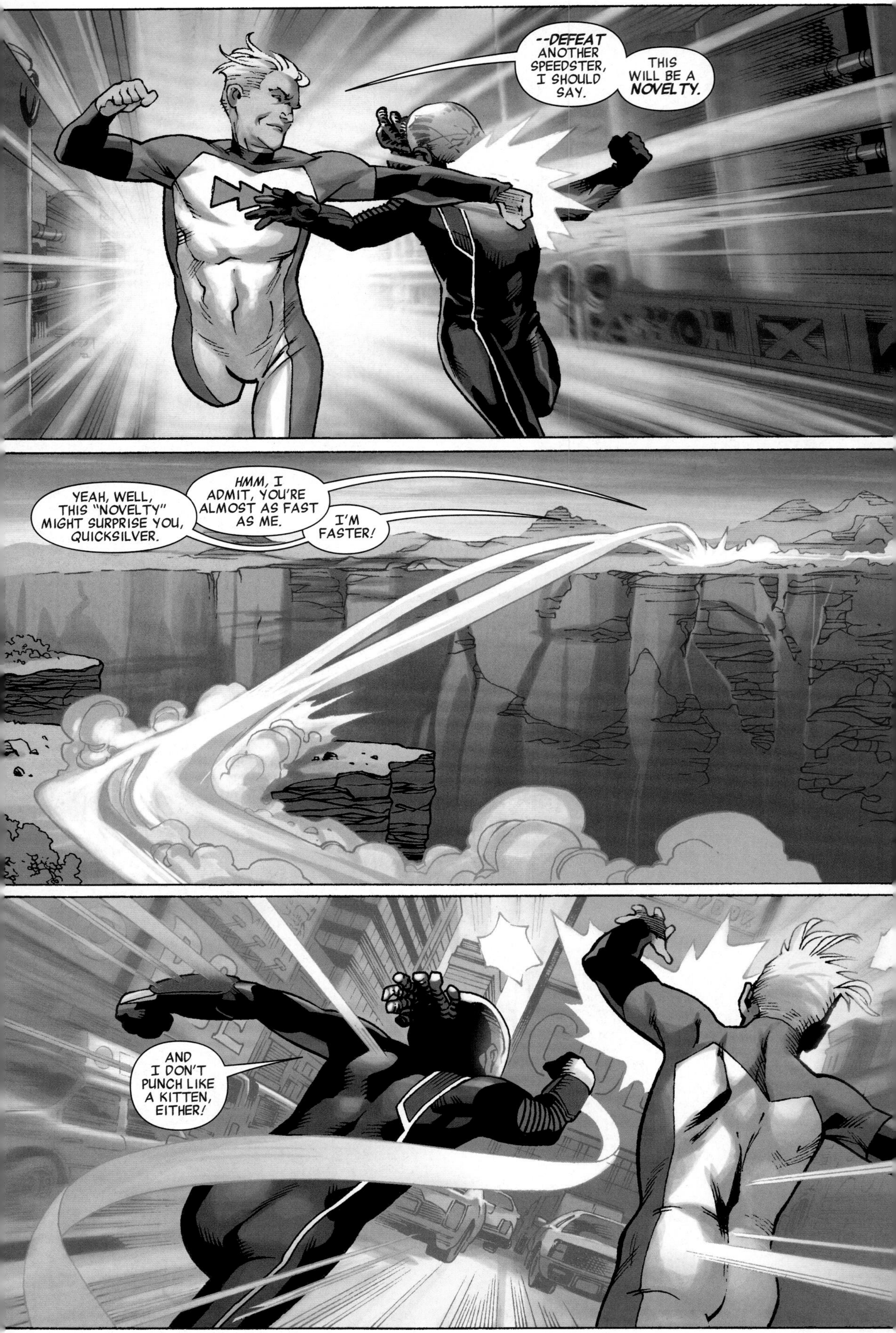
--DEFEAT ANOTHER SPEEDSTER, I SHOULD SAY.
THIS WILL BE A NOVELTY.
YEAH, WELL, THIS "NOVELTY" MIGHT SURPRISE YOU, QUICKSILVER.
HMM, I ADMIT, YOU'RE ALMOST AS FAST AS ME.
I'M FASTER!
AND I DON'T PUNCH LIKE A KITTEN, EITHER!

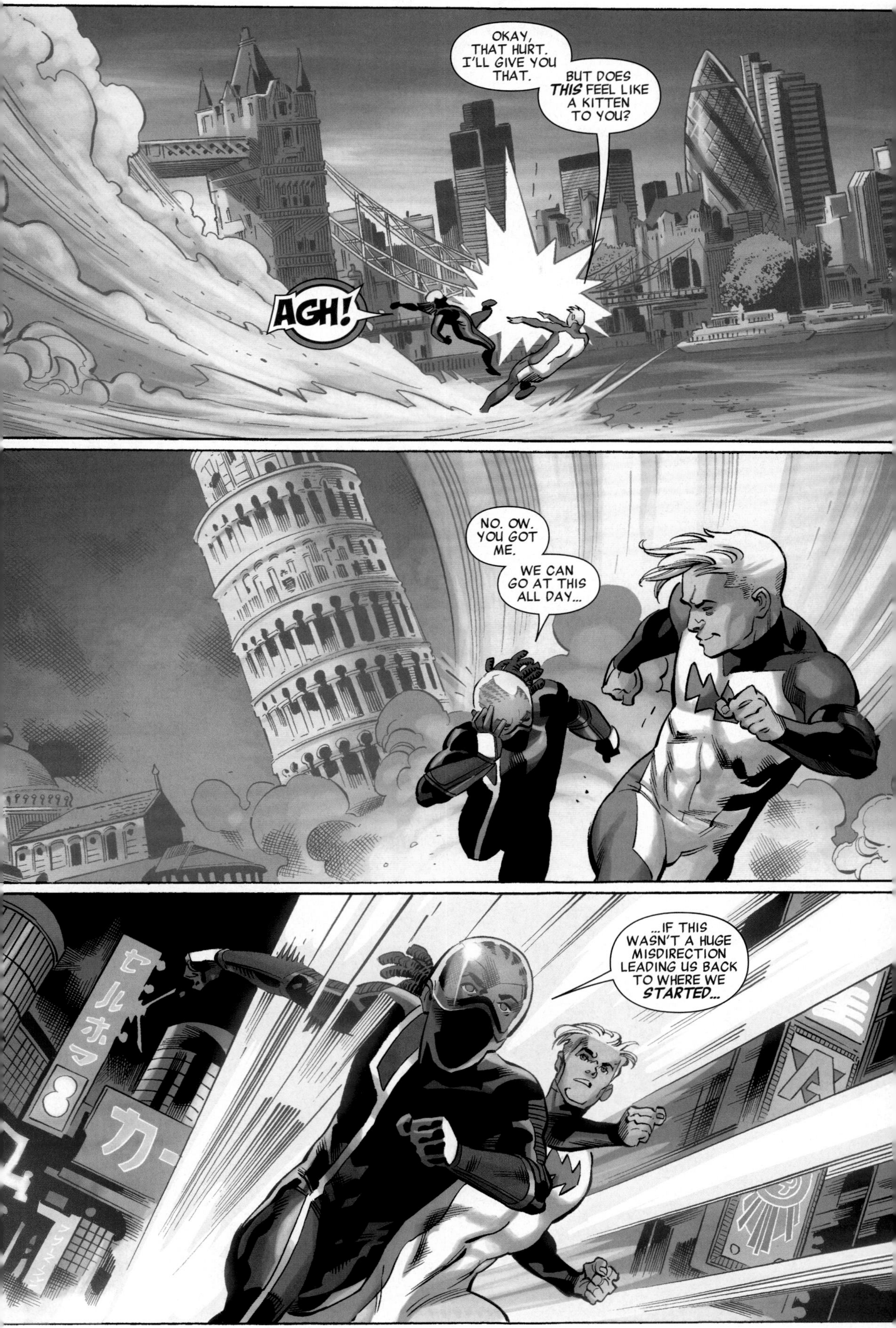
OKAY, THAT HURT. I'LL GIVE YOU THAT.
BUT DOES THIS FEEL LIKE A KITTEN TO YOU?
AGH!
NO. OW. YOU GOT ME.
WE CAN GO AT THIS ALL DAY...
...IF THIS WASN'T A HUGE MISDIRECTION LEADING US BACK TO WHERE WE STARTED...

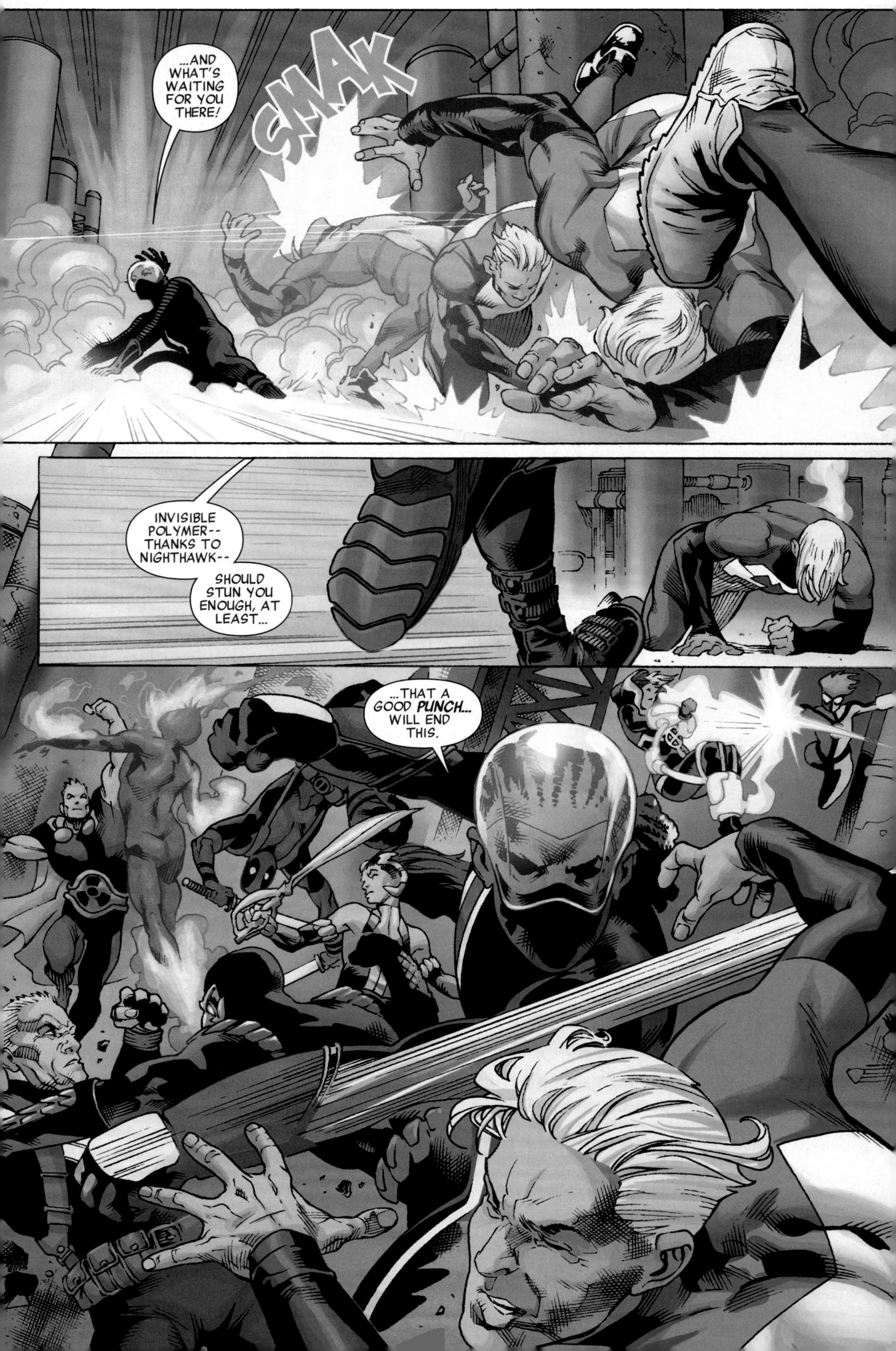
...AND WHAT'S WAITING FOR YOU THERE!
SMAK
INVISIBLE POLYMER--THANKS TO NIGHTHAWK--
SHOULD STUN YOU ENOUGH, AT LEAST...
...THAT A GOOD PUNCH... WILL END THIS.

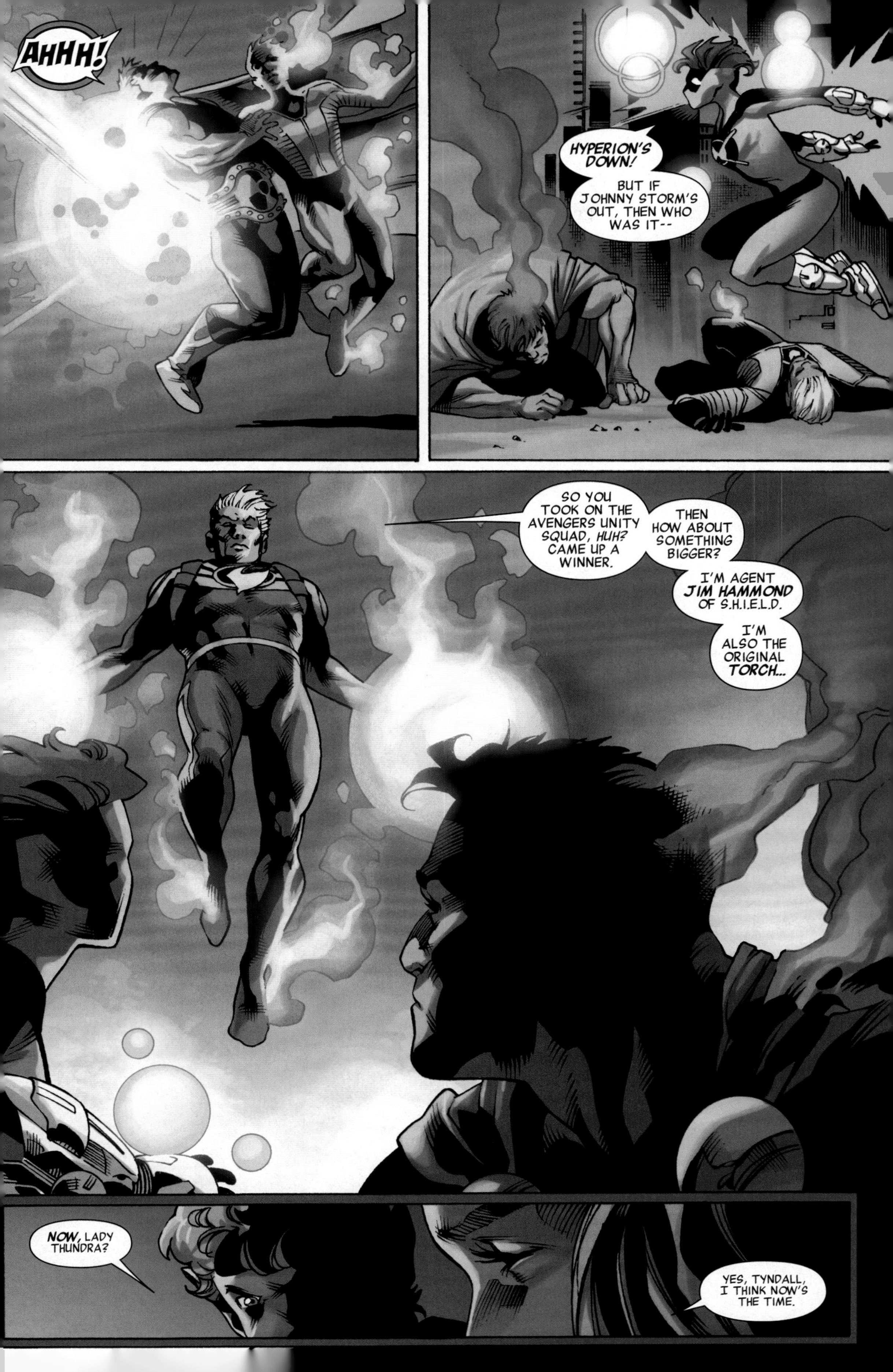

AHHH!
HYPERION'S DOWN!
BUT IF JOHNNY STORM'S OUT, THEN WHO WAS IT--
SO YOU TOOK ON THE AVENGERS UNITY SQUAD, HUH? CAME UP A WINNER.
THEN HOW ABOUT SOMETHING BIGGER?
I'M AGENT JIM HAMMOND OF S.H.I.E.L.D.
I'M ALSO THE ORIGINAL TORCH...
NOW, LADY THUNDRA?
YES, TYNDALL, I THINK NOW'S THE TIME.

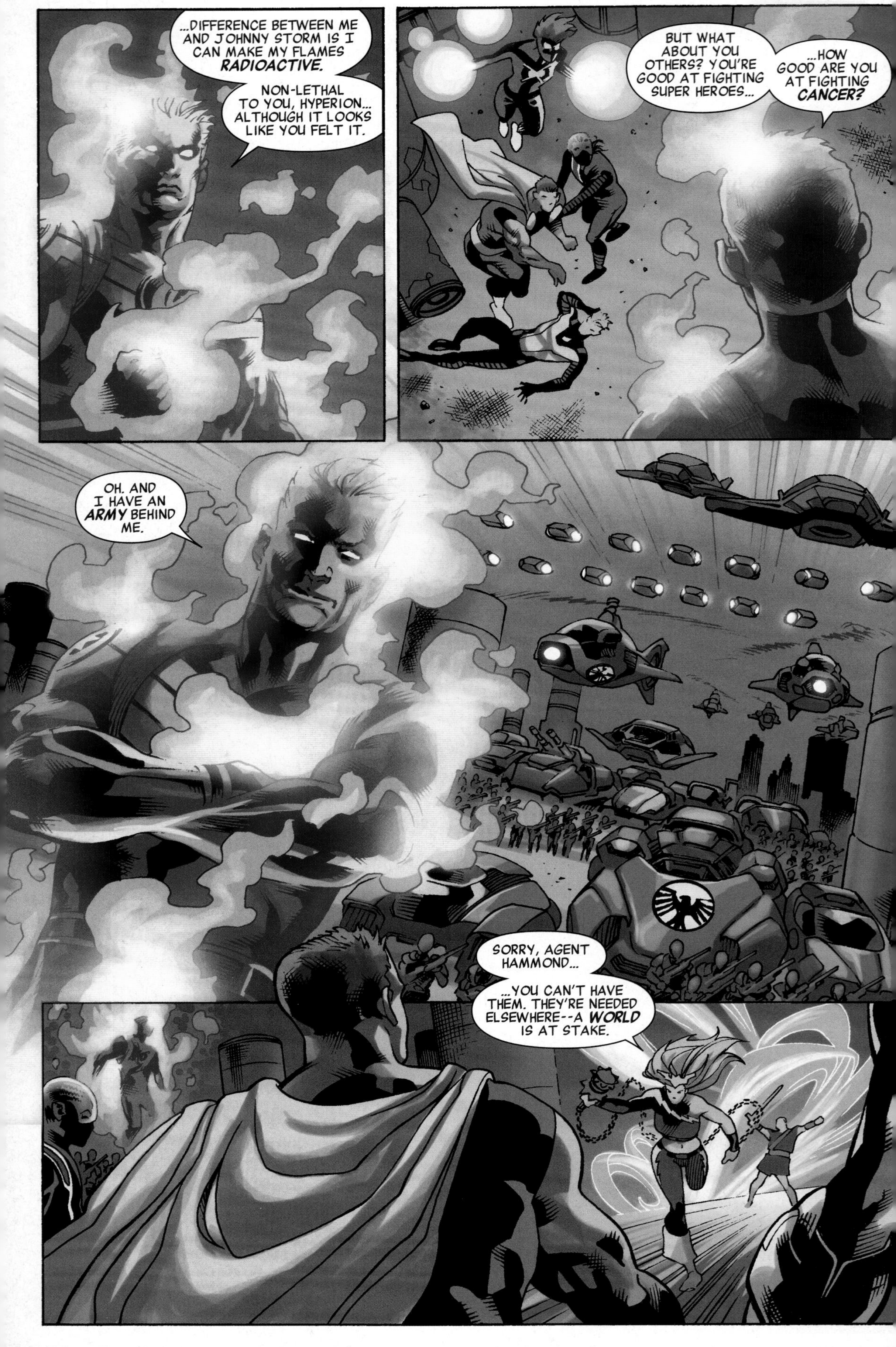
...DIFFERENCE BETWEEN ME AND JOHNNY STORM IS I CAN MAKE MY FLAMES RADIOACTIVE.
NON-LETHAL TO YOU, HYPERION... ALTHOUGH IT LOOKS LIKE YOU FELT IT.
BUT WHAT ABOUT YOU OTHERS? YOU'RE GOOD AT FIGHTING SUPER HEROES...
...HOW GOOD ARE YOU AT FIGHTING CANCER?
OH. AND I HAVE AN ARMY BEHIND ME.
SORRY, AGENT HAMMOND...
...YOU CAN'T HAVE THEM. THEY'RE NEEDED ELSEWHERE--A WORLD IS AT STAKE.

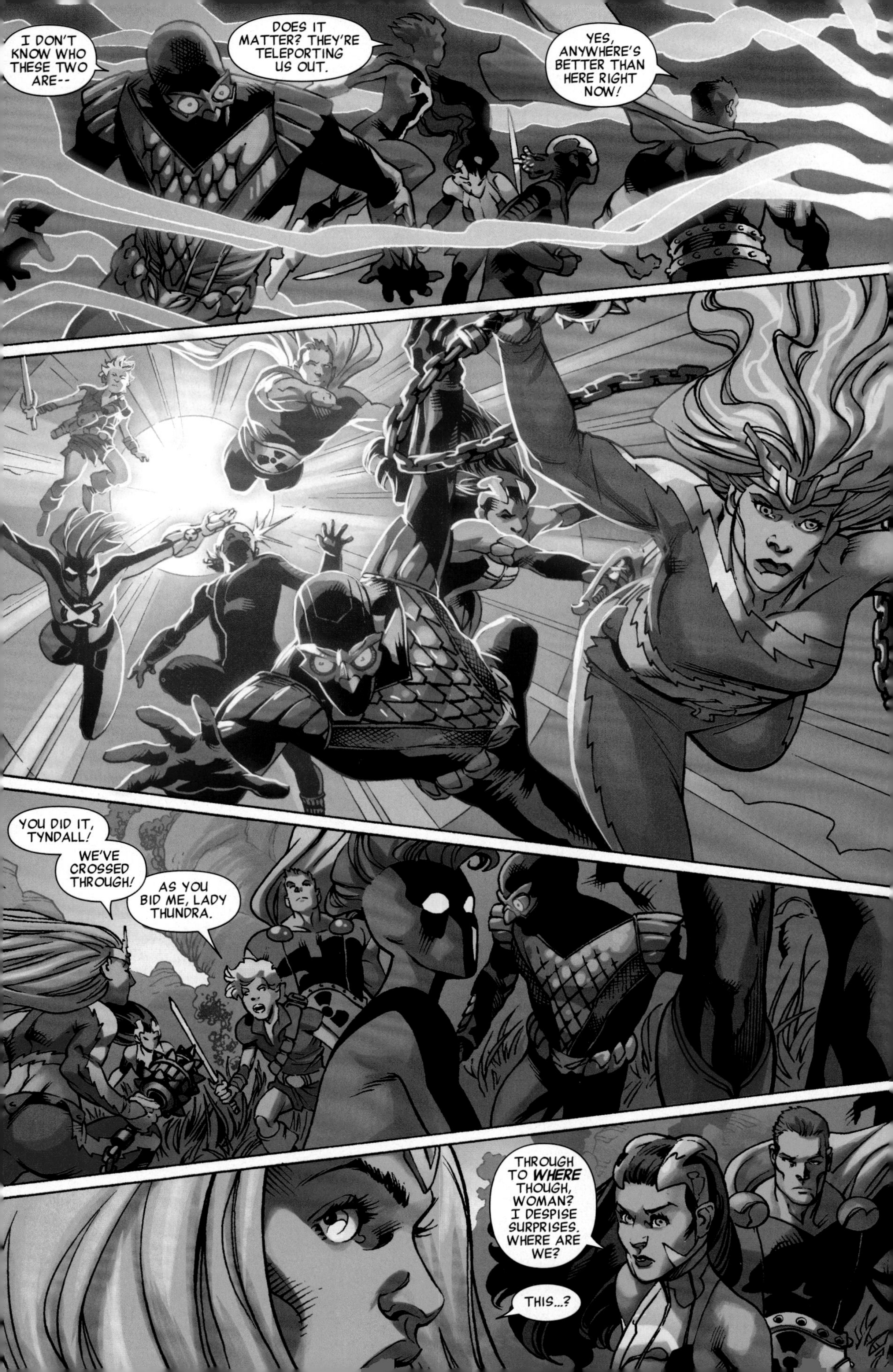
I DON'T KNOW WHO THESE TWO ARE--
DOES IT MATTER? THEY'RE TELEPORTING US OUT.
YES, ANYWHERE'S BETTER THAN HERE RIGHT NOW!
YOU DID IT, TYNDALL!
WE'VE CROSSED THROUGH!
AS YOU BID ME, LADY THUNDRA.
THROUGH TO *WHERE* THOUGH, WOMAN? I DESPISE SURPRISES. WHERE ARE WE?
THIS...?

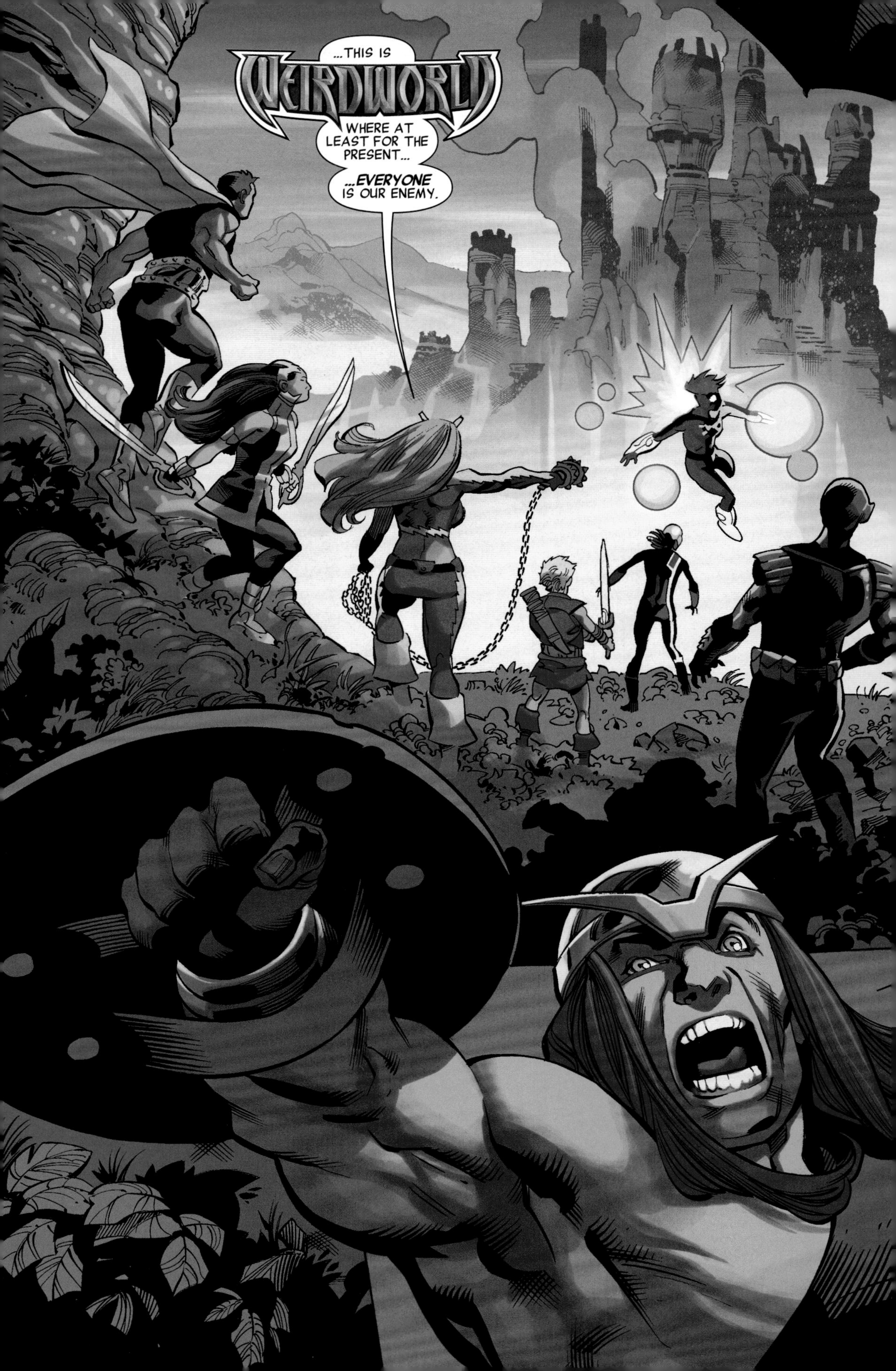
...THIS IS
WEIRDWORLD
WHERE AT LEAST FOR THE PRESENT...
...EVERYONE IS OUR ENEMY.

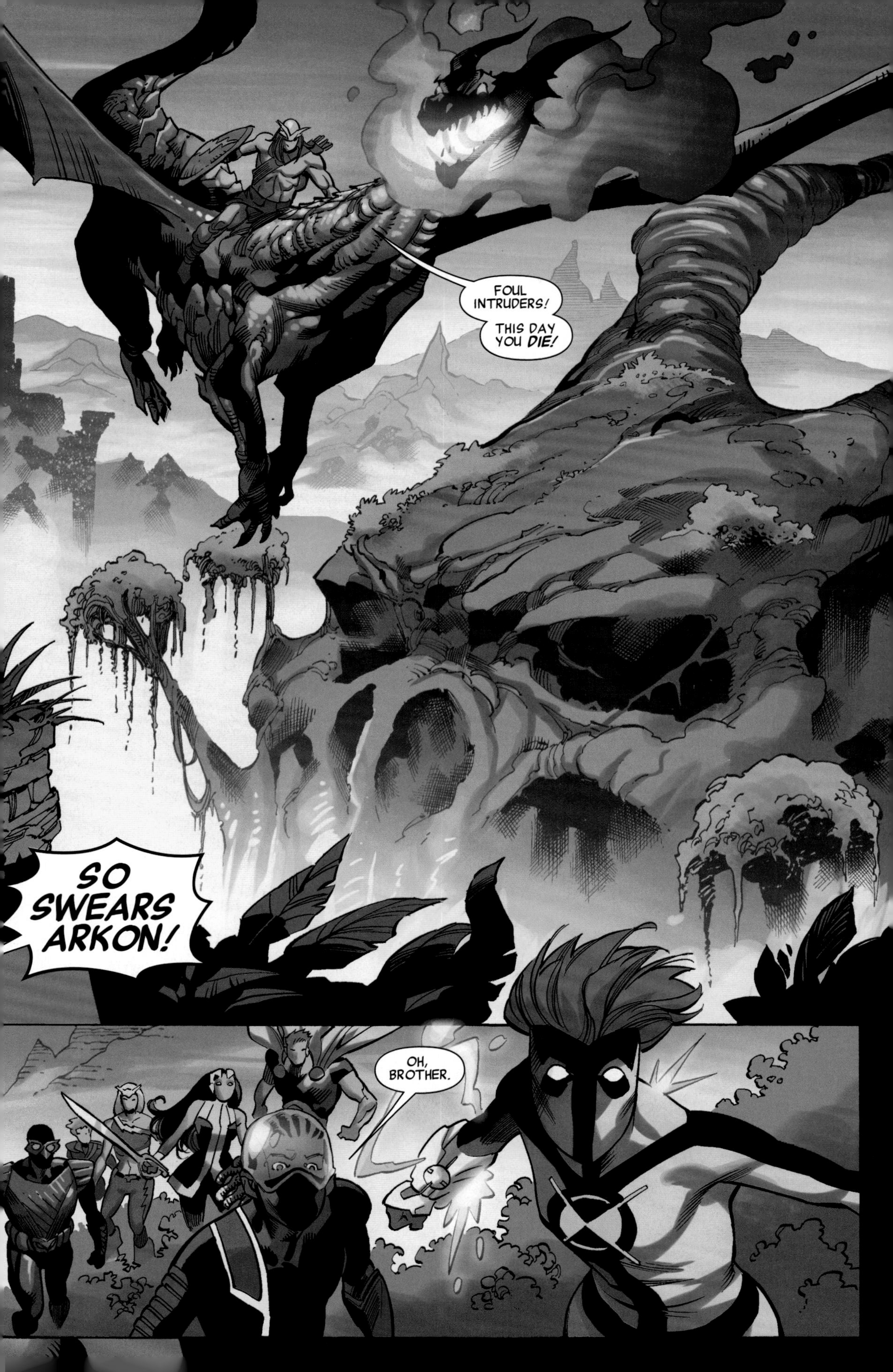
FOUL INTRUDERS!
THIS DAY YOU DIE!
SO SWEARS ARKON!
OH, BROTHER.

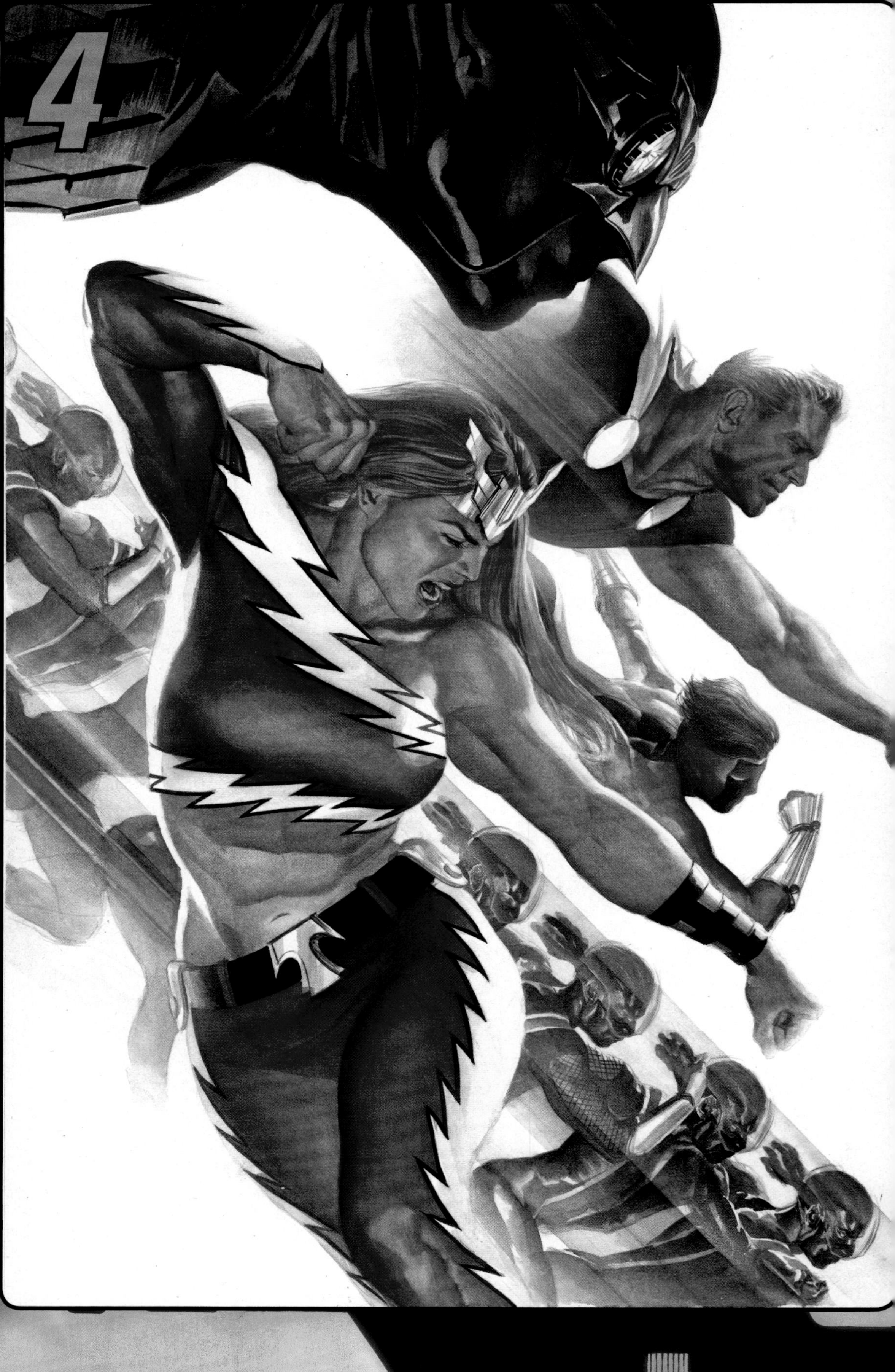
4

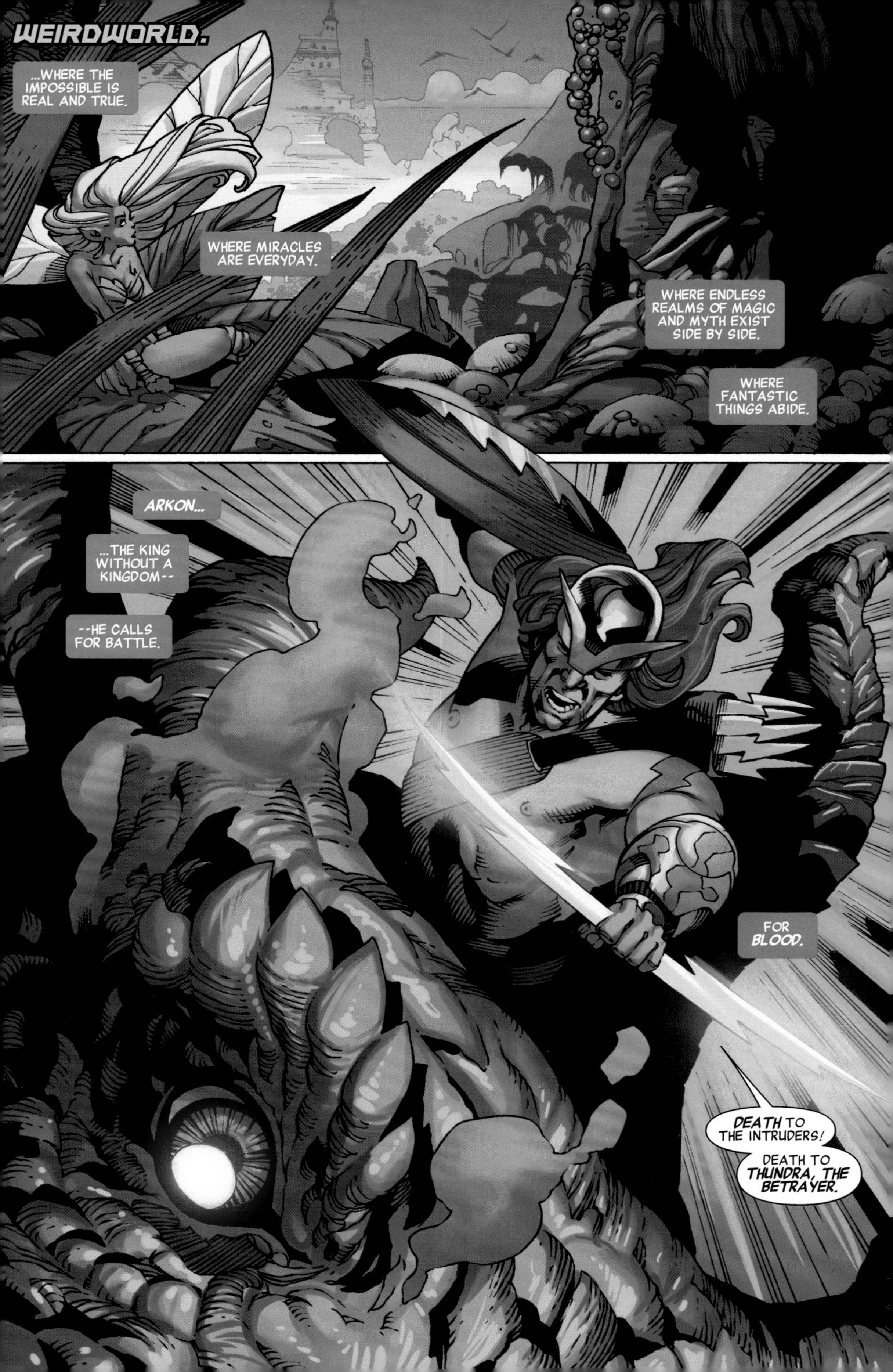
WEIRDWORLD.
...WHERE THE IMPOSSIBLE IS REAL AND TRUE.
WHERE MIRACLES ARE EVERYDAY.
WHERE ENDLESS REALMS OF MAGIC AND MYTH EXIST SIDE BY SIDE.
WHERE FANTASTIC THINGS ABIDE.
ARKON...
...THE KING WITHOUT A KINGDOM--
--HE CALLS FOR BATTLE.
FOR BLOOD.
DEATH TO THE INTRUDERS!
DEATH TO THUNDRA, THE BETRAYER.

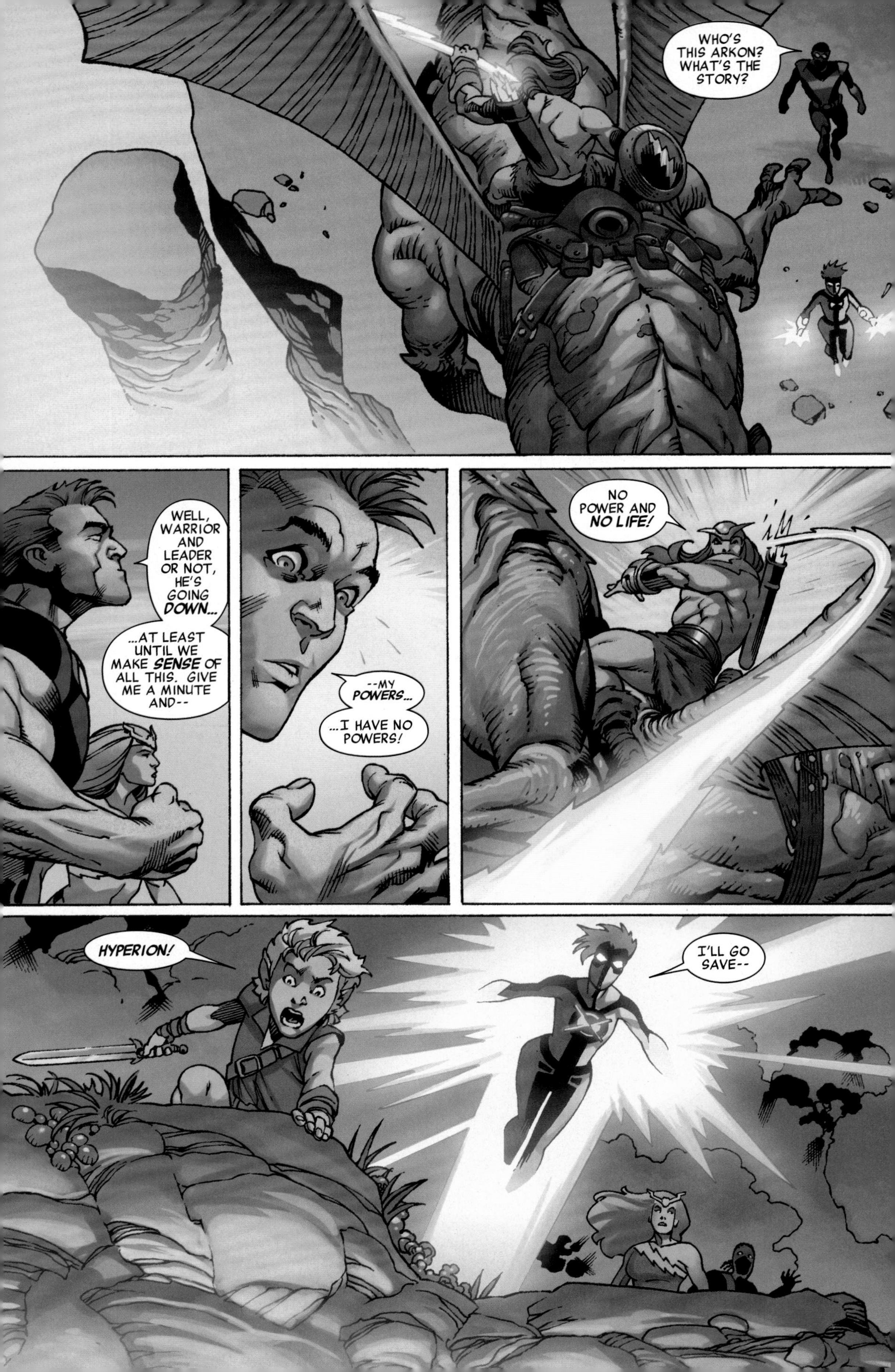
WHO'S THIS ARKON? WHAT'S THE STORY?
WELL, WARRIOR AND LEADER OR NOT, HE'S GOING DOWN...
...AT LEAST UNTIL WE MAKE SENSE OF ALL THIS. GIVE ME A MINUTE AND--
--MY POWERS...
...I HAVE NO POWERS!
NO POWER AND NO LIFE!
HYPERION!
I'LL GO SAVE--

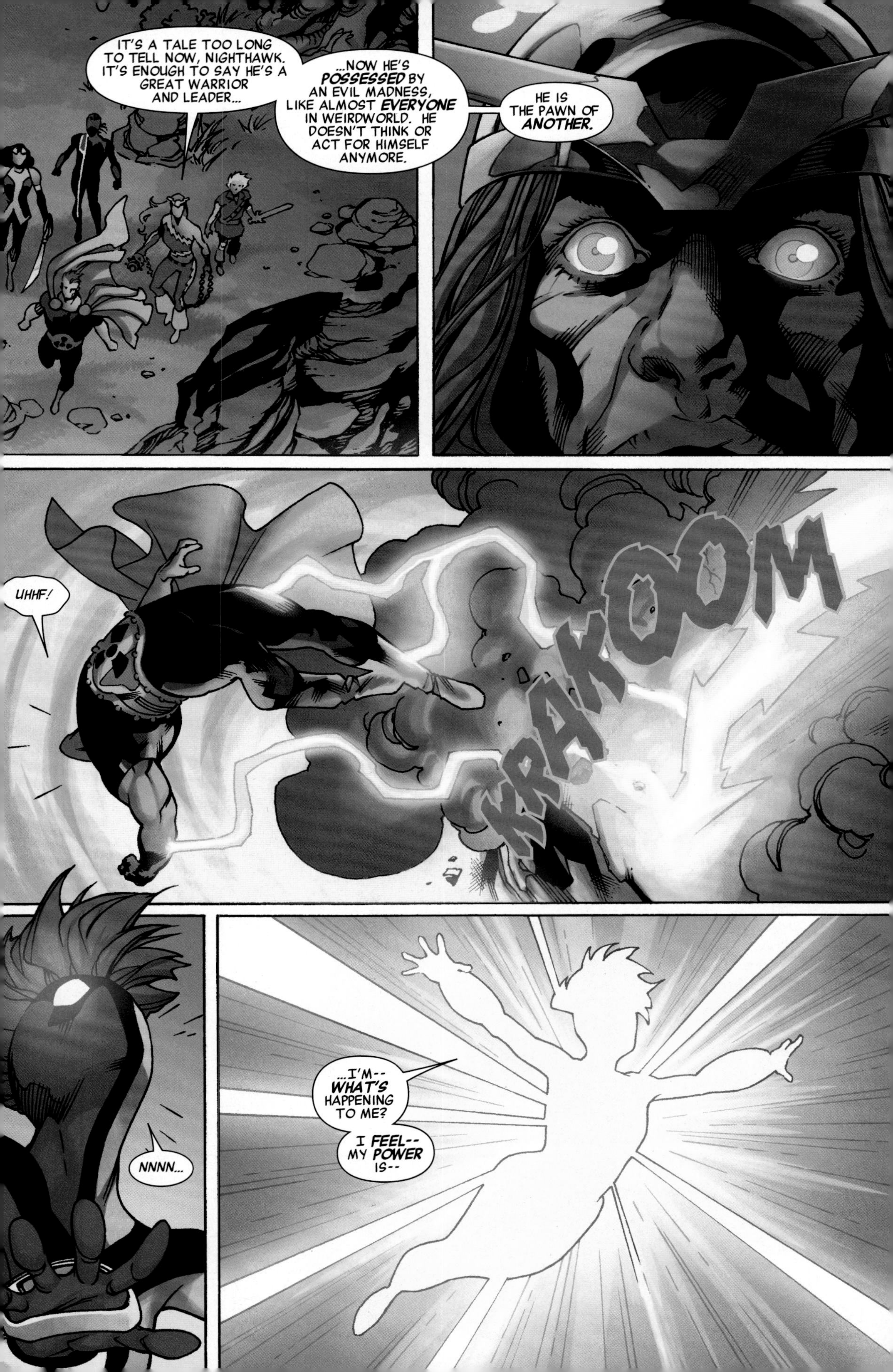
IT'S A TALE TOO LONG TO TELL NOW, NIGHTHAWK. IT'S ENOUGH TO SAY HE'S A GREAT WARRIOR AND LEADER...
...NOW HE'S POSSESSED BY AN EVIL MADNESS, LIKE ALMOST EVERYONE IN WEIRDWORLD. HE DOESN'T THINK OR ACT FOR HIMSELF ANYMORE.
HE IS THE PAWN OF ANOTHER.
UHHF!
KRAKOOM
NNNN...
...I'M-- WHAT'S HAPPENING TO ME?
I FEEL-- MY POWER IS--

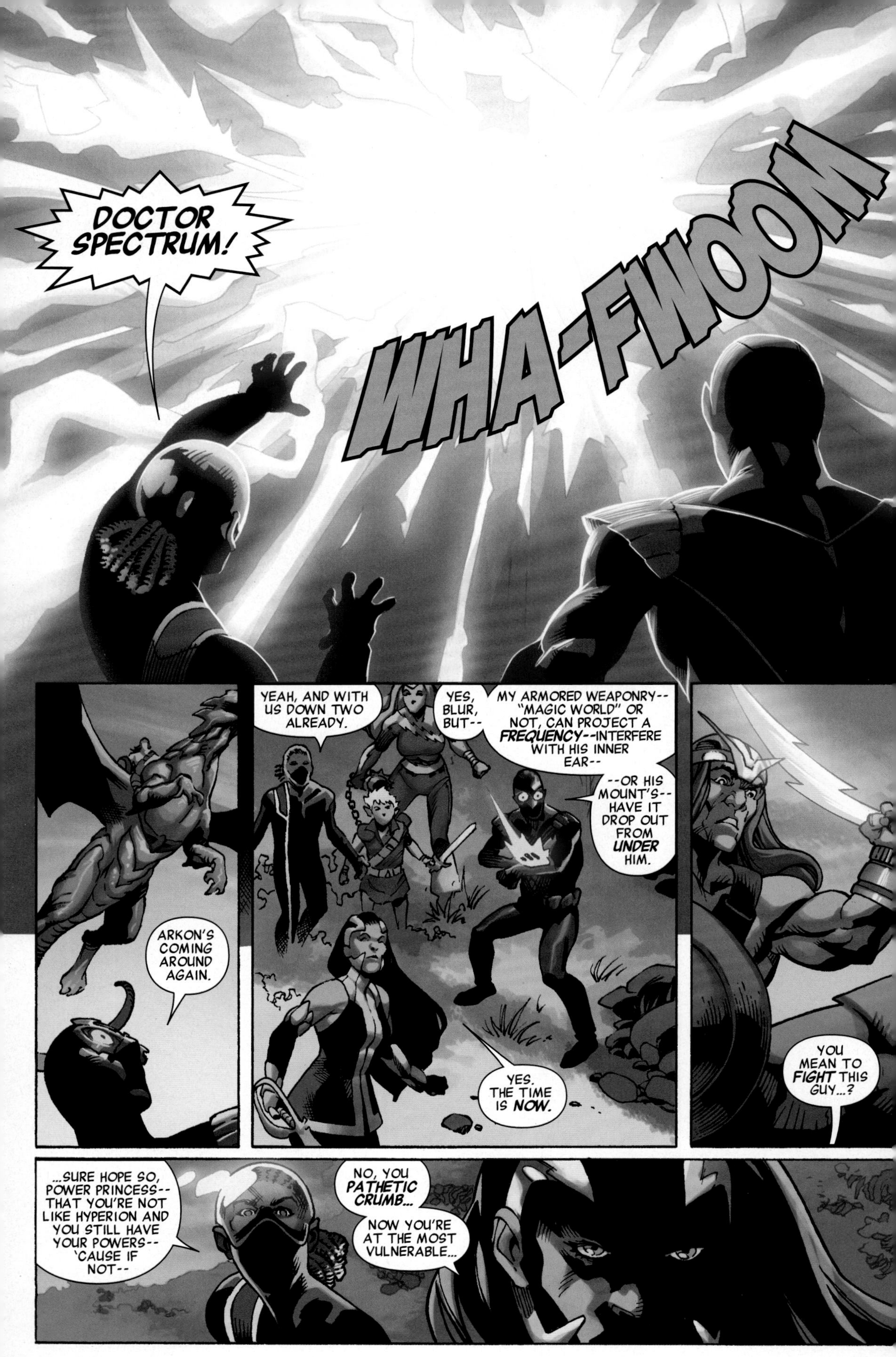
DOCTOR SPECTRUM!
WHA-FWOOM
ARKON'S COMING AROUND AGAIN.
YEAH, AND WITH US DOWN TWO ALREADY.
YES, BLUR, BUT--
MY ARMORED WEAPONRY-- "MAGIC WORLD" OR NOT, CAN PROJECT A FREQUENCY--INTERFERE WITH HIS INNER EAR--
--OR HIS MOUNT'S--HAVE IT DROP OUT FROM UNDER HIM.
YES. THE TIME IS NOW.
YOU MEAN TO FIGHT THIS GUY...?
...SURE HOPE SO, POWER PRINCESS--THAT YOU'RE NOT LIKE HYPERION AND YOU STILL HAVE YOUR POWERS--'CAUSE IF NOT--
NO, YOU PATHETIC CRUMB...
NOW YOU'RE AT THE MOST VULNERABLE...

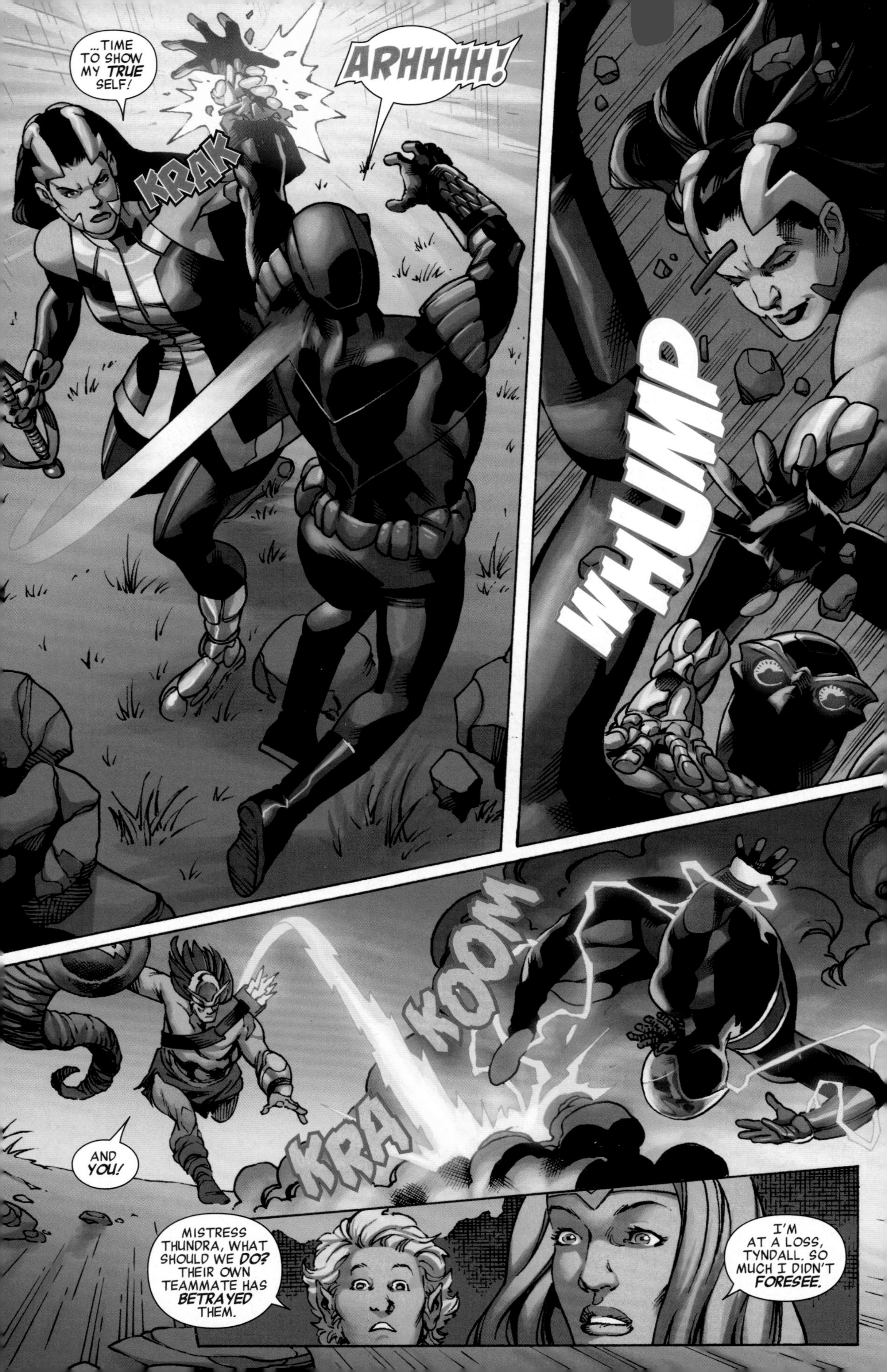
...TIME TO SHOW MY TRUE SELF!
KRAK
ARHHHH!
WHUMP
AND YOU!
KRA
KOOM
MISTRESS THUNDRA, WHAT SHOULD WE DO? THEIR OWN TEAMMATE HAS BETRAYED THEM.
I'M AT A LOSS, TYNDALL. SO MUCH I DIDN'T FORESEE.

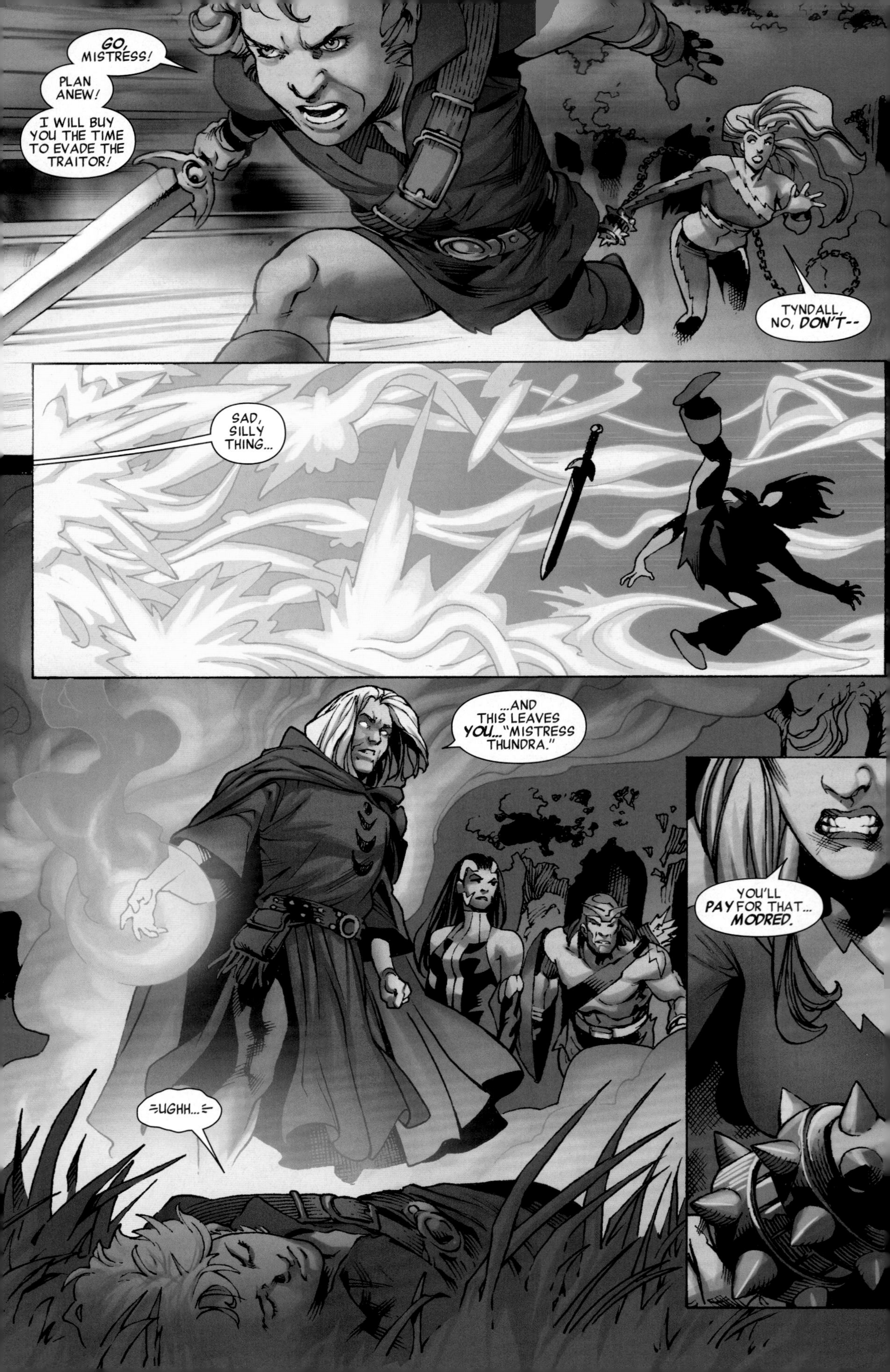
GO, MISTRESS!
PLAN ANEW!
I WILL BUY YOU THE TIME TO EVADE THE TRAITOR!
TYNDALL, NO, DON'T--
SAD, SILLY THING...
...AND THIS LEAVES YOU..."MISTRESS THUNDRA."
YOU'LL PAY FOR THAT... MODRED.
=UGHH...=

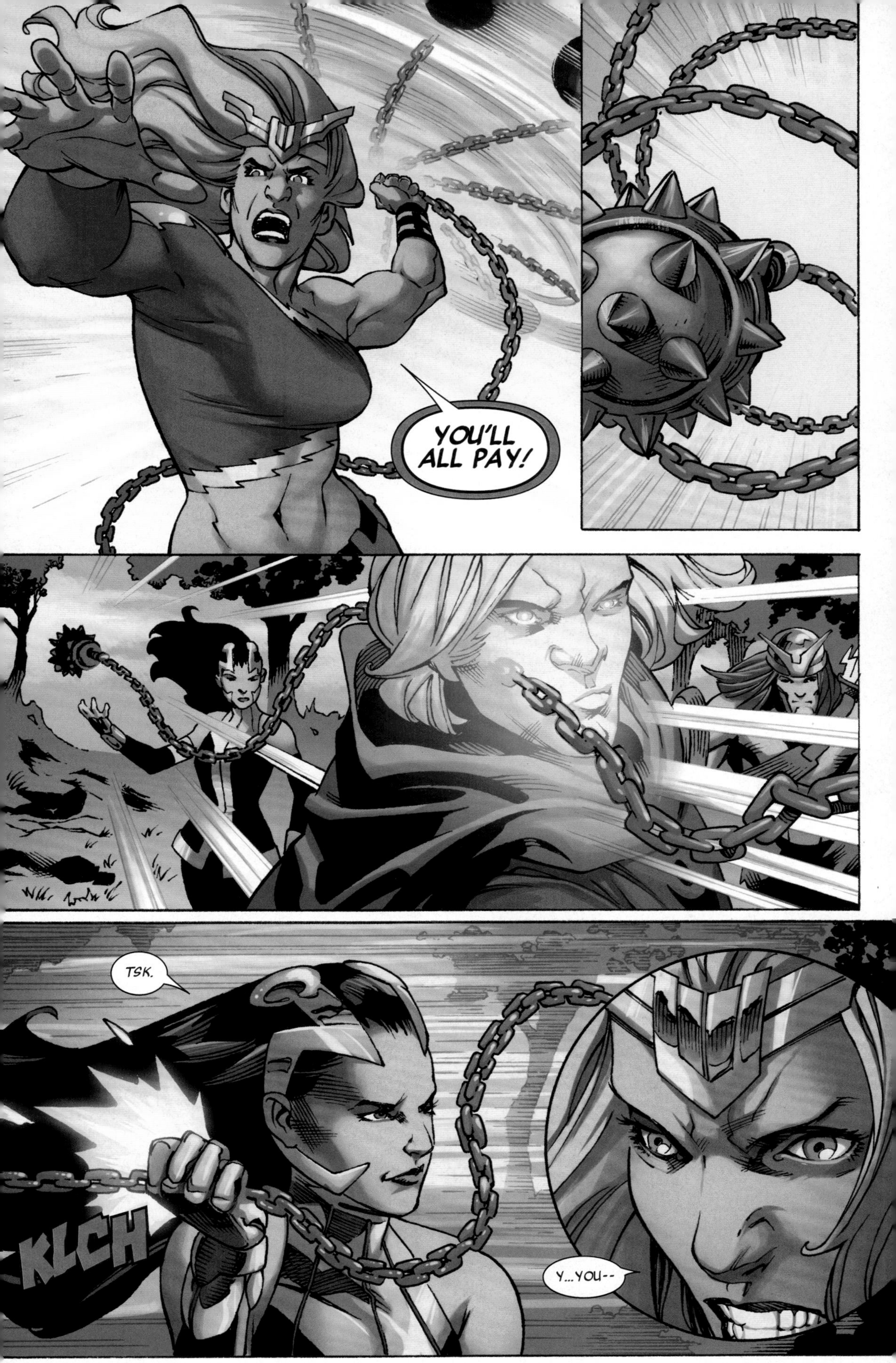
YOU'LL ALL PAY!
TSK.
KLCH
Y...YOU--

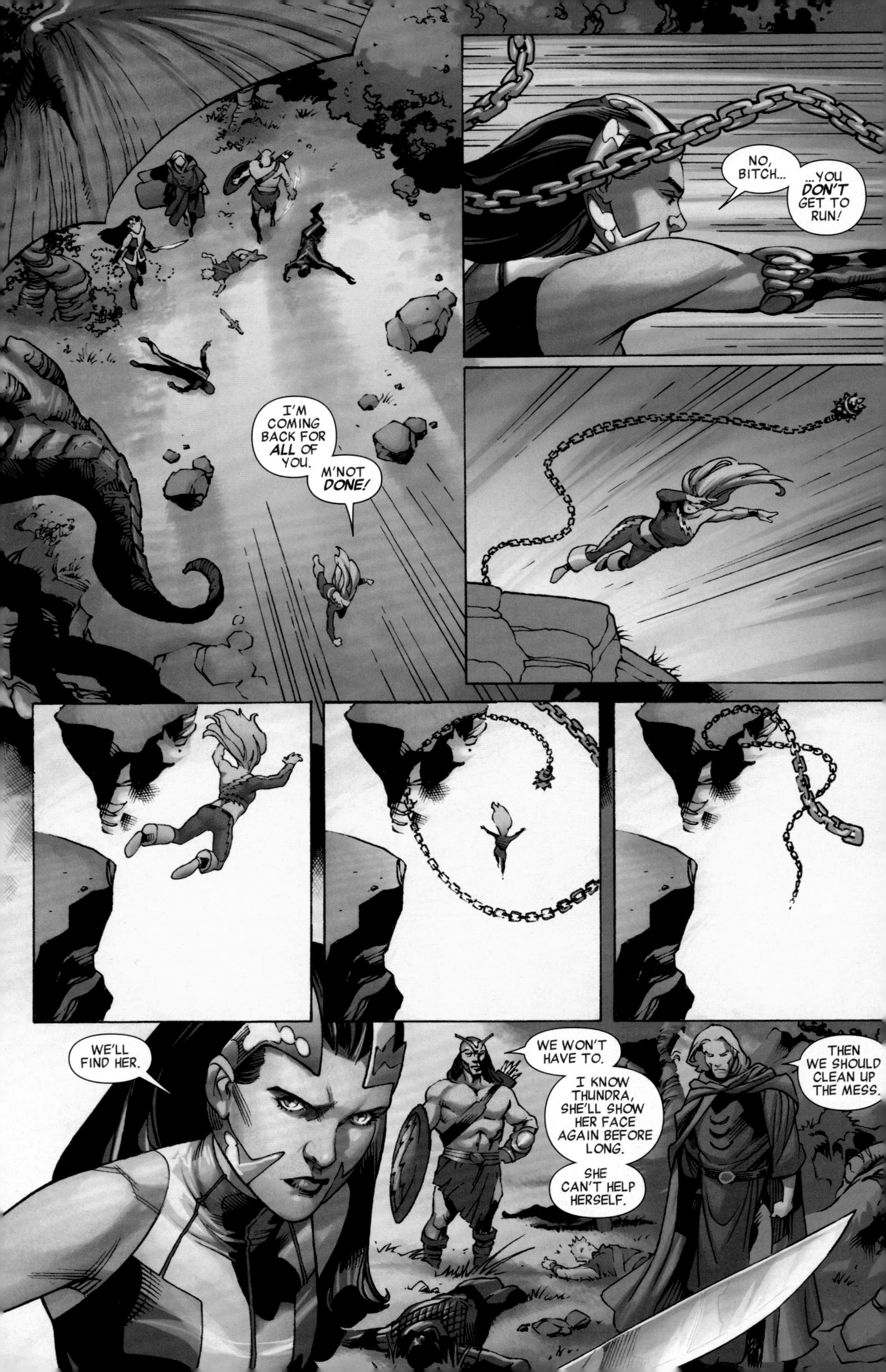
NO, BITCH...
...YOU DON'T GET TO RUN!
I'M COMING BACK FOR ALL OF YOU.
M'NOT DONE!
WE'LL FIND HER.
WE WON'T HAVE TO.
I KNOW THUNDRA, SHE'LL SHOW HER FACE AGAIN BEFORE LONG.
SHE CAN'T HELP HERSELF.
THEN WE SHOULD CLEAN UP THE MESS.

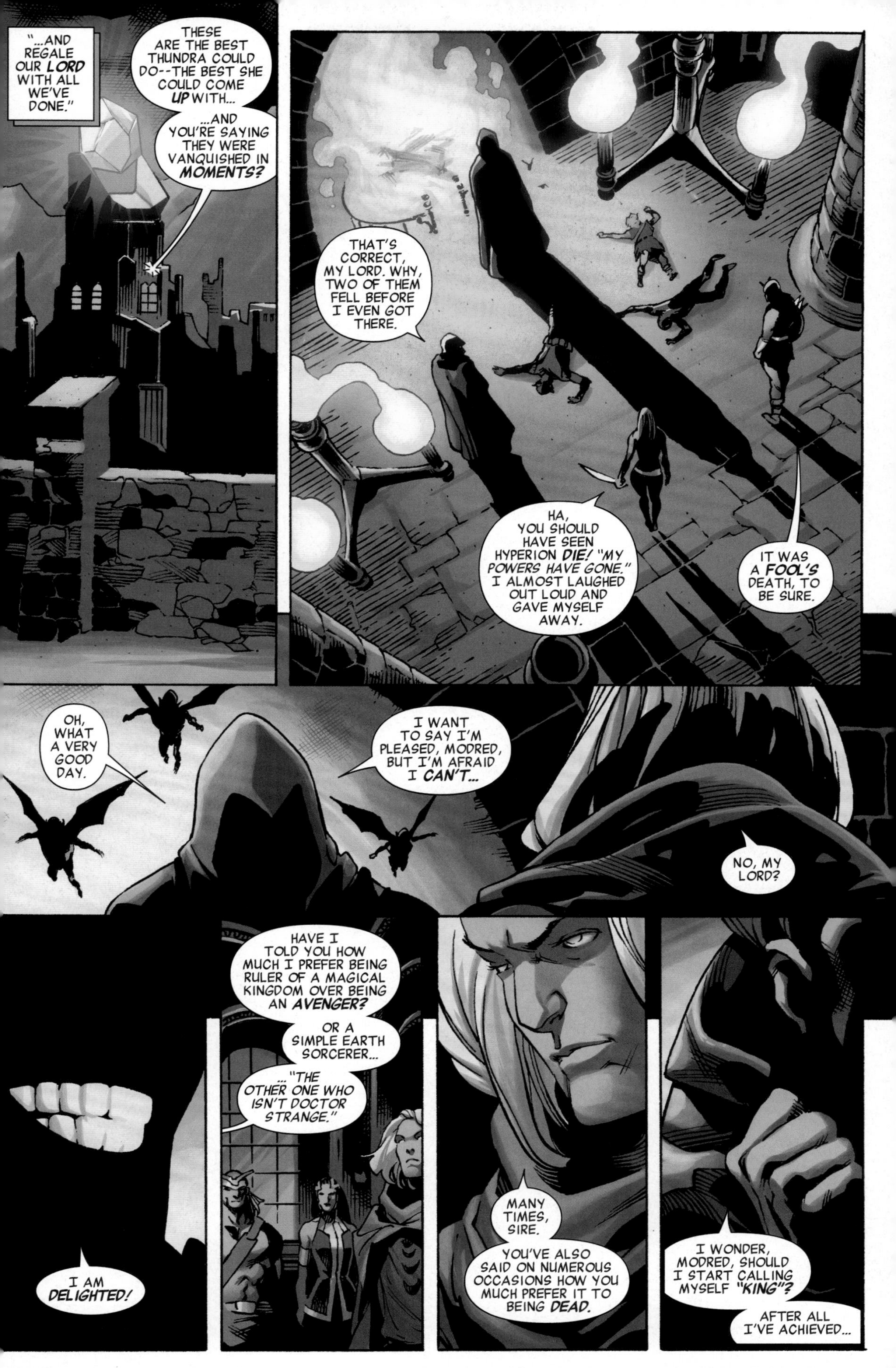
"...AND REGALE OUR LORD WITH ALL WE'VE DONE."
THESE ARE THE BEST THUNDRA COULD DO--THE BEST SHE COULD COME UP WITH...
...AND YOU'RE SAYING THEY WERE VANQUISHED IN MOMENTS?
THAT'S CORRECT, MY LORD. WHY, TWO OF THEM FELL BEFORE I EVEN GOT THERE.
HA, YOU SHOULD HAVE SEEN HYPERION DIE! "MY POWERS HAVE GONE." I ALMOST LAUGHED OUT LOUD AND GAVE MYSELF AWAY.
IT WAS A FOOL'S DEATH, TO BE SURE.
OH, WHAT A VERY GOOD DAY.
I WANT TO SAY I'M PLEASED, MODRED, BUT I'M AFRAID I CAN'T...
NO, MY LORD?
I AM DELIGHTED!
HAVE I TOLD YOU HOW MUCH I PREFER BEING RULER OF A MAGICAL KINGDOM OVER BEING AN AVENGER?
OR A SIMPLE EARTH SORCERER...
..."THE OTHER ONE WHO ISN'T DOCTOR STRANGE."
MANY TIMES, SIRE.
YOU'VE ALSO SAID ON NUMEROUS OCCASIONS HOW YOU MUCH PREFER IT TO BEING DEAD.
I WONDER, MODRED, SHOULD I START CALLING MYSELF "KING"?
AFTER ALL I'VE ACHIEVED...

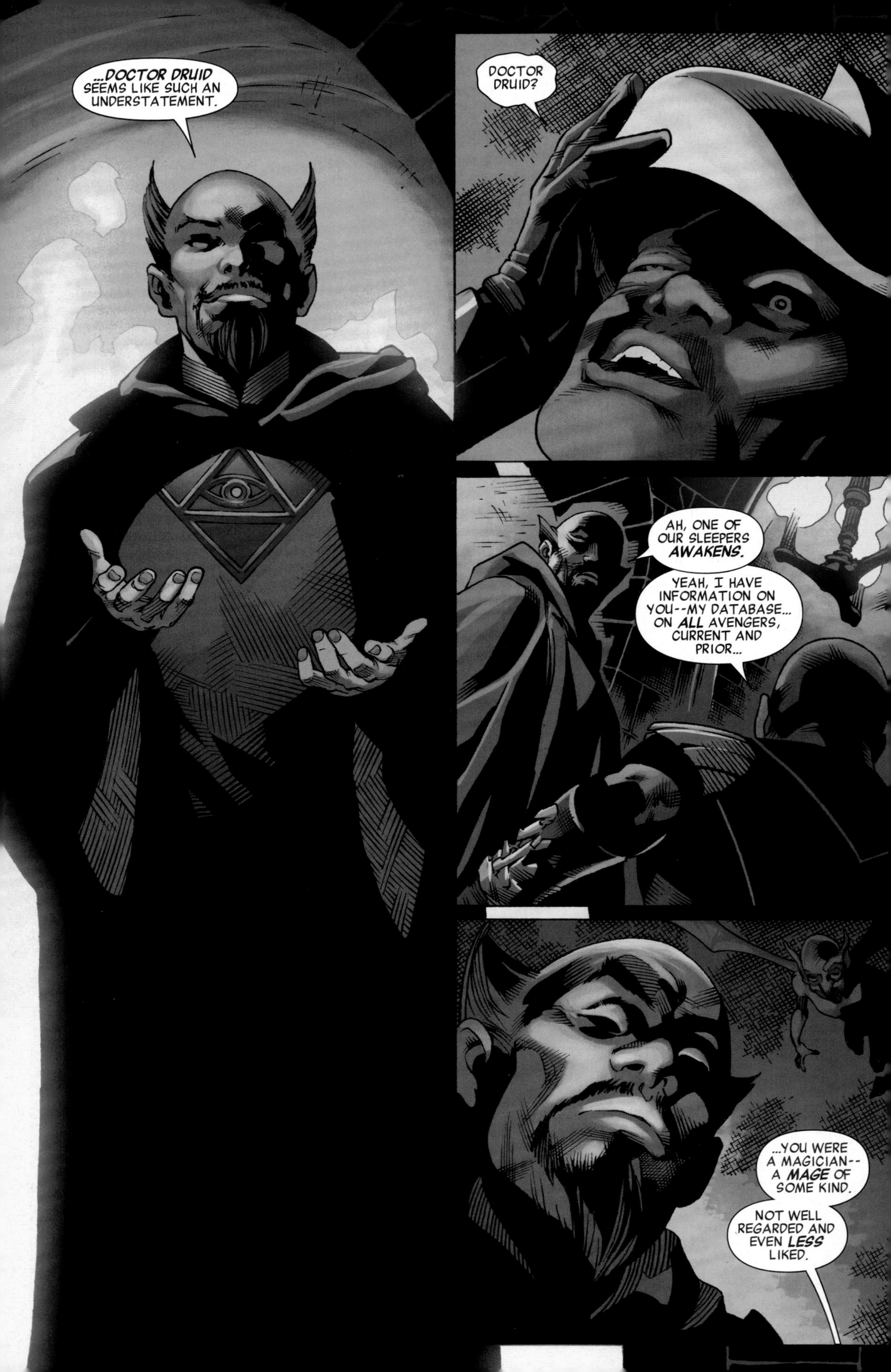
...DOCTOR DRUID SEEMS LIKE SUCH AN UNDERSTATEMENT.
DOCTOR DRUID?
AH, ONE OF OUR SLEEPERS AWAKENS.
YEAH, I HAVE INFORMATION ON YOU--MY DATABASE... ON ALL AVENGERS, CURRENT AND PRIOR...
...YOU WERE A MAGICIAN-- A MAGE OF SOME KIND.
NOT WELL REGARDED AND EVEN LESS LIKED.

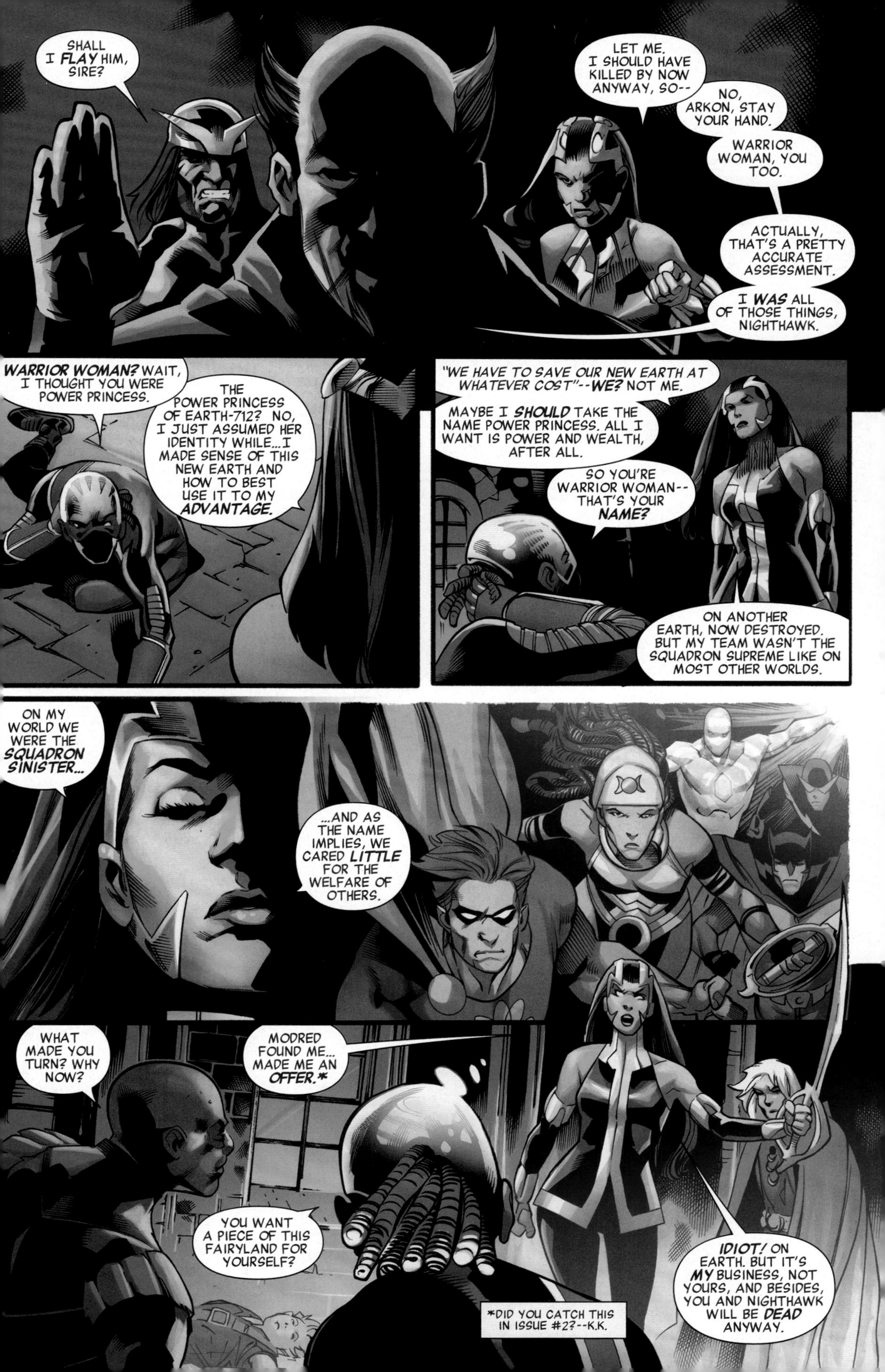
SHALL I **FLAY** HIM, SIRE?
LET ME. I SHOULD HAVE KILLED BY NOW ANYWAY, SO--
NO, ARKON, STAY YOUR HAND.
WARRIOR WOMAN, YOU TOO.
ACTUALLY, THAT'S A PRETTY ACCURATE ASSESSMENT.
I **WAS** ALL OF THOSE THINGS, NIGHTHAWK.
WARRIOR WOMAN? WAIT, I THOUGHT YOU WERE POWER PRINCESS.
THE POWER PRINCESS OF EARTH-712? NO, I JUST ASSUMED HER IDENTITY WHILE...I MADE SENSE OF THIS NEW EARTH AND HOW TO BEST USE IT TO MY **ADVANTAGE.**
"WE HAVE TO SAVE OUR NEW EARTH AT WHATEVER COST"--**WE?** NOT ME.
MAYBE I **SHOULD** TAKE THE NAME POWER PRINCESS. ALL I WANT IS POWER AND WEALTH, AFTER ALL.
SO YOU'RE WARRIOR WOMAN--THAT'S YOUR **NAME?**
ON ANOTHER EARTH, NOW DESTROYED. BUT MY TEAM WASN'T THE SQUADRON SUPREME LIKE ON MOST OTHER WORLDS.
ON MY WORLD WE WERE THE **SQUADRON SINISTER...**
...AND AS THE NAME IMPLIES, WE CARED **LITTLE** FOR THE WELFARE OF OTHERS.
WHAT MADE YOU TURN? WHY NOW?
MODRED FOUND ME... MADE ME AN **OFFER.***
YOU WANT A PIECE OF THIS FAIRYLAND FOR YOURSELF?
IDIOT! ON EARTH. BUT IT'S **MY** BUSINESS, NOT YOURS, AND BESIDES, YOU AND NIGHTHAWK WILL BE **DEAD** ANYWAY.
*DID YOU CATCH THIS IN ISSUE #2?--K.K.

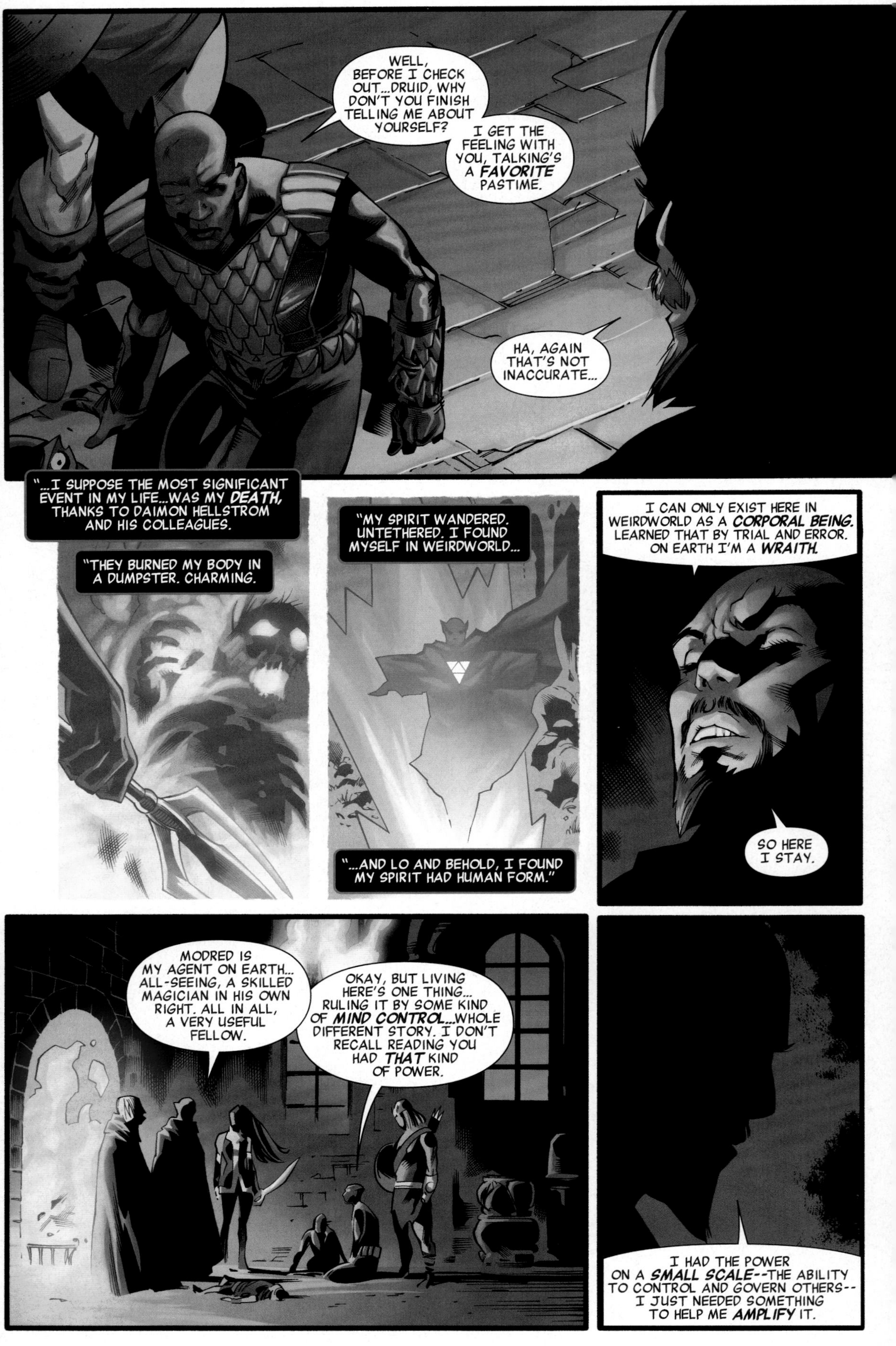
WELL, BEFORE I CHECK OUT...DRUID, WHY DON'T YOU FINISH TELLING ME ABOUT YOURSELF?
I GET THE FEELING WITH YOU, TALKING'S A FAVORITE PASTIME.
HA, AGAIN THAT'S NOT INACCURATE...
"...I SUPPOSE THE MOST SIGNIFICANT EVENT IN MY LIFE...WAS MY DEATH, THANKS TO DAIMON HELLSTROM AND HIS COLLEAGUES.
"THEY BURNED MY BODY IN A DUMPSTER. CHARMING.
"MY SPIRIT WANDERED. UNTETHERED. I FOUND MYSELF IN WEIRDWORLD...
"...AND LO AND BEHOLD, I FOUND MY SPIRIT HAD HUMAN FORM."
I CAN ONLY EXIST HERE IN WEIRDWORLD AS A CORPORAL BEING. LEARNED THAT BY TRIAL AND ERROR. ON EARTH I'M A WRAITH.
SO HERE I STAY.
MODRED IS MY AGENT ON EARTH... ALL-SEEING, A SKILLED MAGICIAN IN HIS OWN RIGHT. ALL IN ALL, A VERY USEFUL FELLOW.
OKAY, BUT LIVING HERE'S ONE THING... RULING IT BY SOME KIND OF MIND CONTROL...WHOLE DIFFERENT STORY. I DON'T RECALL READING YOU HAD THAT KIND OF POWER.
I HAD THE POWER ON A SMALL SCALE--THE ABILITY TO CONTROL AND GOVERN OTHERS--I JUST NEEDED SOMETHING TO HELP ME AMPLIFY IT.

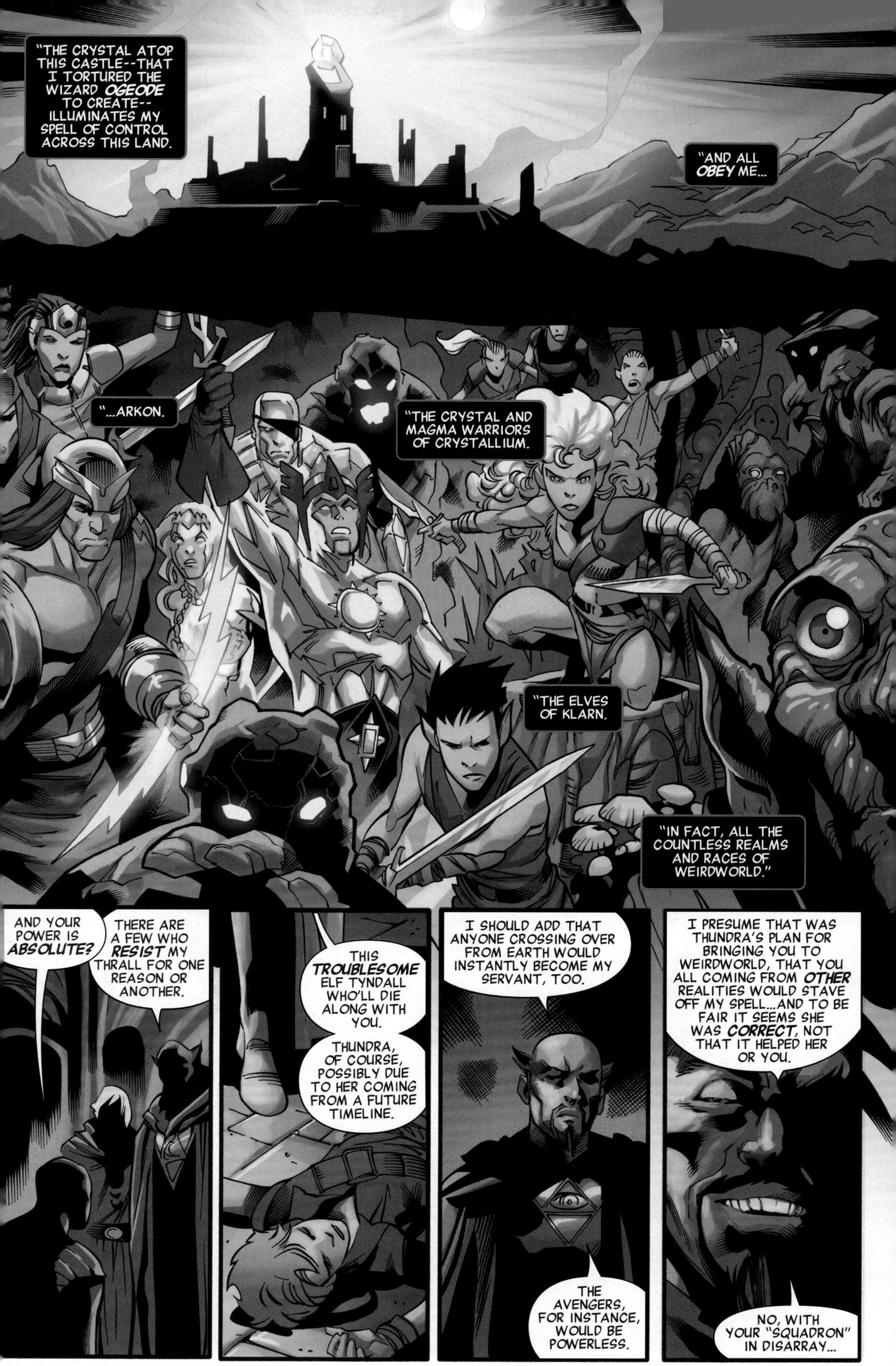
"THE CRYSTAL ATOP THIS CASTLE--THAT I TORTURED THE WIZARD OGEODE TO CREATE--ILLUMINATES MY SPELL OF CONTROL ACROSS THIS LAND.
"AND ALL OBEY ME...
"...ARKON.
"THE CRYSTAL AND MAGMA WARRIORS OF CRYSTALLIUM.
"THE ELVES OF KLARN.
"IN FACT, ALL THE COUNTLESS REALMS AND RACES OF WEIRDWORLD."
AND YOUR POWER IS ABSOLUTE?
THERE ARE A FEW WHO RESIST MY THRALL FOR ONE REASON OR ANOTHER.
THIS TROUBLESOME ELF TYNDALL WHO'LL DIE ALONG WITH YOU.
THUNDRA, OF COURSE, POSSIBLY DUE TO HER COMING FROM A FUTURE TIMELINE.
I SHOULD ADD THAT ANYONE CROSSING OVER FROM EARTH WOULD INSTANTLY BECOME MY SERVANT, TOO.
THE AVENGERS, FOR INSTANCE, WOULD BE POWERLESS.
I PRESUME THAT WAS THUNDRA'S PLAN FOR BRINGING YOU TO WEIRDWORLD, THAT YOU ALL COMING FROM OTHER REALITIES WOULD STAVE OFF MY SPELL...AND TO BE FAIR IT SEEMS SHE WAS CORRECT, NOT THAT IT HELPED HER OR YOU.
NO, WITH YOUR "SQUADRON" IN DISARRAY...

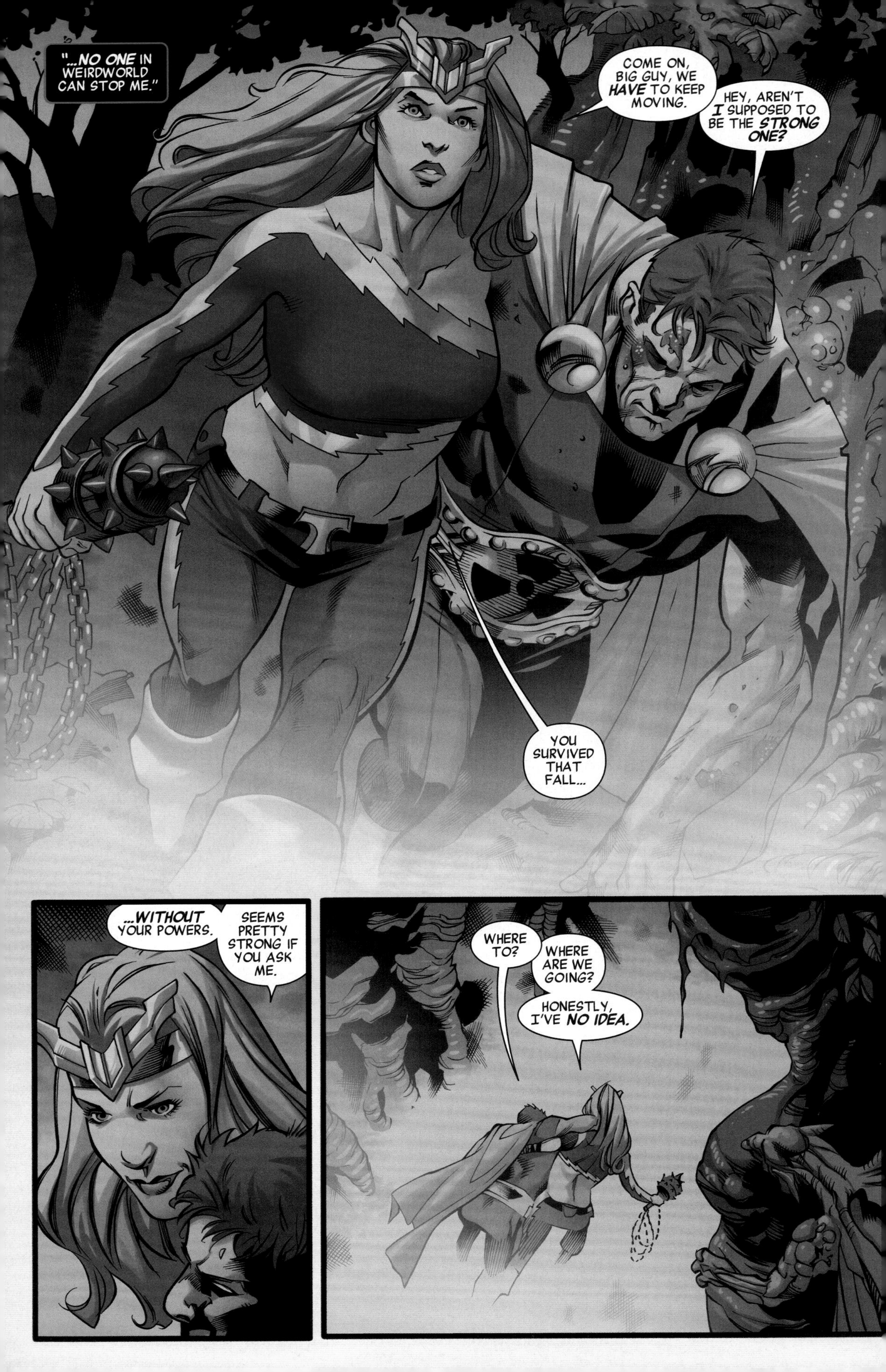
"...NO ONE IN WEIRDWORLD CAN STOP ME."
COME ON, BIG GUY, WE HAVE TO KEEP MOVING.
HEY, AREN'T I SUPPOSED TO BE THE STRONG ONE?
YOU SURVIVED THAT FALL...
...WITHOUT YOUR POWERS.
SEEMS PRETTY STRONG IF YOU ASK ME.
WHERE TO?
WHERE ARE WE GOING?
HONESTLY, I'VE NO IDEA.

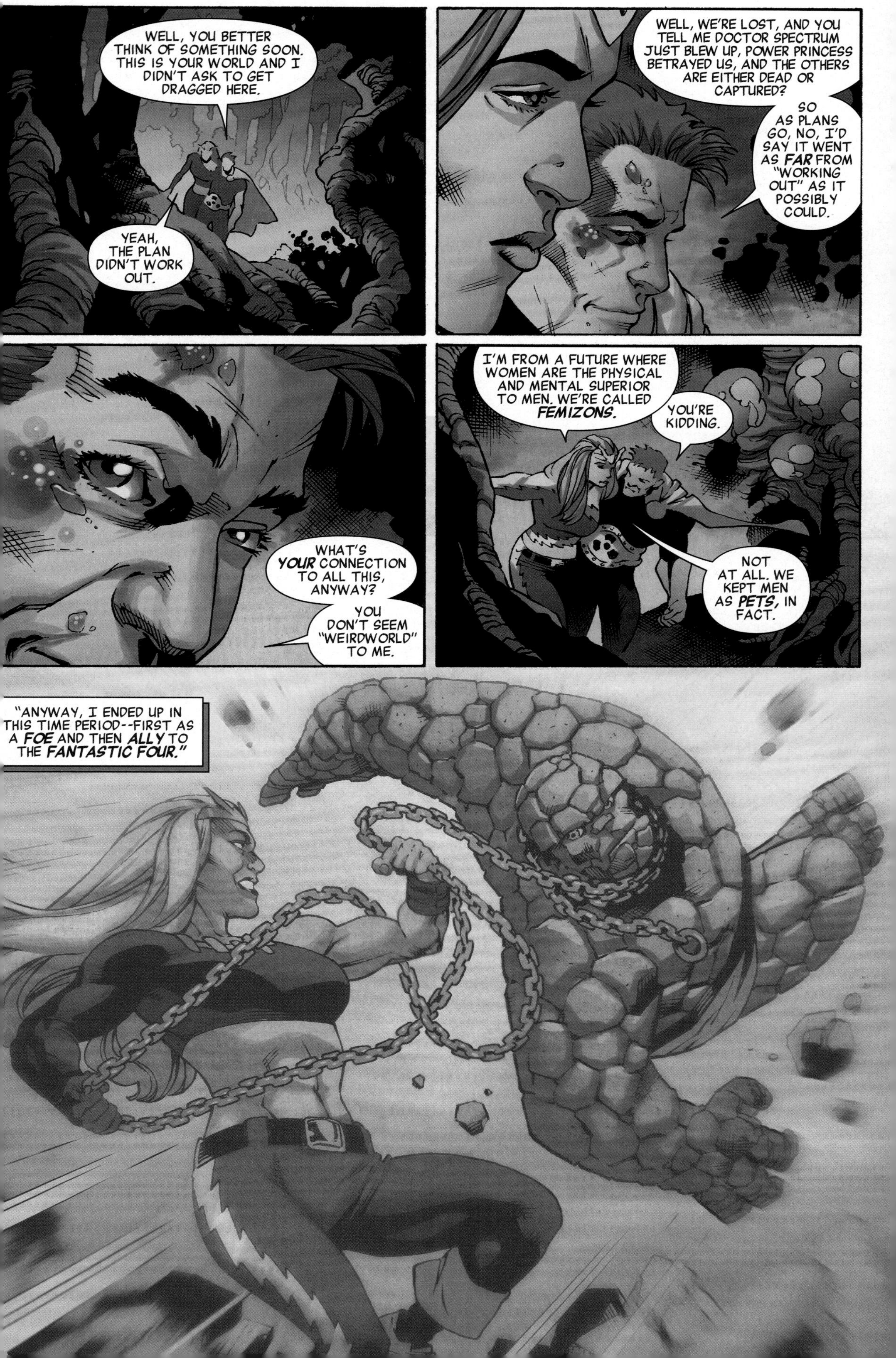
WELL, YOU BETTER THINK OF SOMETHING SOON. THIS IS YOUR WORLD AND I DIDN'T ASK TO GET DRAGGED HERE.
YEAH, THE PLAN DIDN'T WORK OUT.
WELL, WE'RE LOST, AND YOU TELL ME DOCTOR SPECTRUM JUST BLEW UP, POWER PRINCESS BETRAYED US, AND THE OTHERS ARE EITHER DEAD OR CAPTURED?
SO AS PLANS GO, NO, I'D SAY IT WENT AS FAR FROM "WORKING OUT" AS IT POSSIBLY COULD.
WHAT'S YOUR CONNECTION TO ALL THIS, ANYWAY?
YOU DON'T SEEM "WEIRDWORLD" TO ME.
I'M FROM A FUTURE WHERE WOMEN ARE THE PHYSICAL AND MENTAL SUPERIOR TO MEN. WE'RE CALLED FEMIZONS.
YOU'RE KIDDING.
NOT AT ALL. WE KEPT MEN AS PETS, IN FACT.
"ANYWAY, I ENDED UP IN THIS TIME PERIOD--FIRST AS A FOE AND THEN ALLY TO THE FANTASTIC FOUR."

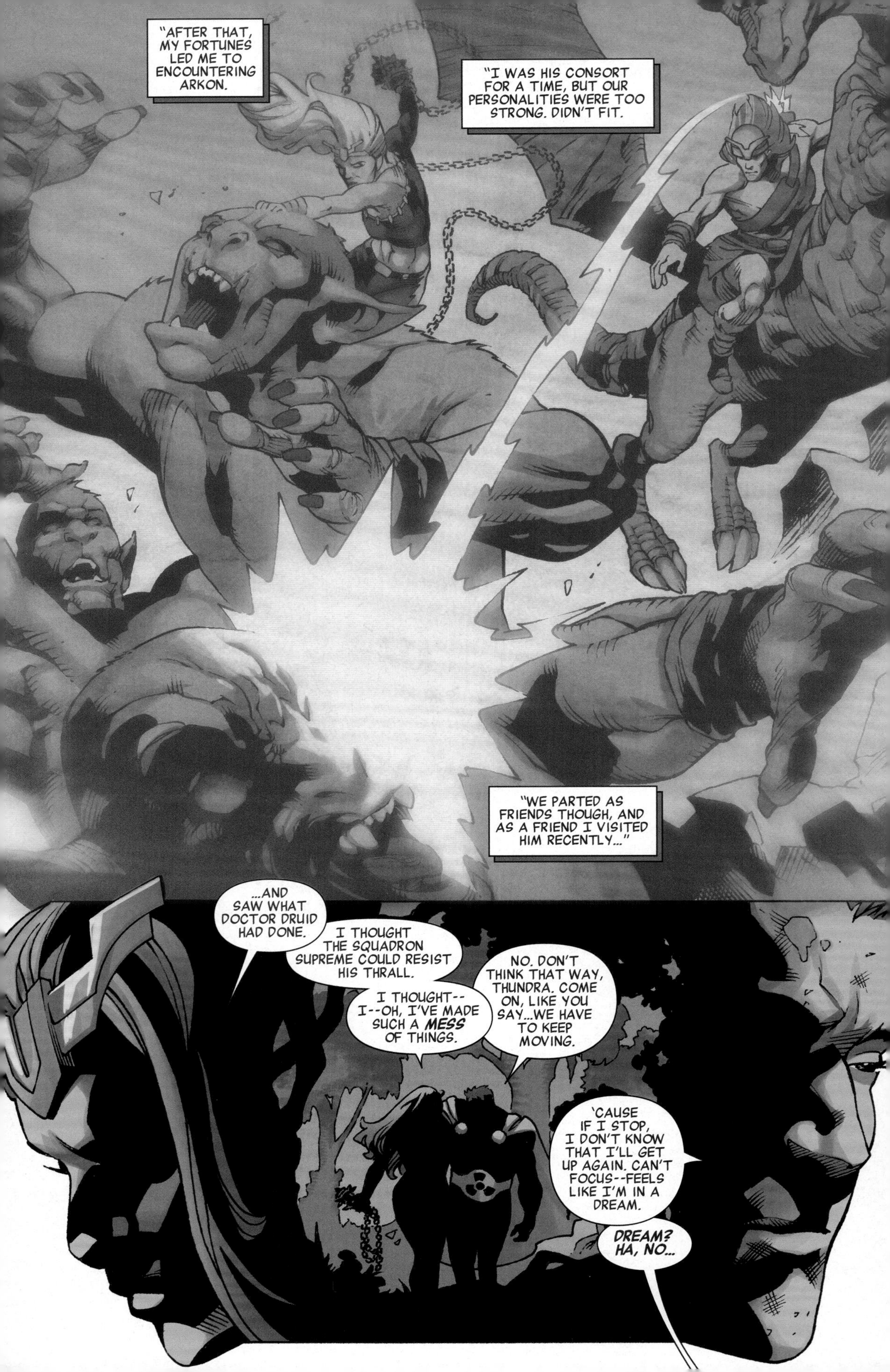
"AFTER THAT, MY FORTUNES LED ME TO ENCOUNTERING ARKON.
"I WAS HIS CONSORT FOR A TIME, BUT OUR PERSONALITIES WERE TOO STRONG. DIDN'T FIT.
"WE PARTED AS FRIENDS THOUGH, AND AS A FRIEND I VISITED HIM RECENTLY..."
...AND SAW WHAT DOCTOR DRUID HAD DONE.
I THOUGHT THE SQUADRON SUPREME COULD RESIST HIS THRALL.
I THOUGHT-- I--OH, I'VE MADE SUCH A MESS OF THINGS.
NO. DON'T THINK THAT WAY, THUNDRA. COME ON, LIKE YOU SAY...WE HAVE TO KEEP MOVING.
'CAUSE IF I STOP, I DON'T KNOW THAT I'LL GET UP AGAIN. CAN'T FOCUS--FEELS LIKE I'M IN A DREAM.
DREAM? HA, NO...

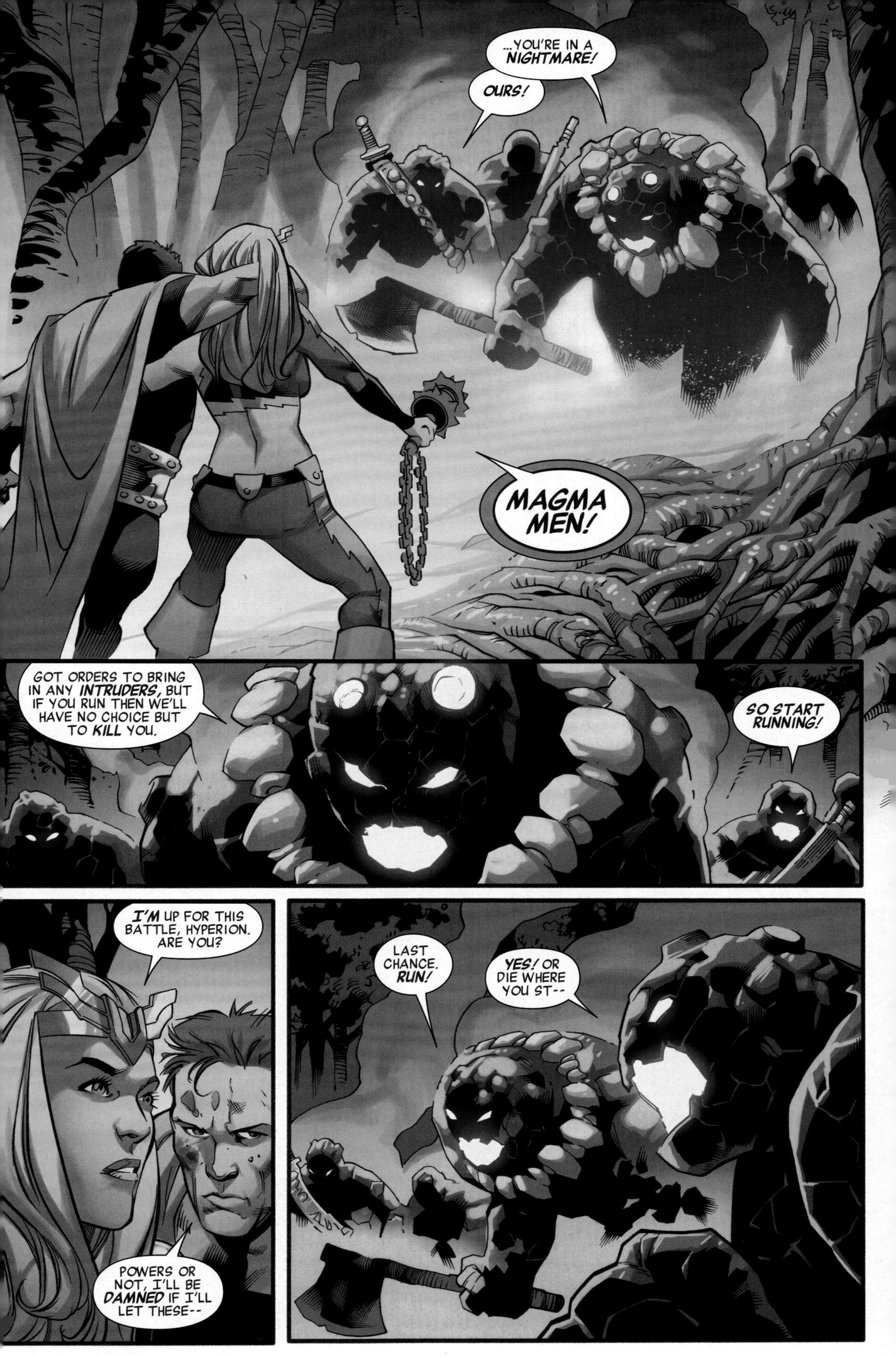
...YOU'RE IN A NIGHTMARE!
OURS!
MAGMA MEN!
GOT ORDERS TO BRING IN ANY INTRUDERS, BUT IF YOU RUN THEN WE'LL HAVE NO CHOICE BUT TO KILL YOU.
SO START RUNNING!
I'M UP FOR THIS BATTLE, HYPERION. ARE YOU?
POWERS OR NOT, I'LL BE DAMNED IF I'LL LET THESE--
LAST CHANCE. RUN!
YES! OR DIE WHERE YOU ST--

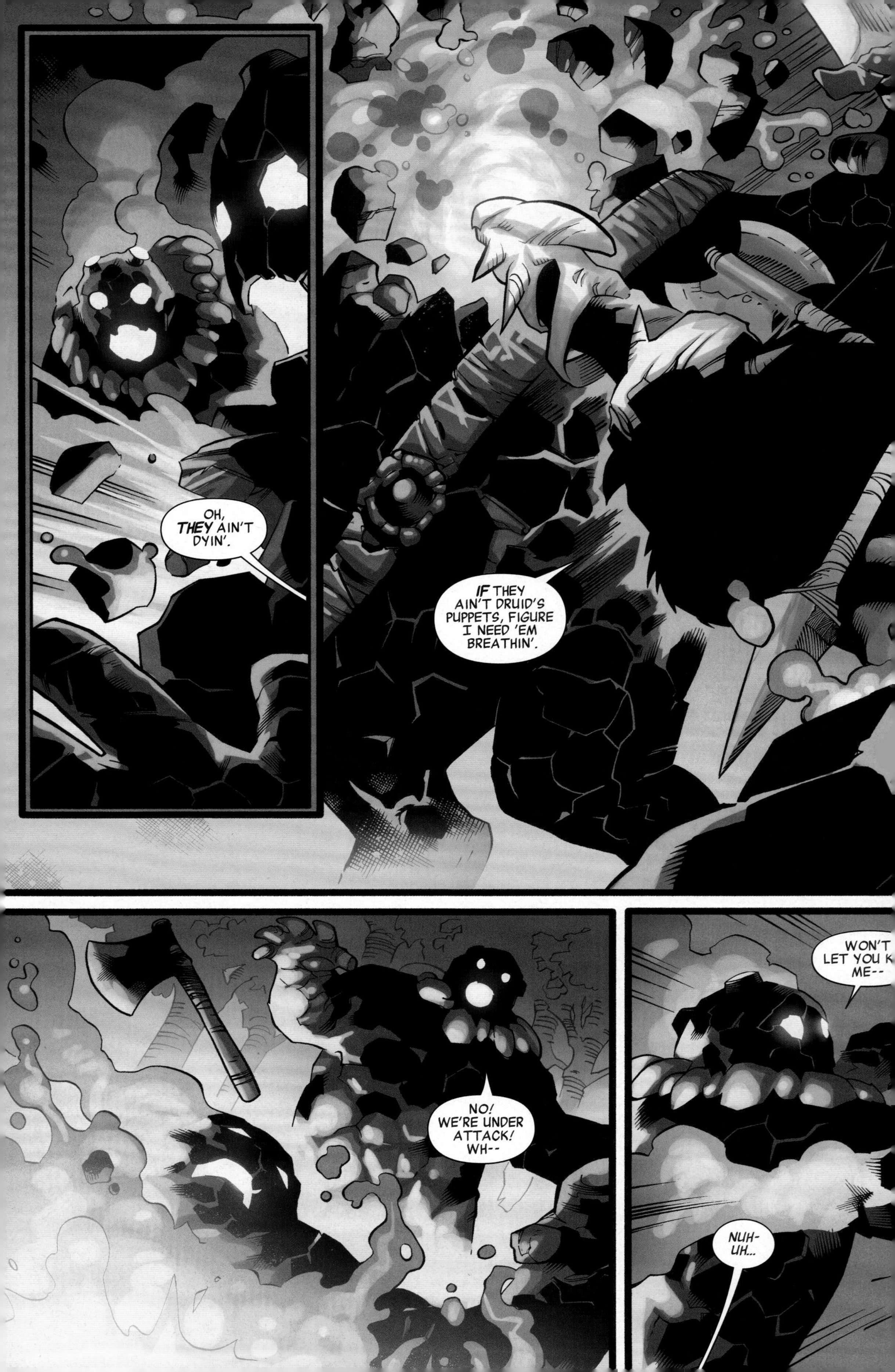
OH, THEY AIN'T DYIN'.
IF THEY AIN'T DRUID'S PUPPETS, FIGURE I NEED 'EM BREATHIN'.
NO! WE'RE UNDER ATTACK! WH--
WON'T LET YOU K ME--
NUH-UH...

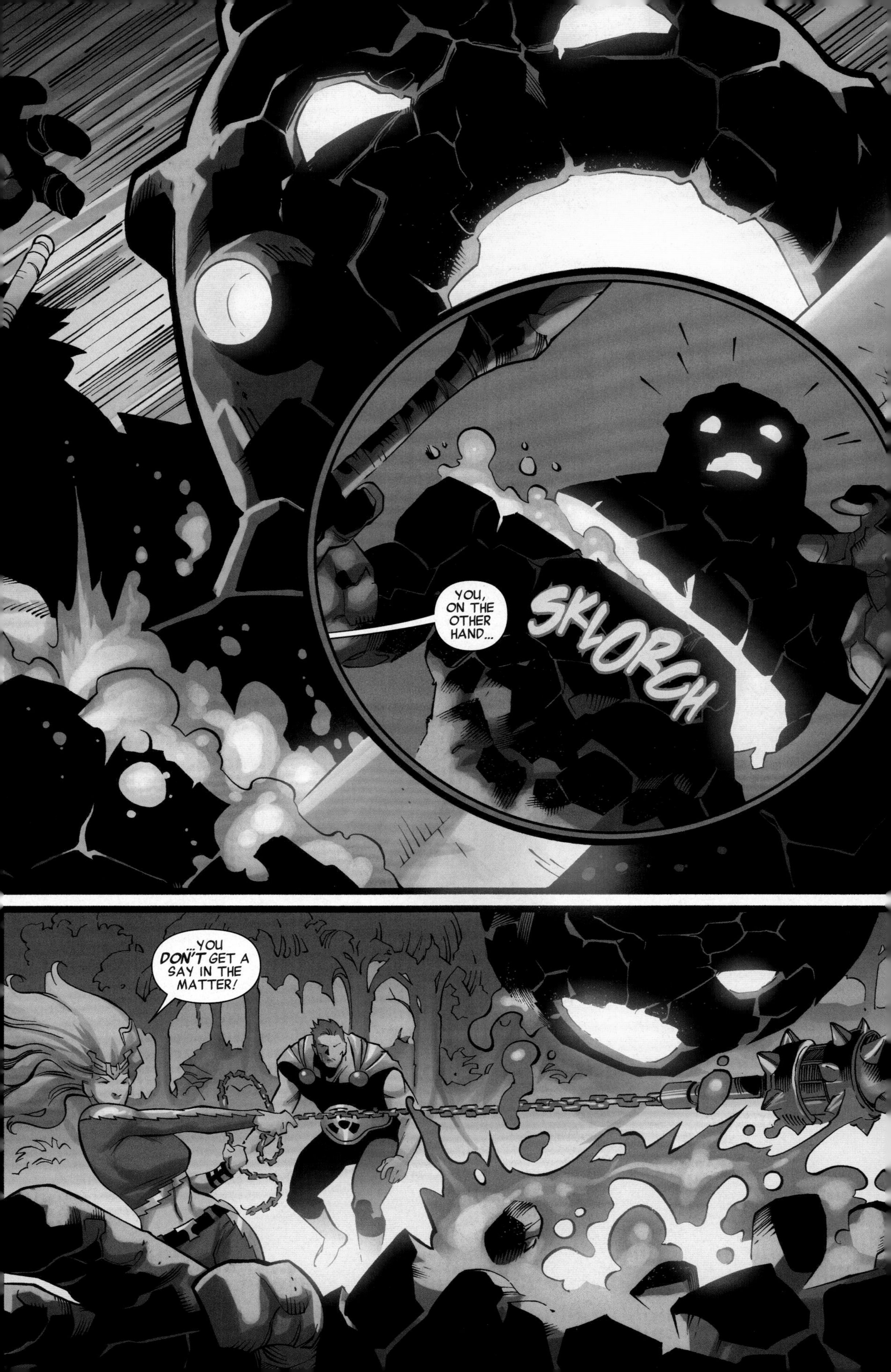
YOU, ON THE OTHER HAND...
SKLORCH
...YOU DON'T GET A SAY IN THE MATTER!

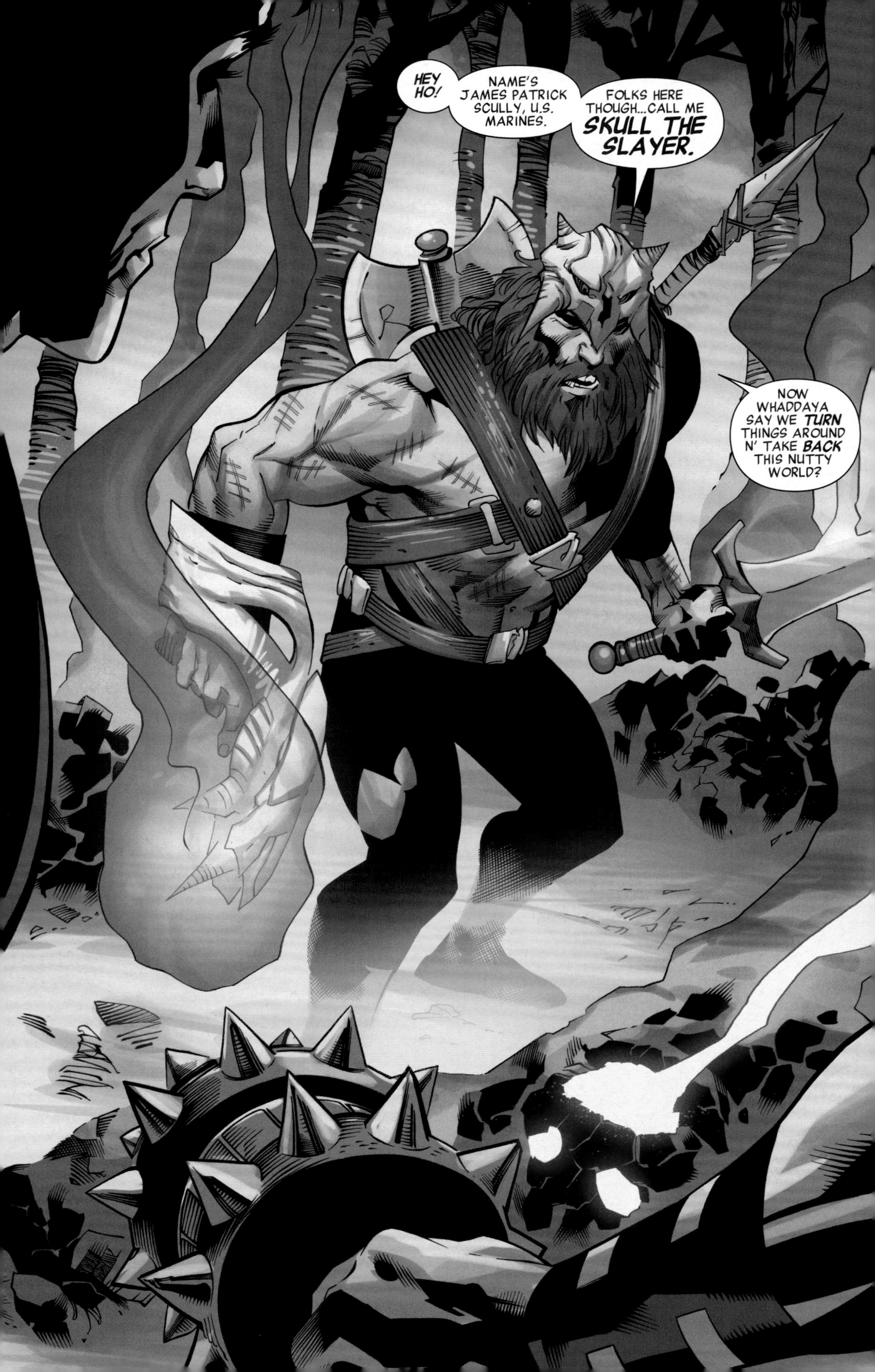
HEY HO!
NAME'S JAMES PATRICK SCULLY, U.S. MARINES.
FOLKS HERE THOUGH...CALL ME SKULL THE SLAYER.
NOW WHADDAYA SAY WE TURN THINGS AROUND N' TAKE BACK THIS NUTTY WORLD?

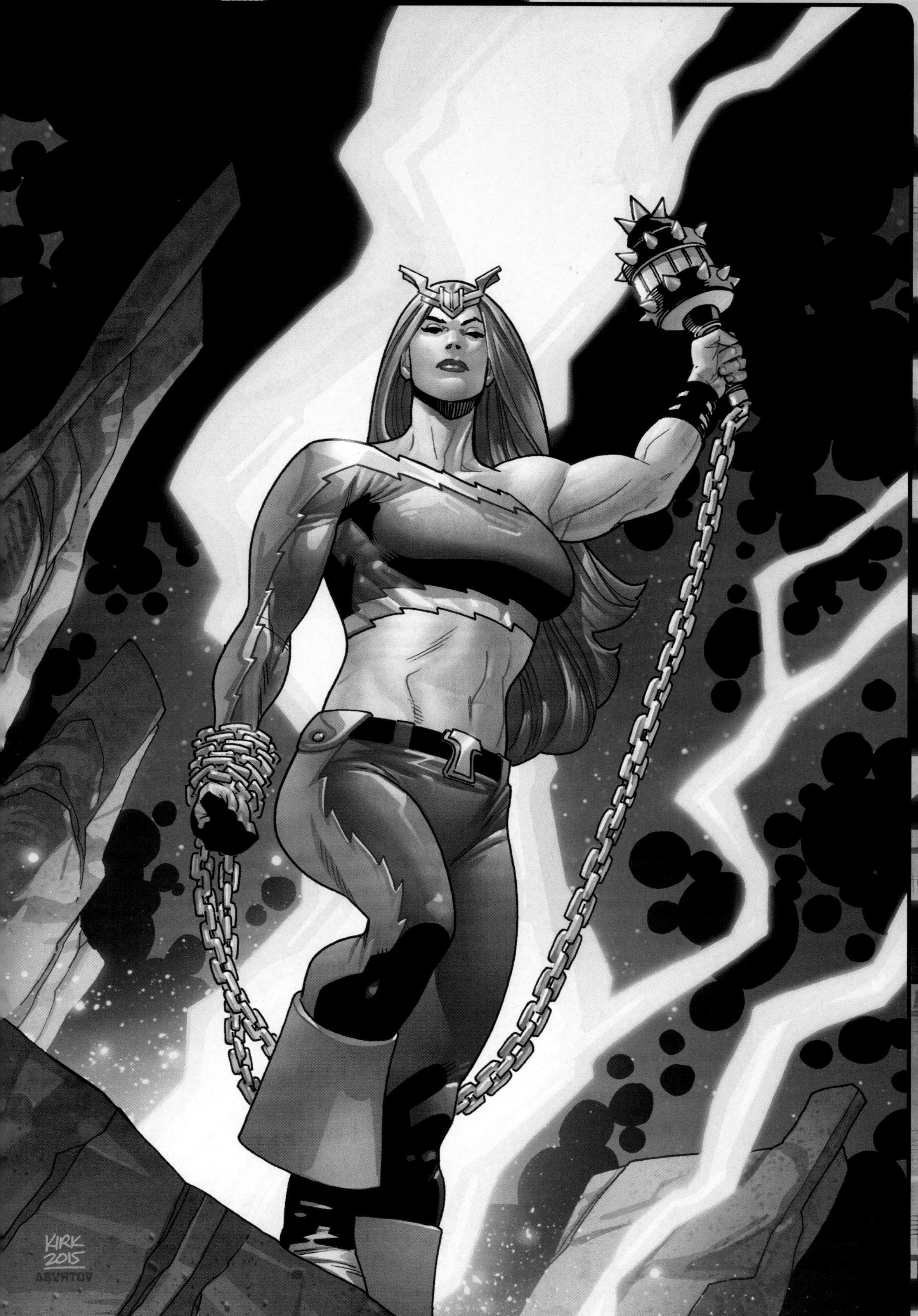
KIRK
2015

#4 VARIANT BY LEONARD KIRK & JESUS ABURTOV

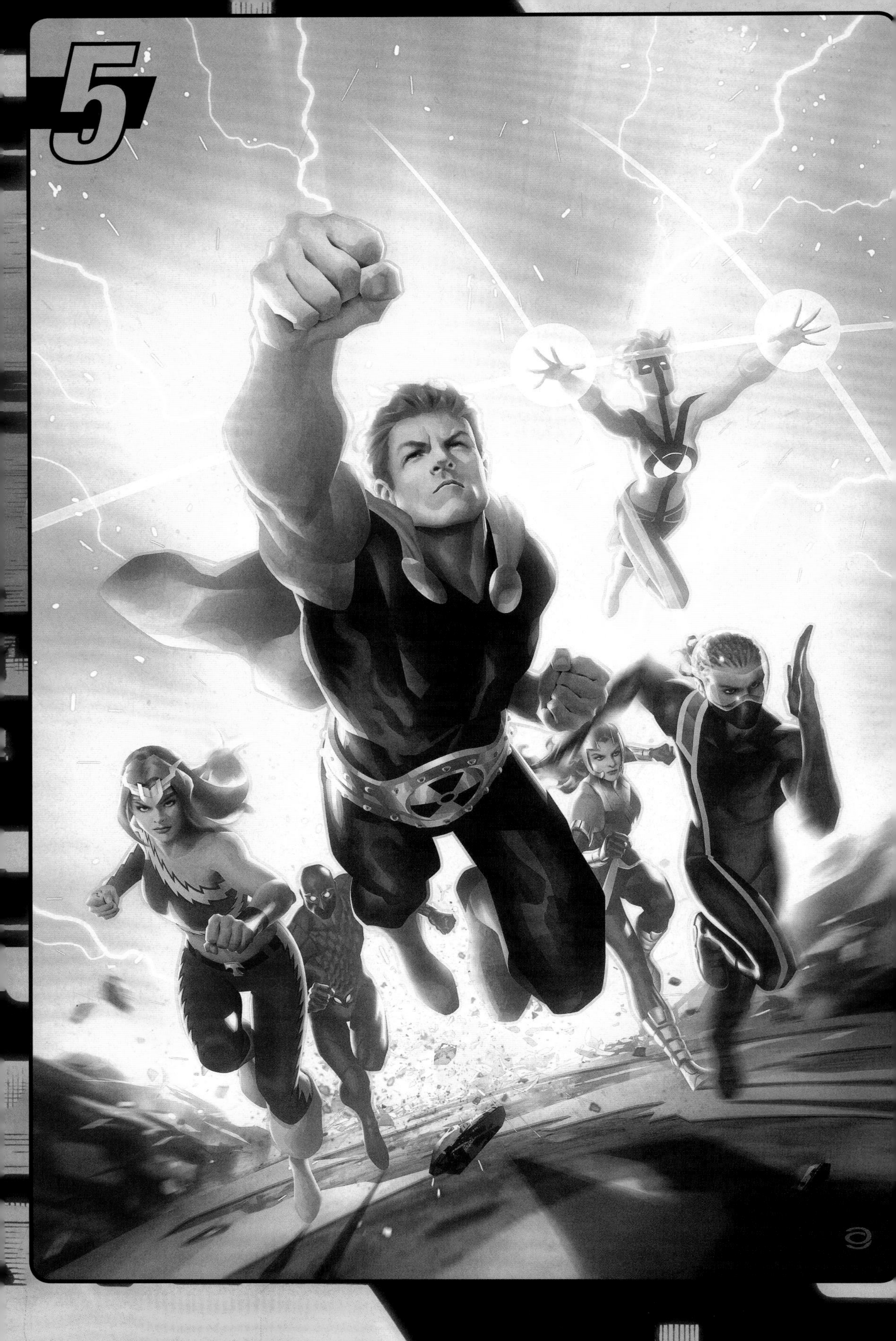
5

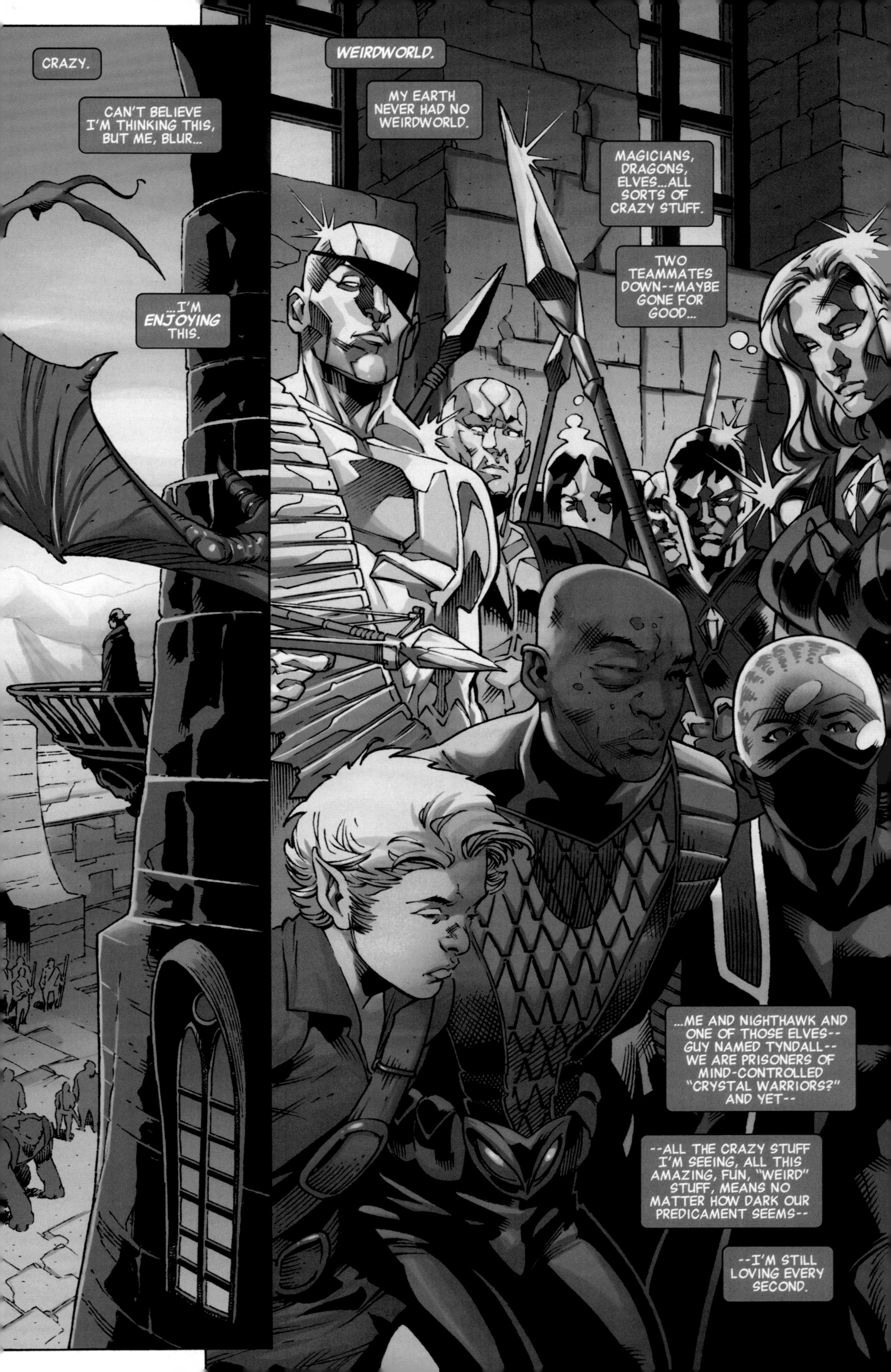
CRAZY.
CAN'T BELIEVE I'M THINKING THIS, BUT ME, BLUR...
...I'M ENJOYING THIS.
WEIRDWORLD.
MY EARTH NEVER HAD NO WEIRDWORLD.
MAGICIANS, DRAGONS, ELVES...ALL SORTS OF CRAZY STUFF.
TWO TEAMMATES DOWN--MAYBE GONE FOR GOOD...
...ME AND NIGHTHAWK AND ONE OF THOSE ELVES--GUY NAMED TYNDALL--WE ARE PRISONERS OF MIND-CONTROLLED "CRYSTAL WARRIORS?" AND YET--
--ALL THE CRAZY STUFF I'M SEEING, ALL THIS AMAZING, FUN, "WEIRD" STUFF, MEANS NO MATTER HOW DARK OUR PREDICAMENT SEEMS--
--I'M STILL LOVING EVERY SECOND.

N' NOW WE ESCAPE, I GUESS--YEAH, FROM NIGHTHAWK BLINKING HE'S TELLING ME THAT'S THE PLAN.

NIGHTHAWK--THE MOST GROUNDED ONE ON THE TEAM--THE MOST *REAL*-- LIKE ON MY WORLD. MAYBE THAT'S WHY WE BONDED--

--WHY WHEN THE OTHERS WERE OFF DOING WHATEVER THEY DO WHEN THEY'RE NOT AROUND EACH OTHER--

--IN ZARDA'S CASE PLANNING TO BETRAY US, I GUESS--

--ME AND HIM WERE TRAINING. MANEUVERS. TEAMWORK.

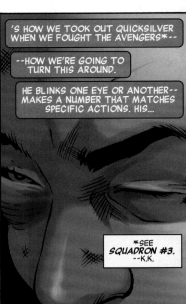

'S HOW WE TOOK OUT QUICKSILVER WHEN WE FOUGHT THE AVENGERS*--

--HOW WE'RE GOING TO TURN THIS AROUND.

HE BLINKS ONE EYE OR ANOTHER-- MAKES A NUMBER THAT MATCHES SPECIFIC ACTIONS. HIS...

*SEE
SQUADRON #3.
--K.K.

...AND MINE!

DO IT, BLUR! *FASTER!*

YOU GOT IT!

WITH THE FREQUENCY MY SUIT IS EMITTING COMBINED WITH YOUR VORTEX THINNING THE AIR AROUND THEM...

...THE CRYSTAL WARRIORS WILL *SHATTER.*

FASTER! THAT'S IT!

MASTER NIGHTHAWK! NO...!

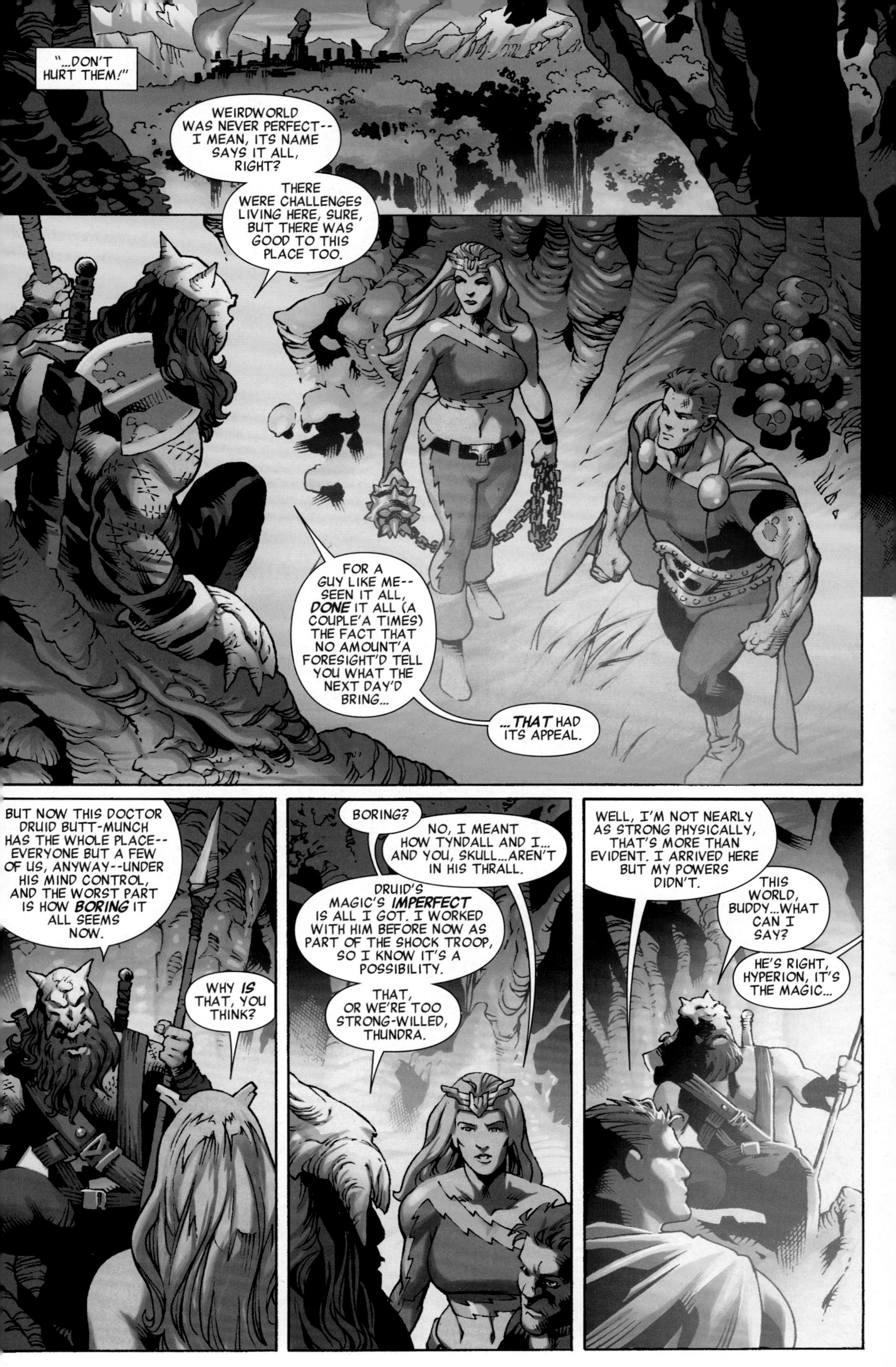
"...DON'T HURT THEM!"
WEIRDWORLD WAS NEVER PERFECT-- I MEAN, ITS NAME SAYS IT ALL, RIGHT?
THERE WERE CHALLENGES LIVING HERE, SURE, BUT THERE WAS GOOD TO THIS PLACE TOO.
FOR A GUY LIKE ME-- SEEN IT ALL, DONE IT ALL (A COUPLE'A TIMES) THE FACT THAT NO AMOUNT'A FORESIGHT'D TELL YOU WHAT THE NEXT DAY'D BRING...
...THAT HAD ITS APPEAL.
BUT NOW THIS DOCTOR DRUID BUTT-MUNCH HAS THE WHOLE PLACE-- EVERYONE BUT A FEW OF US, ANYWAY--UNDER HIS MIND CONTROL, AND THE WORST PART IS HOW BORING IT ALL SEEMS NOW.
WHY IS THAT, YOU THINK?
BORING?
NO, I MEANT HOW TYNDALL AND I... AND YOU, SKULL...AREN'T IN HIS THRALL.
DRUID'S MAGIC'S IMPERFECT IS ALL I GOT. I WORKED WITH HIM BEFORE NOW AS PART OF THE SHOCK TROOP, SO I KNOW IT'S A POSSIBILITY.
THAT, OR WE'RE TOO STRONG-WILLED, THUNDRA.
WELL, I'M NOT NEARLY AS STRONG PHYSICALLY, THAT'S MORE THAN EVIDENT. I ARRIVED HERE BUT MY POWERS DIDN'T.
THIS WORLD, BUDDY...WHAT CAN I SAY?
HE'S RIGHT, HYPERION, IT'S THE MAGIC...

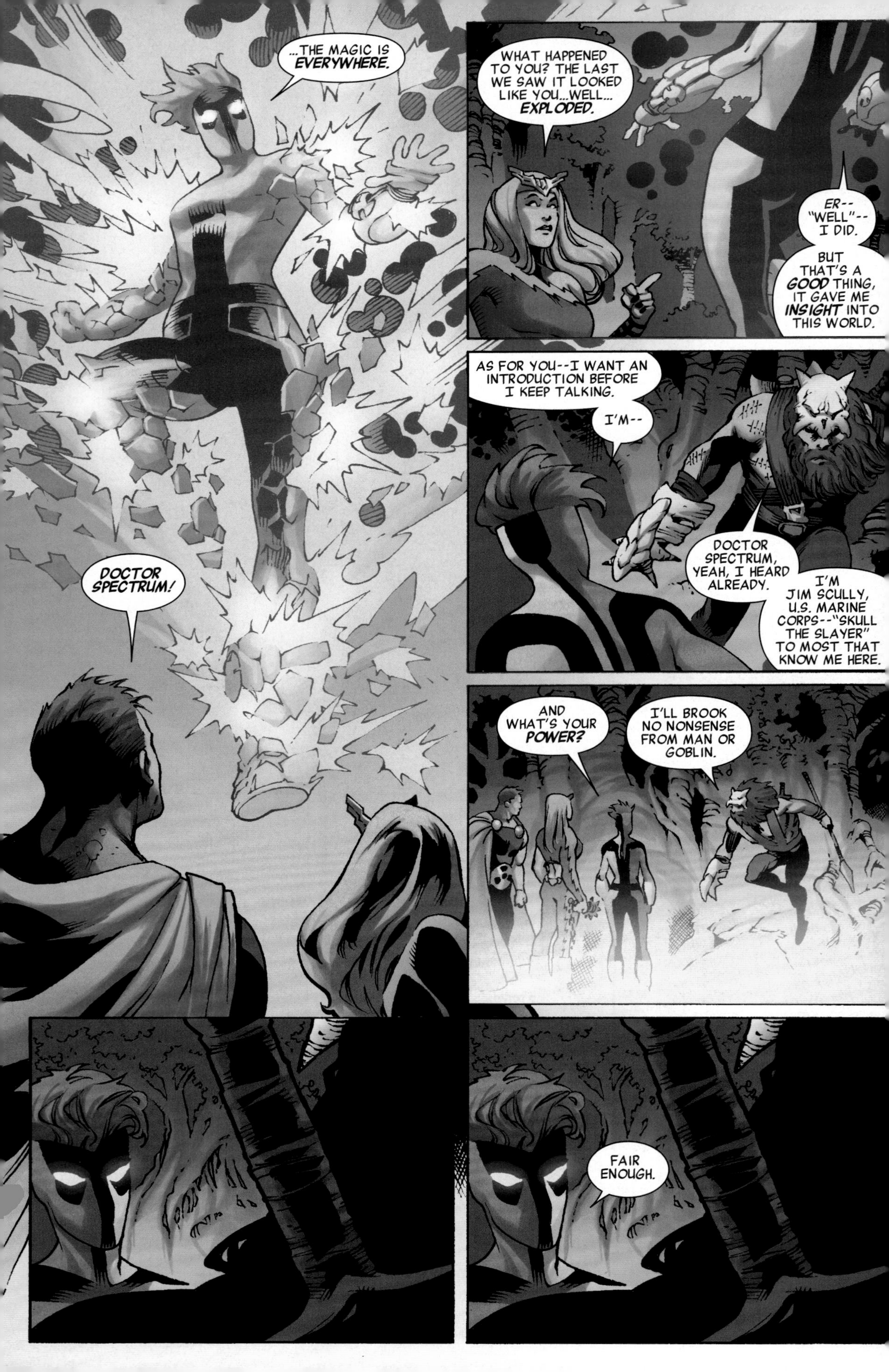
...THE MAGIC IS *EVERYWHERE.*
DOCTOR SPECTRUM!
WHAT HAPPENED TO YOU? THE LAST WE SAW IT LOOKED LIKE YOU...WELL... *EXPLODED.*
ER-- "WELL"-- I DID.
BUT THAT'S A *GOOD* THING, IT GAVE ME *INSIGHT* INTO THIS WORLD.
AS FOR YOU--I WANT AN INTRODUCTION BEFORE I KEEP TALKING.
I'M--
DOCTOR SPECTRUM, YEAH, I HEARD ALREADY.
I'M JIM SCULLY, U.S. MARINE CORPS--"SKULL THE SLAYER" TO MOST THAT KNOW ME HERE.
AND WHAT'S YOUR *POWER?*
I'LL BROOK NO NONSENSE FROM MAN OR GOBLIN.
FAIR ENOUGH.

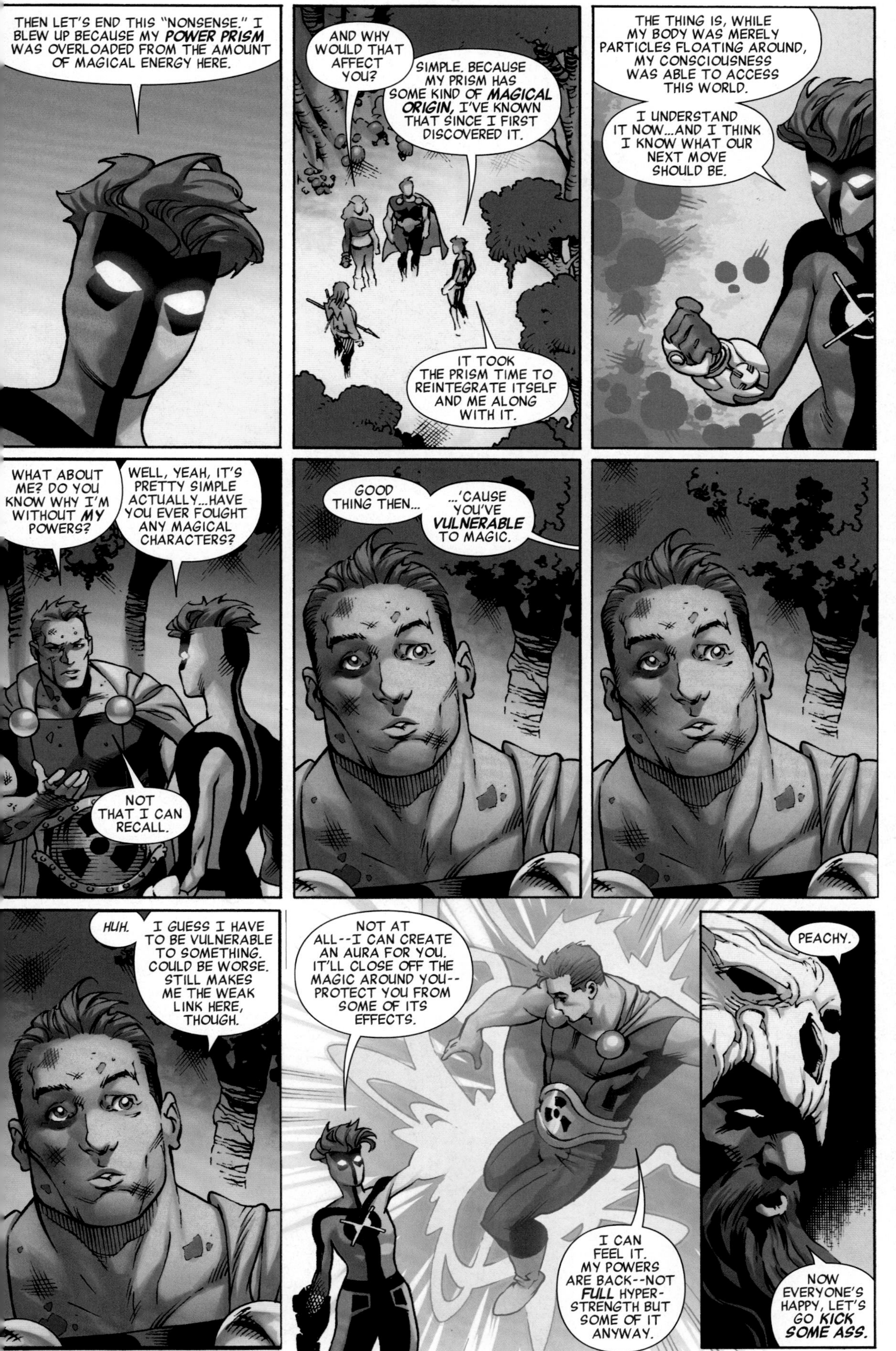
THEN LET'S END THIS "NONSENSE." I BLEW UP BECAUSE MY POWER PRISM WAS OVERLOADED FROM THE AMOUNT OF MAGICAL ENERGY HERE.
AND WHY WOULD THAT AFFECT YOU?
SIMPLE. BECAUSE MY PRISM HAS SOME KIND OF MAGICAL ORIGIN, I'VE KNOWN THAT SINCE I FIRST DISCOVERED IT.
IT TOOK THE PRISM TIME TO REINTEGRATE ITSELF AND ME ALONG WITH IT.
THE THING IS, WHILE MY BODY WAS MERELY PARTICLES FLOATING AROUND, MY CONSCIOUSNESS WAS ABLE TO ACCESS THIS WORLD.
I UNDERSTAND IT NOW...AND I THINK I KNOW WHAT OUR NEXT MOVE SHOULD BE.
WHAT ABOUT ME? DO YOU KNOW WHY I'M WITHOUT MY POWERS?
WELL, YEAH, IT'S PRETTY SIMPLE ACTUALLY...HAVE YOU EVER FOUGHT ANY MAGICAL CHARACTERS?
NOT THAT I CAN RECALL.
GOOD THING THEN...
...'CAUSE YOU'VE VULNERABLE TO MAGIC.
HUH.
I GUESS I HAVE TO BE VULNERABLE TO SOMETHING. COULD BE WORSE. STILL MAKES ME THE WEAK LINK HERE, THOUGH.
NOT AT ALL--I CAN CREATE AN AURA FOR YOU. IT'LL CLOSE OFF THE MAGIC AROUND YOU--PROTECT YOU FROM SOME OF ITS EFFECTS.
I CAN FEEL IT. MY POWERS ARE BACK--NOT FULL HYPER-STRENGTH BUT SOME OF IT ANYWAY.
PEACHY.
NOW EVERYONE'S HAPPY, LET'S GO KICK SOME ASS.

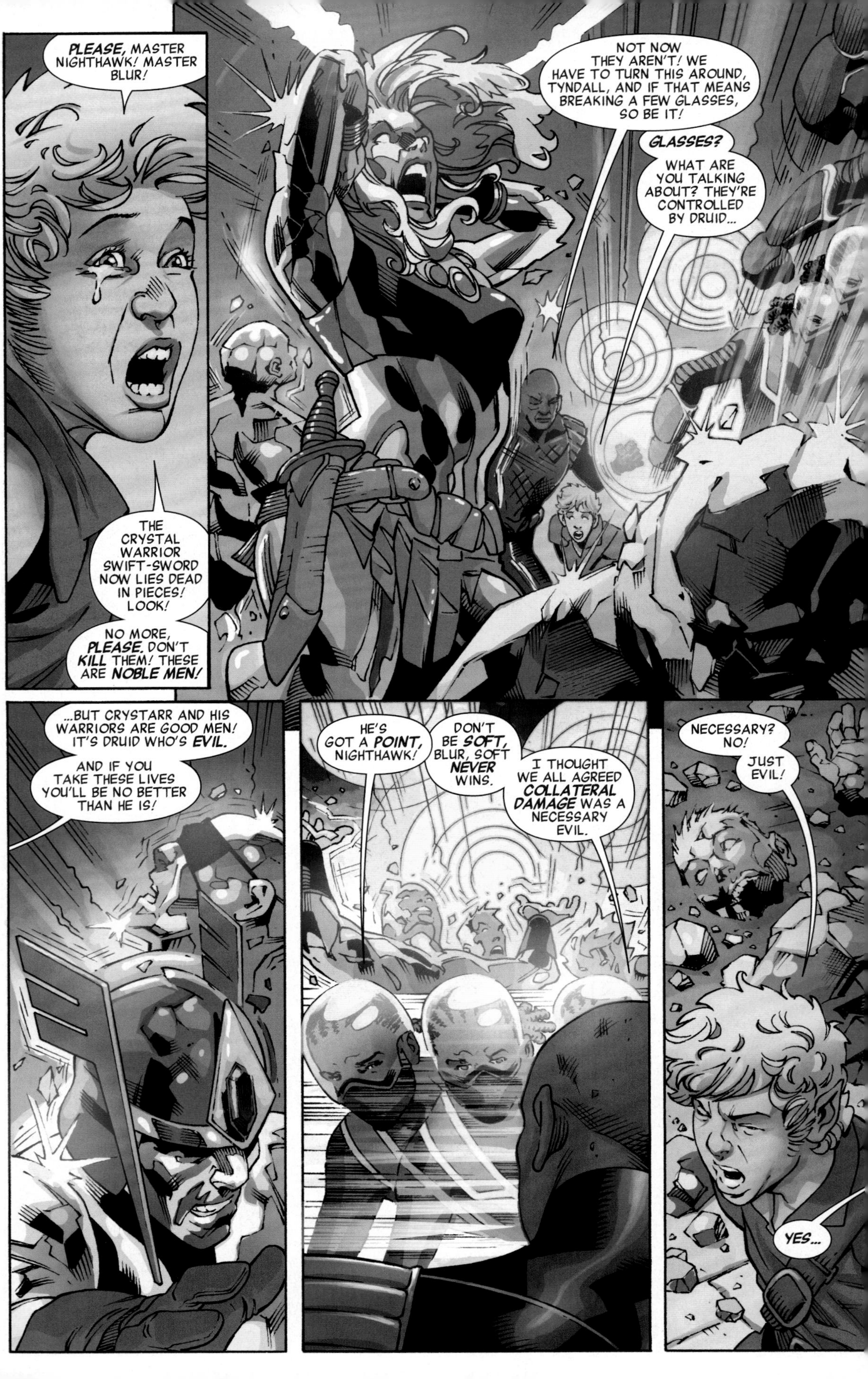
PLEASE, MASTER NIGHTHAWK! MASTER BLUR!
NOT NOW THEY AREN'T! WE HAVE TO TURN THIS AROUND, TYNDALL, AND IF THAT MEANS BREAKING A FEW GLASSES, SO BE IT!
GLASSES?
WHAT ARE YOU TALKING ABOUT? THEY'RE CONTROLLED BY DRUID...
THE CRYSTAL WARRIOR SWIFT-SWORD NOW LIES DEAD IN PIECES! LOOK!
NO MORE, PLEASE. DON'T KILL THEM! THESE ARE NOBLE MEN!
...BUT CRYSTARR AND HIS WARRIORS ARE GOOD MEN! IT'S DRUID WHO'S EVIL.
AND IF YOU TAKE THESE LIVES YOU'LL BE NO BETTER THAN HE IS!
HE'S GOT A POINT, NIGHTHAWK!
DON'T BE SOFT, BLUR, SOFT NEVER WINS.
I THOUGHT WE ALL AGREED COLLATERAL DAMAGE WAS A NECESSARY EVIL.
NECESSARY? NO!
JUST EVIL!
YES...

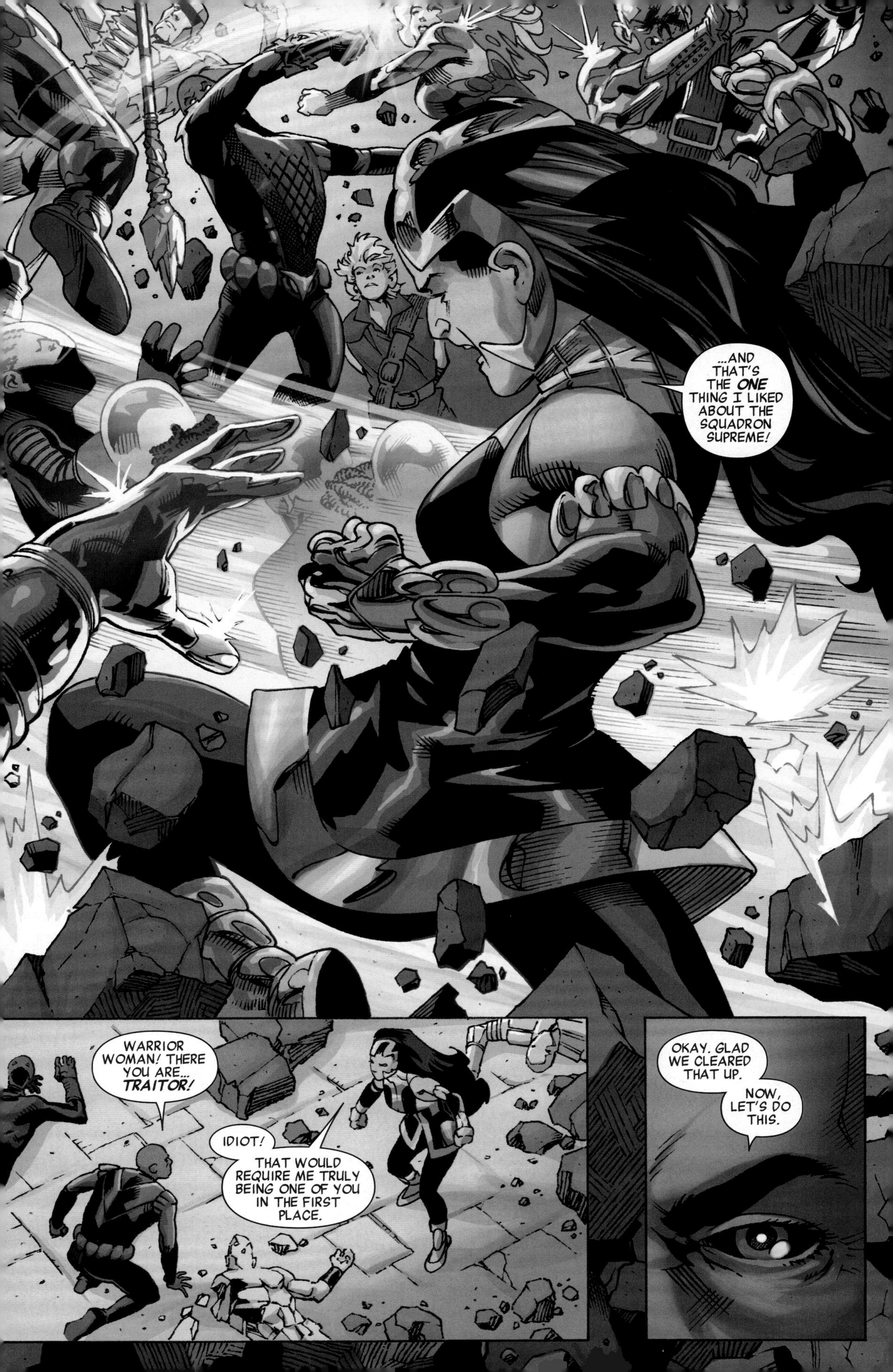
...AND THAT'S THE ONE THING I LIKED ABOUT THE SQUADRON SUPREME!
WARRIOR WOMAN! THERE YOU ARE... TRAITOR!
IDIOT!
THAT WOULD REQUIRE ME TRULY BEING ONE OF YOU IN THE FIRST PLACE.
OKAY. GLAD WE CLEARED THAT UP.
NOW, LET'S DO THIS.

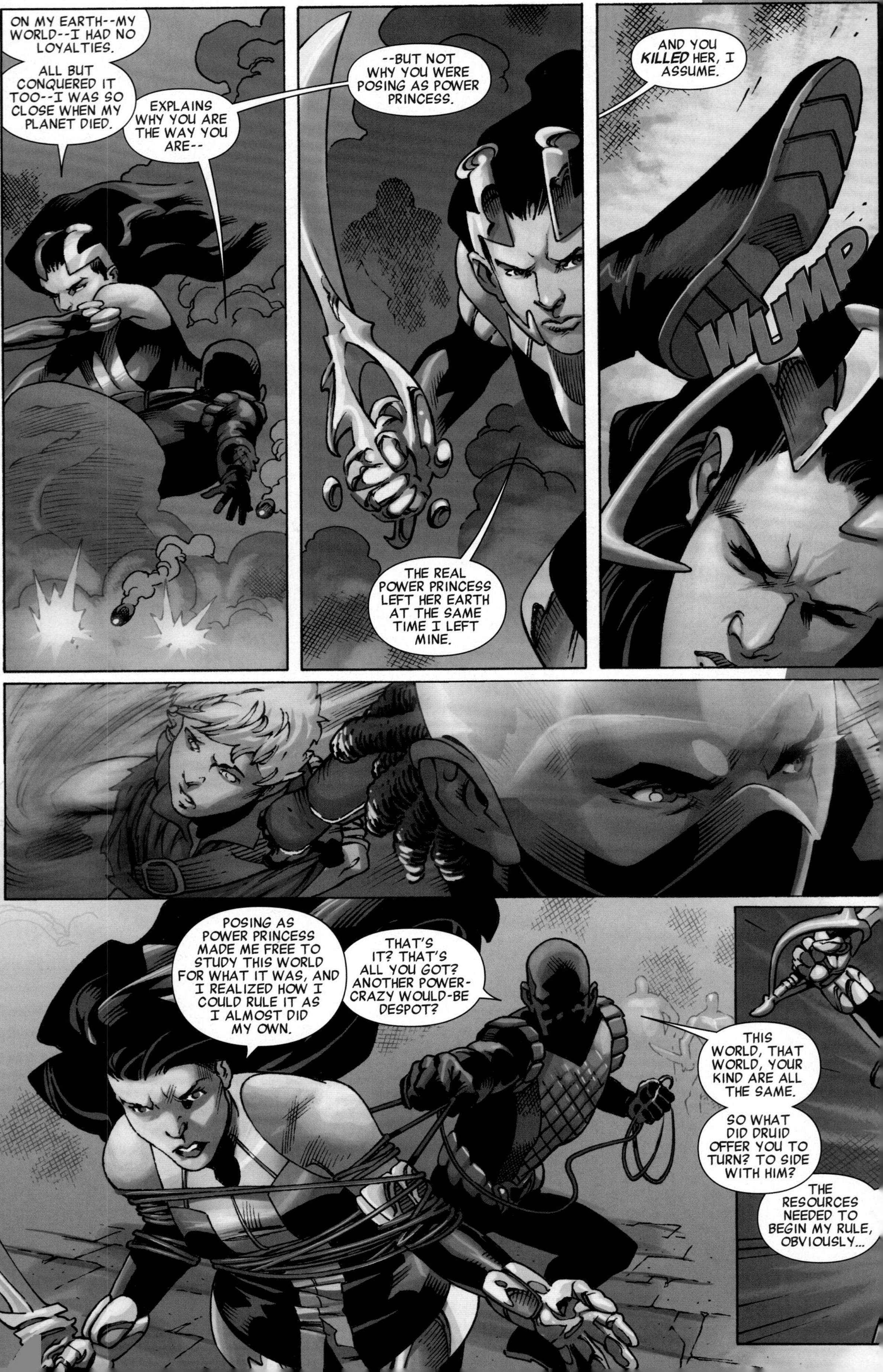

ON MY EARTH--MY WORLD--I HAD NO LOYALTIES.
ALL BUT CONQUERED IT TOO--I WAS SO CLOSE WHEN MY PLANET DIED.
EXPLAINS WHY YOU ARE THE WAY YOU ARE--
--BUT NOT WHY YOU WERE POSING AS POWER PRINCESS.
THE REAL POWER PRINCESS LEFT HER EARTH AT THE SAME TIME I LEFT MINE.
AND YOU KILLED HER, I ASSUME.
WUMP
POSING AS POWER PRINCESS MADE ME FREE TO STUDY THIS WORLD FOR WHAT IT WAS, AND I REALIZED HOW I COULD RULE IT AS I ALMOST DID MY OWN.
THAT'S IT? THAT'S ALL YOU GOT? ANOTHER POWER-CRAZY WOULD-BE DESPOT?
THIS WORLD, THAT WORLD, YOUR KIND ARE ALL THE SAME.
SO WHAT DID DRUID OFFER YOU TO TURN? TO SIDE WITH HIM?
THE RESOURCES NEEDED TO BEGIN MY RULE, OBVIOUSLY...

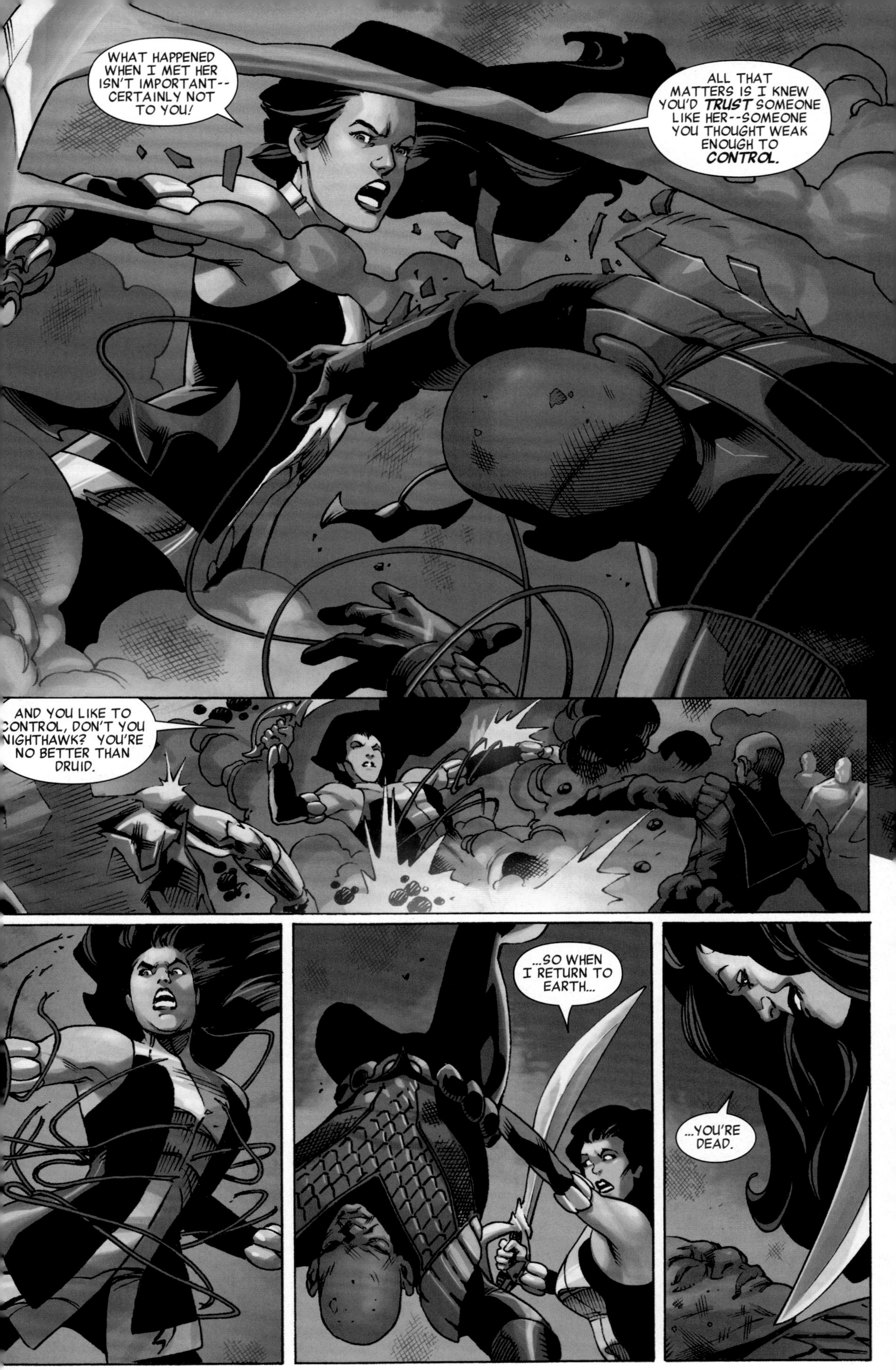
WHAT HAPPENED WHEN I MET HER ISN'T IMPORTANT-- CERTAINLY NOT TO YOU!
ALL THAT MATTERS IS I KNEW YOU'D TRUST SOMEONE LIKE HER--SOMEONE YOU THOUGHT WEAK ENOUGH TO CONTROL.
AND YOU LIKE TO CONTROL, DON'T YOU NIGHTHAWK? YOU'RE NO BETTER THAN DRUID.
...SO WHEN I RETURN TO EARTH...
...YOU'RE DEAD.

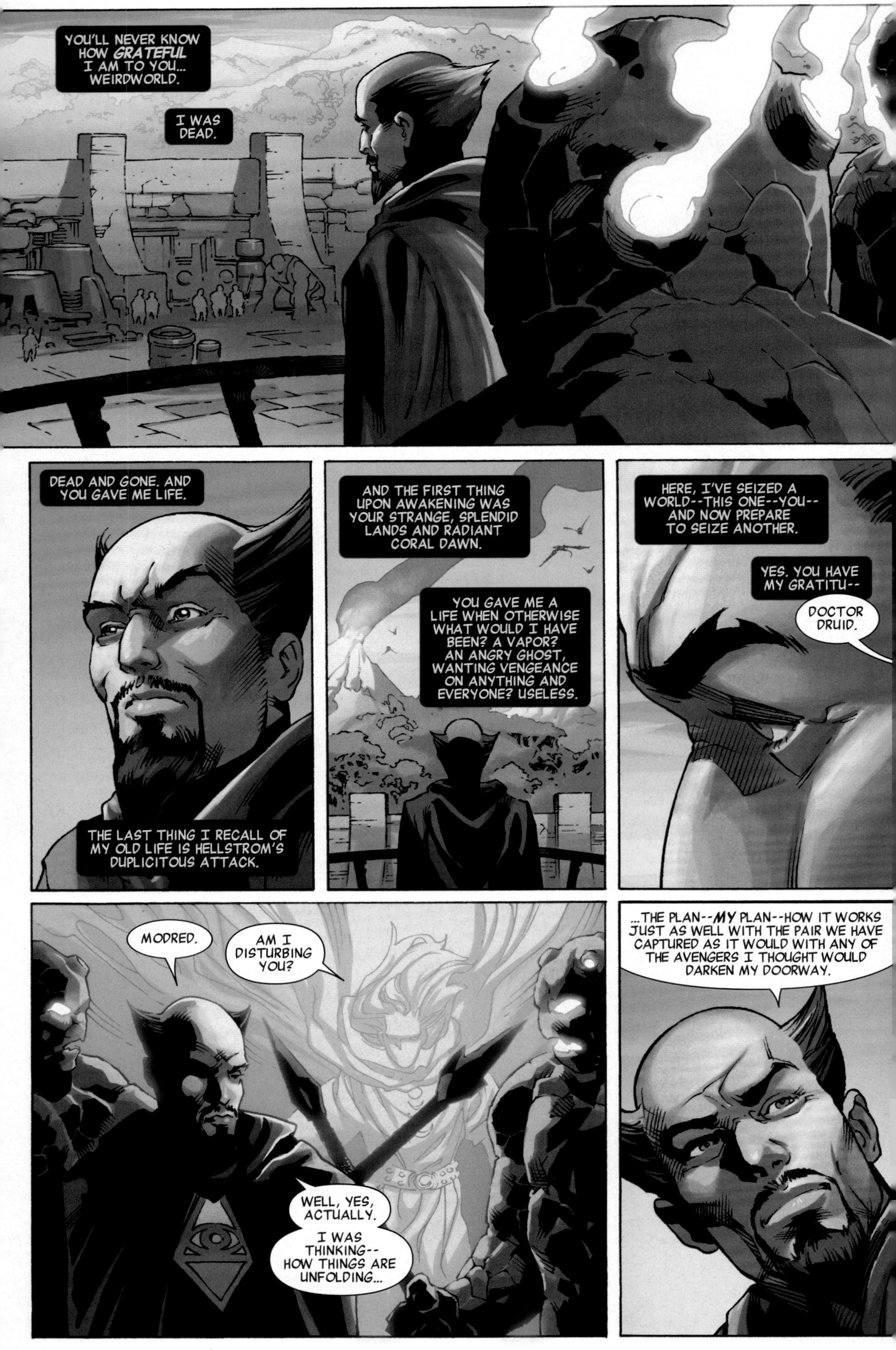

YOU'LL NEVER KNOW HOW GRATEFUL I AM TO YOU... WEIRDWORLD.
I WAS DEAD.
DEAD AND GONE. AND YOU GAVE ME LIFE.
THE LAST THING I RECALL OF MY OLD LIFE IS HELLSTROM'S DUPLICITOUS ATTACK.
AND THE FIRST THING UPON AWAKENING WAS YOUR STRANGE, SPLENDID LANDS AND RADIANT CORAL DAWN.
YOU GAVE ME A LIFE WHEN OTHERWISE WHAT WOULD I HAVE BEEN? A VAPOR? AN ANGRY GHOST, WANTING VENGEANCE ON ANYTHING AND EVERYONE? USELESS.
HERE, I'VE SEIZED A WORLD--THIS ONE--YOU--AND NOW PREPARE TO SEIZE ANOTHER.
YES. YOU HAVE MY GRATITU--
DOCTOR DRUID.
MODRED.
AM I DISTURBING YOU?
WELL, YES, ACTUALLY.
I WAS THINKING--HOW THINGS ARE UNFOLDING...
...THE PLAN--MY PLAN--HOW IT WORKS JUST AS WELL WITH THE PAIR WE HAVE CAPTURED AS IT WOULD WITH ANY OF THE AVENGERS I THOUGHT WOULD DARKEN MY DOORWAY.

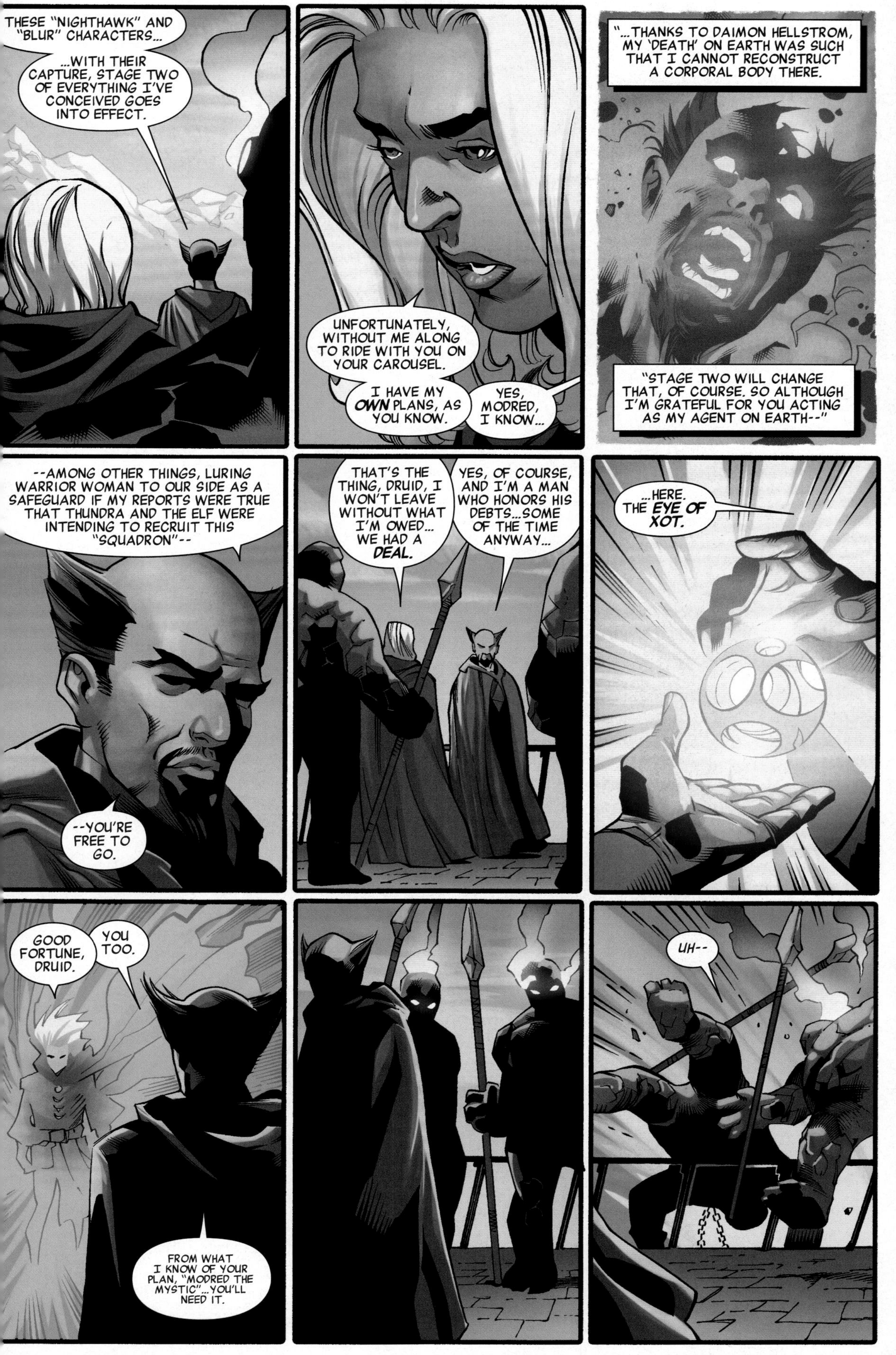
THESE "NIGHTHAWK" AND "BLUR" CHARACTERS...
...WITH THEIR CAPTURE, STAGE TWO OF EVERYTHING I'VE CONCEIVED GOES INTO EFFECT.
UNFORTUNATELY, WITHOUT ME ALONG TO RIDE WITH YOU ON YOUR CAROUSEL.
I HAVE MY OWN PLANS, AS YOU KNOW.
YES, MODRED, I KNOW...
"...THANKS TO DAIMON HELLSTROM, MY 'DEATH' ON EARTH WAS SUCH THAT I CANNOT RECONSTRUCT A CORPORAL BODY THERE.
"STAGE TWO WILL CHANGE THAT, OF COURSE. SO ALTHOUGH I'M GRATEFUL FOR YOU ACTING AS MY AGENT ON EARTH--"
--AMONG OTHER THINGS, LURING WARRIOR WOMAN TO OUR SIDE AS A SAFEGUARD IF MY REPORTS WERE TRUE THAT THUNDRA AND THE ELF WERE INTENDING TO RECRUIT THIS "SQUADRON"--
--YOU'RE FREE TO GO.
THAT'S THE THING, DRUID, I WON'T LEAVE WITHOUT WHAT I'M OWED... WE HAD A DEAL.
YES, OF COURSE, AND I'M A MAN WHO HONORS HIS DEBTS...SOME OF THE TIME ANYWAY...
...HERE. THE EYE OF XOT.
GOOD FORTUNE, DRUID.
YOU TOO.
FROM WHAT I KNOW OF YOUR PLAN, "MODRED THE MYSTIC"...YOU'LL NEED IT.
UH--

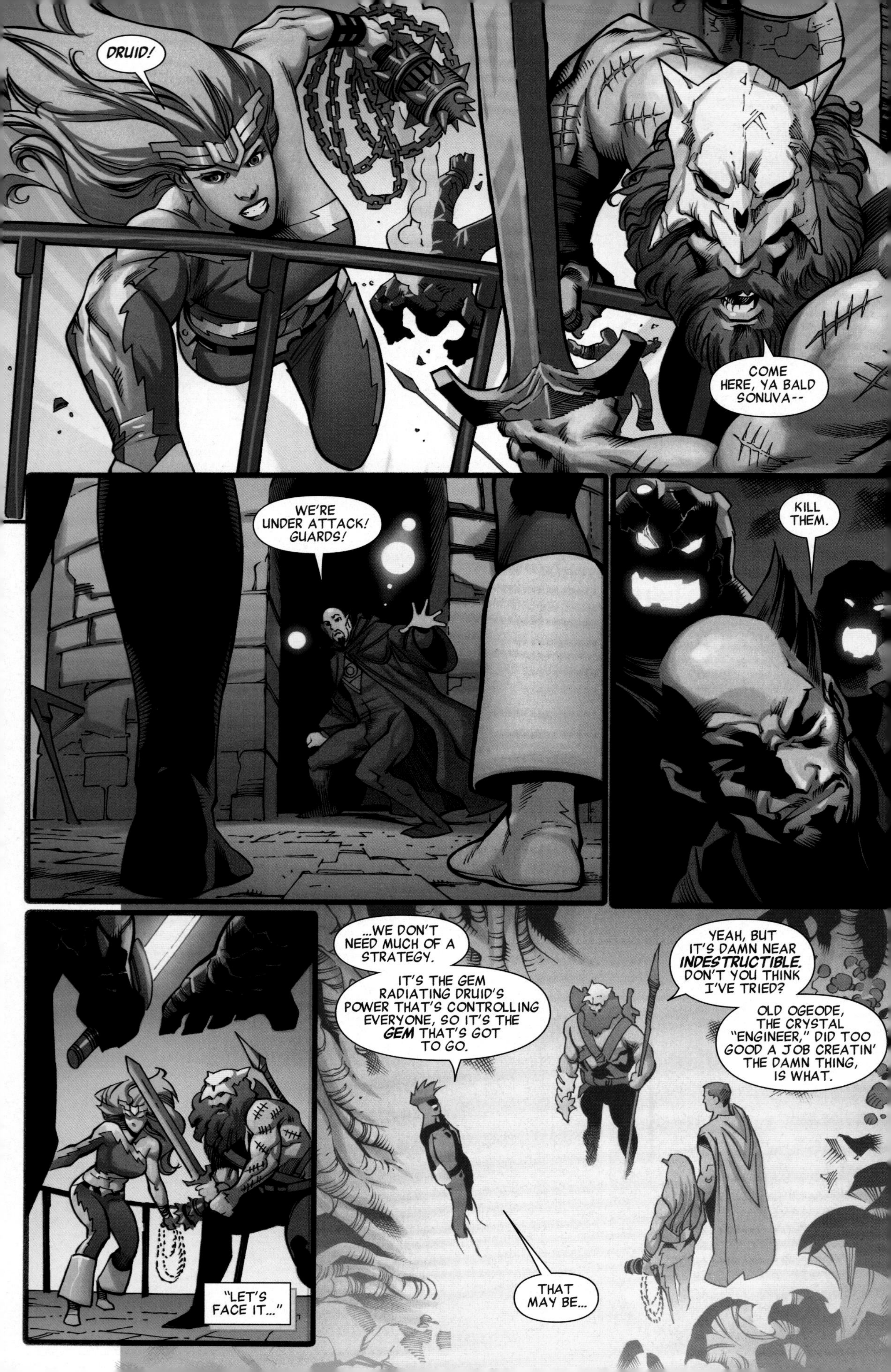
DRUID!
COME HERE, YA BALD SONUVA--
WE'RE UNDER ATTACK! GUARDS!
KILL THEM.
"LET'S FACE IT..."
...WE DON'T NEED MUCH OF A STRATEGY.
IT'S THE GEM RADIATING DRUID'S POWER THAT'S CONTROLLING EVERYONE, SO IT'S THE GEM THAT'S GOT TO GO.
THAT MAY BE...
YEAH, BUT IT'S DAMN NEAR INDESTRUCTIBLE. DON'T YOU THINK I'VE TRIED?
OLD OGEODE, THE CRYSTAL "ENGINEER," DID TOO GOOD A JOB CREATIN' THE DAMN THING, IS WHAT.

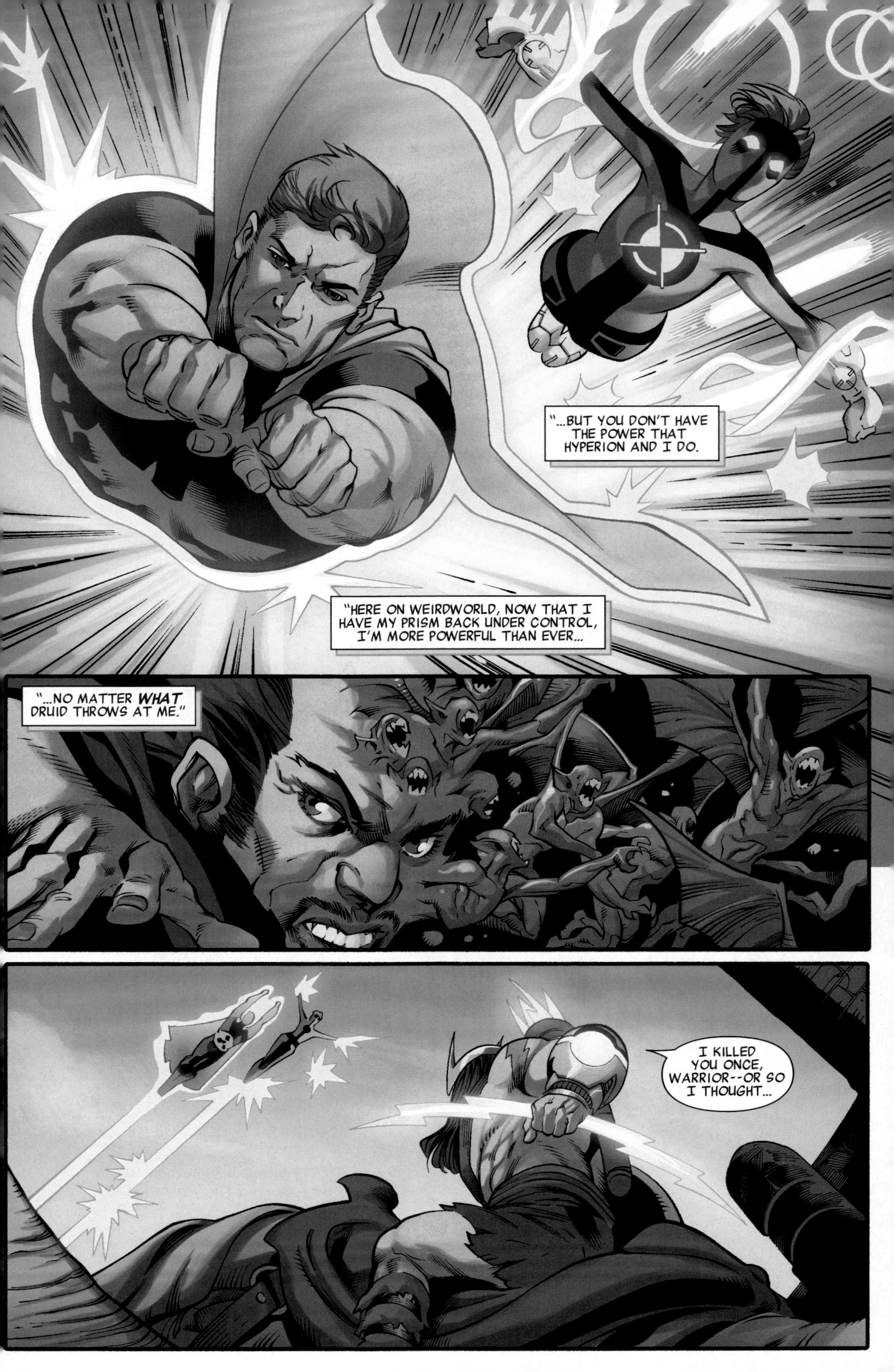
"...BUT YOU DON'T HAVE THE POWER THAT HYPERION AND I DO.
"HERE ON WEIRDWORLD, NOW THAT I HAVE MY PRISM BACK UNDER CONTROL, I'M MORE POWERFUL THAN EVER...
"...NO MATTER WHAT DRUID THROWS AT ME."
I KILLED YOU ONCE, WARRIOR--OR SO I THOUGHT...

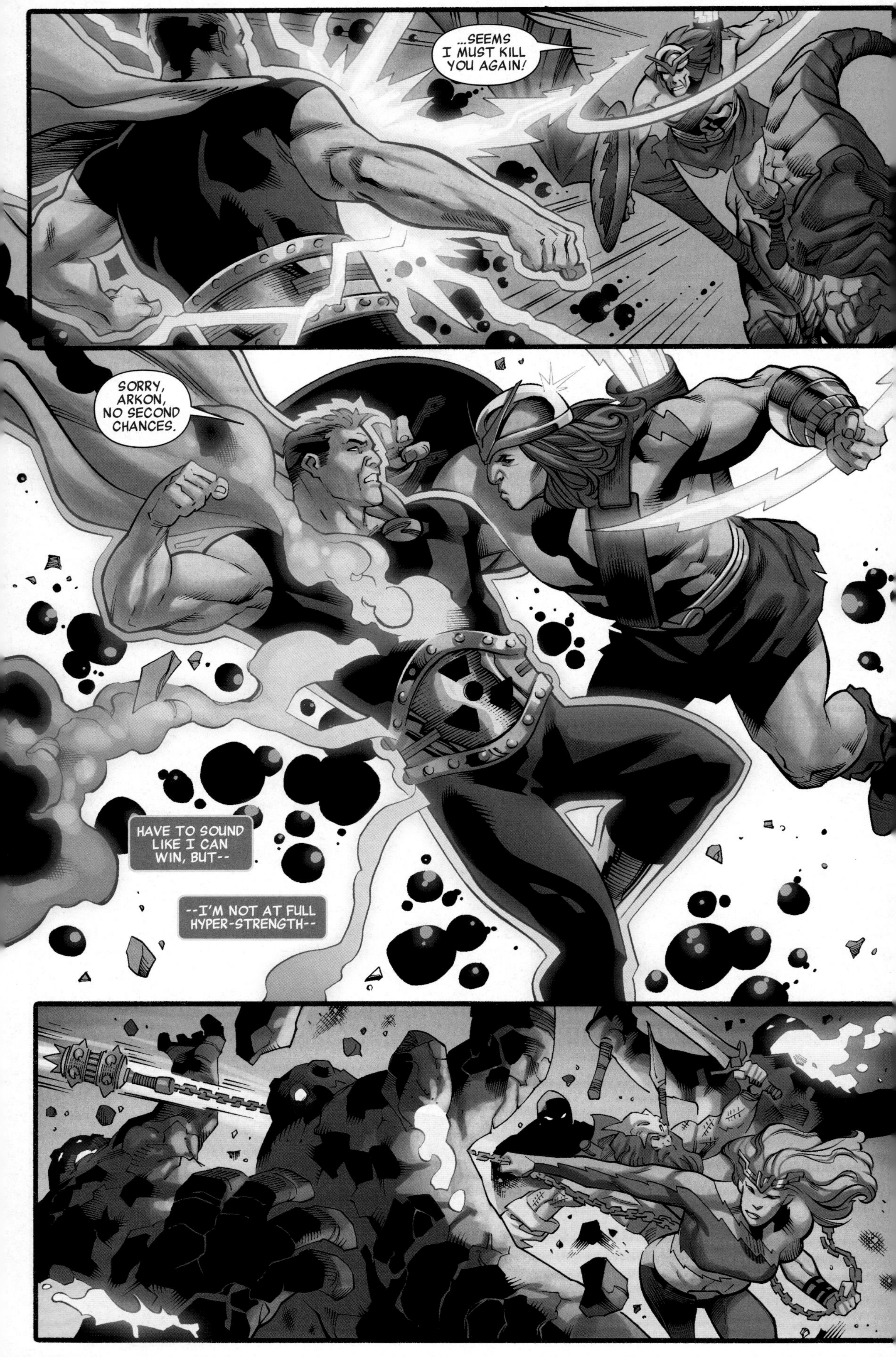
...SEEMS I MUST KILL YOU AGAIN!
SORRY, ARKON, NO SECOND CHANCES.
HAVE TO SOUND LIKE I CAN WIN, BUT--
--I'M NOT AT FULL HYPER-STRENGTH--

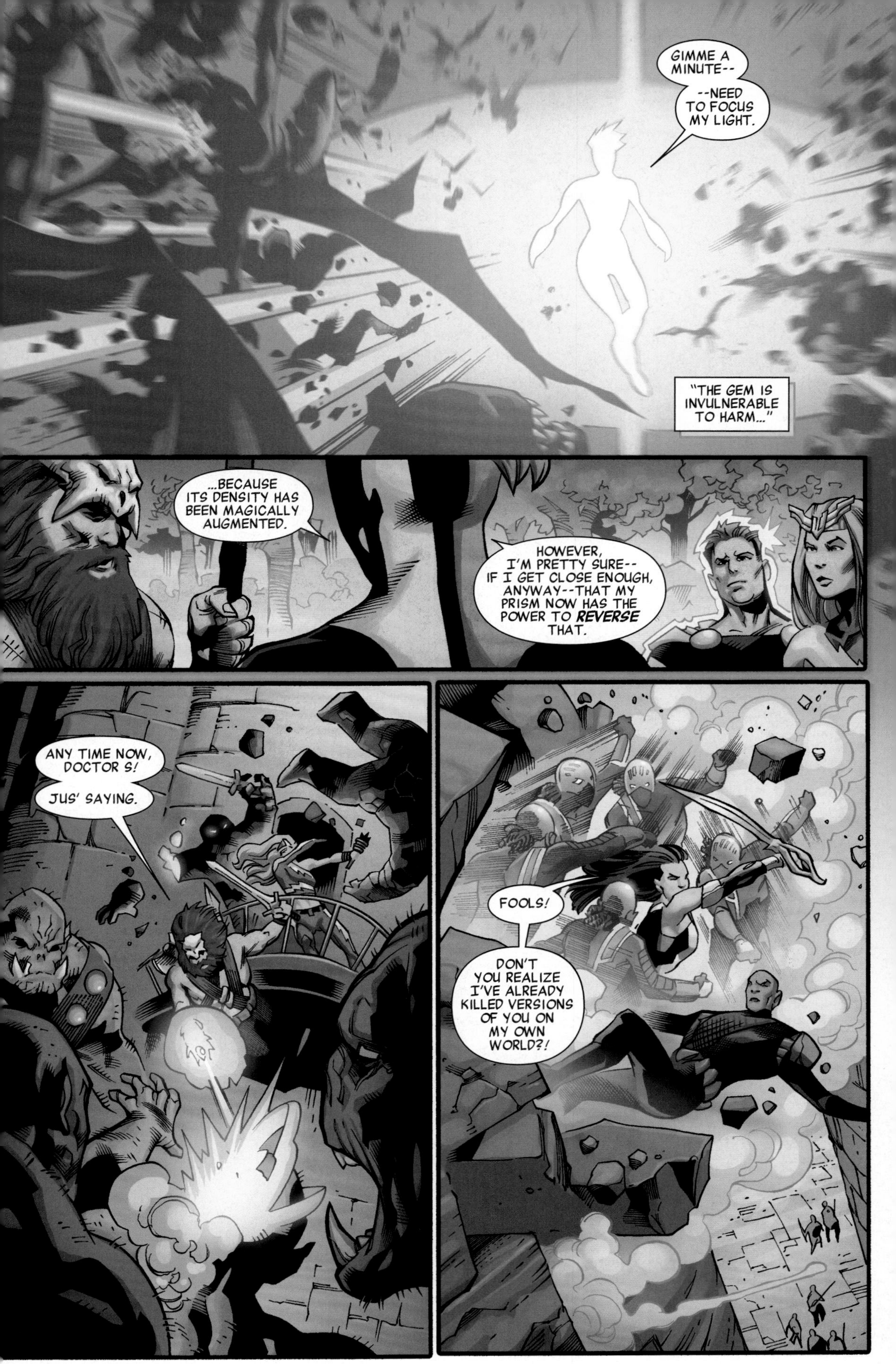
GIMME A MINUTE--
--NEED TO FOCUS MY LIGHT.
"THE GEM IS INVULNERABLE TO HARM..."
...BECAUSE ITS DENSITY HAS BEEN MAGICALLY AUGMENTED.
HOWEVER, I'M PRETTY SURE-- IF I GET CLOSE ENOUGH, ANYWAY--THAT MY PRISM NOW HAS THE POWER TO REVERSE THAT.
ANY TIME NOW, DOCTOR S!
JUS' SAYING.
FOOLS!
DON'T YOU REALIZE I'VE ALREADY KILLED VERSIONS OF YOU ON MY OWN WORLD?!

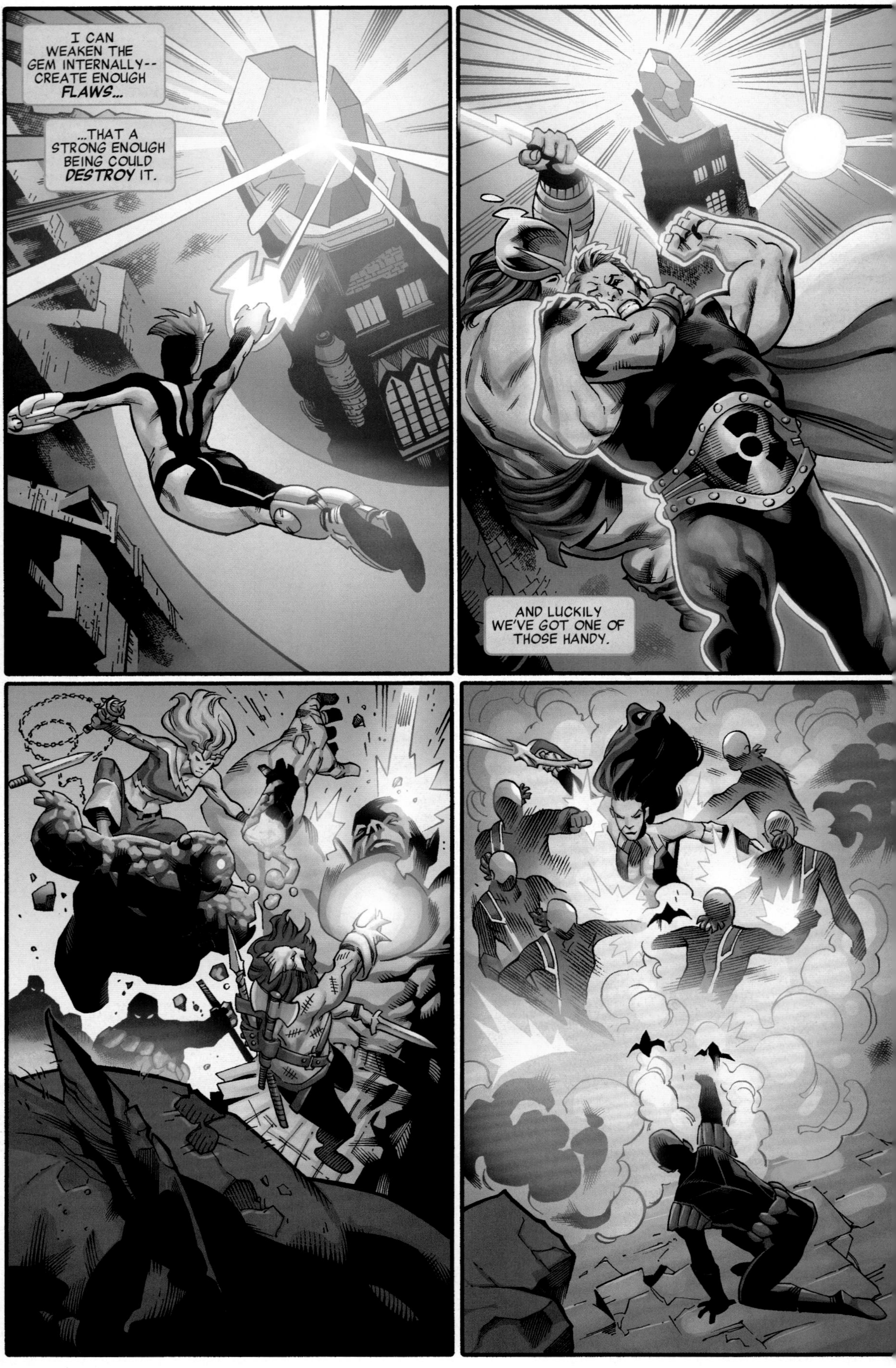
I CAN WEAKEN THE GEM INTERNALLY-- CREATE ENOUGH FLAWS...
...THAT A STRONG ENOUGH BEING COULD DESTROY IT.
AND LUCKILY WE'VE GOT ONE OF THOSE HANDY.

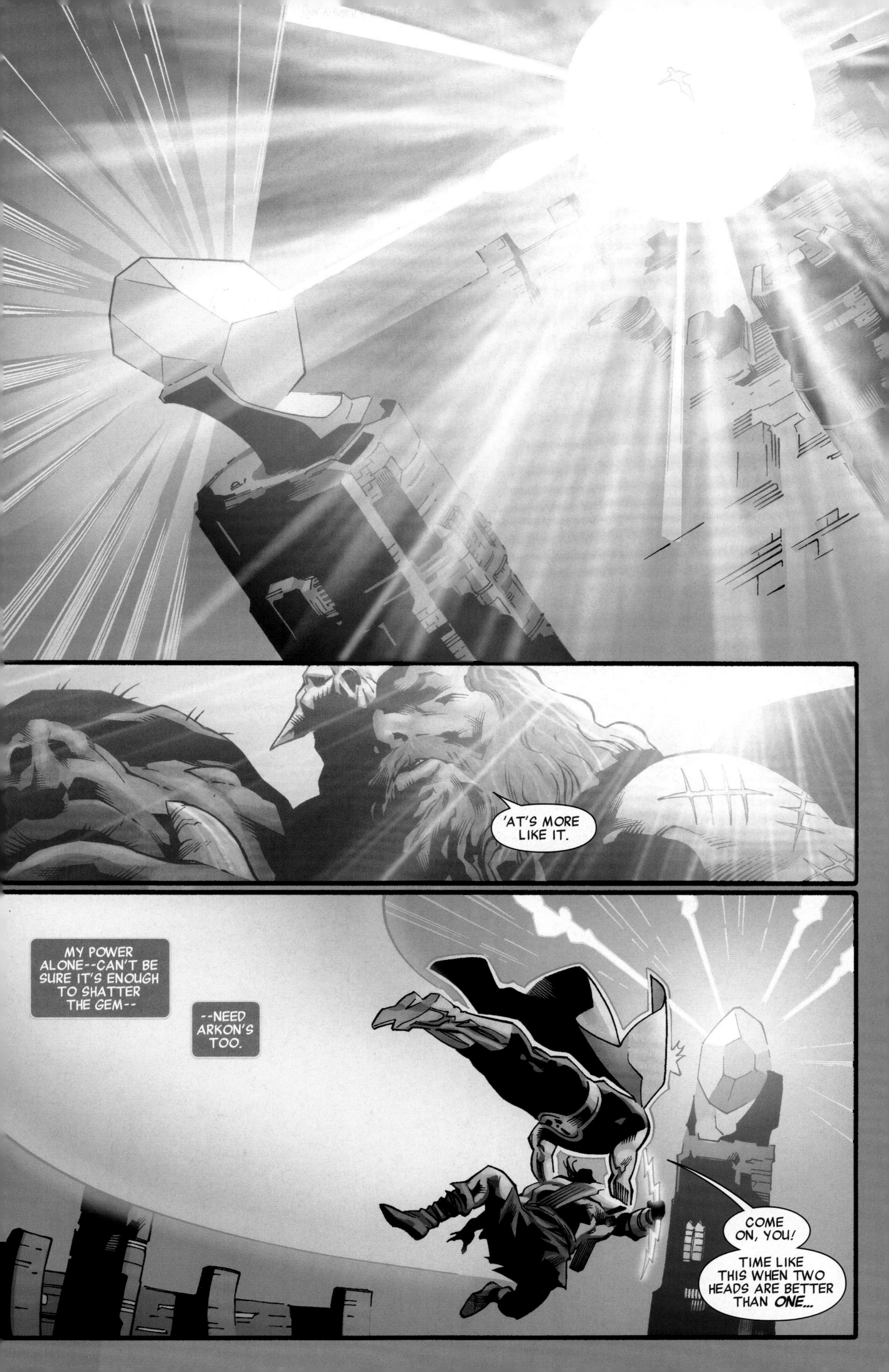
'AT'S MORE LIKE IT.
MY POWER ALONE--CAN'T BE SURE IT'S ENOUGH TO SHATTER THE GEM--
--NEED ARKON'S TOO.
COME ON, YOU!
TIME LIKE THIS WHEN TWO HEADS ARE BETTER THAN ONE...

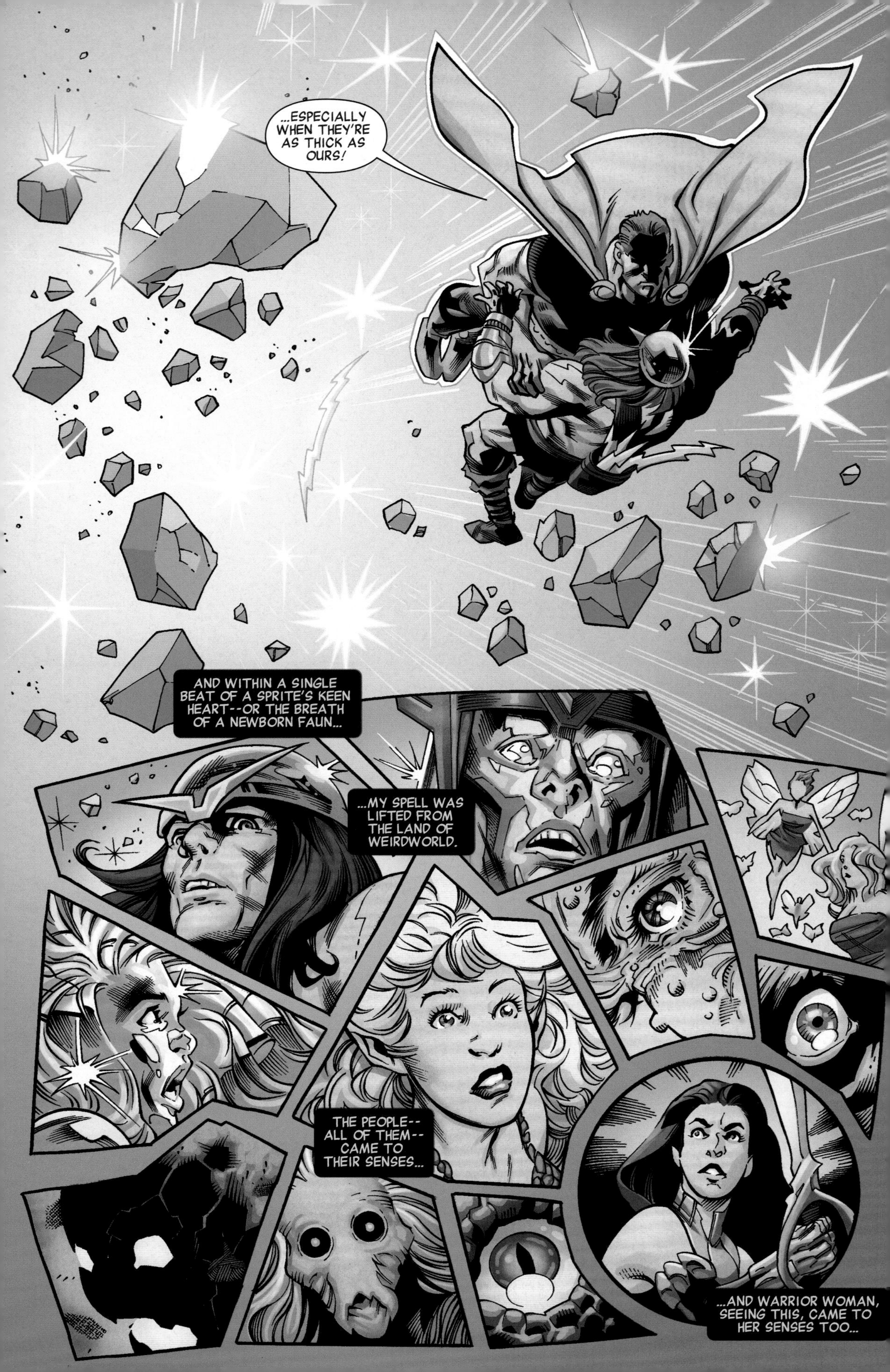
...ESPECIALLY WHEN THEY'RE AS THICK AS OURS!
AND WITHIN A SINGLE BEAT OF A SPRITE'S KEEN HEART--OR THE BREATH OF A NEWBORN FAUN...
...MY SPELL WAS LIFTED FROM THE LAND OF WEIRDWORLD.
THE PEOPLE-- ALL OF THEM-- CAME TO THEIR SENSES...
...AND WARRIOR WOMAN, SEEING THIS, CAME TO HER SENSES TOO...

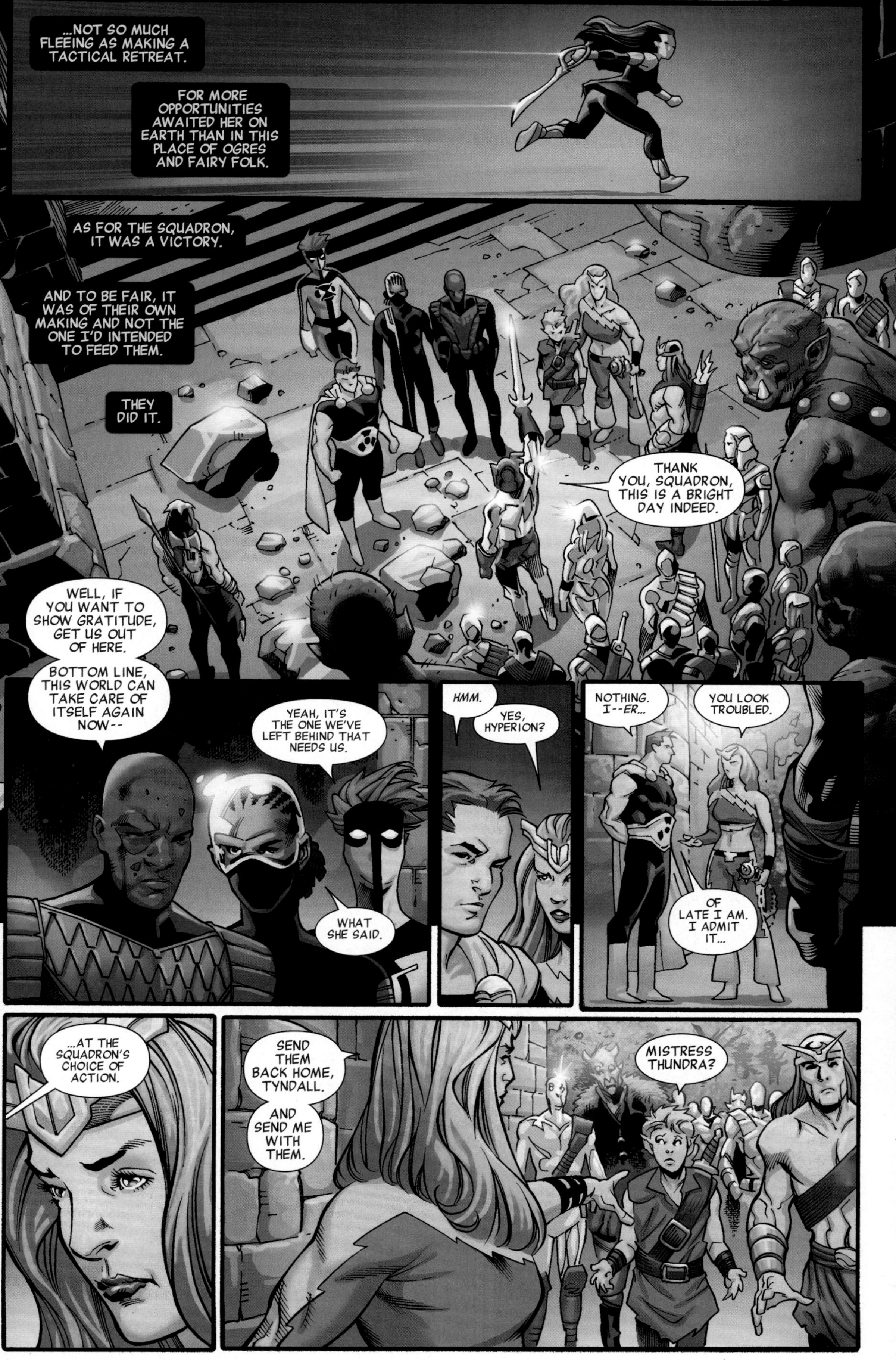
...NOT SO MUCH FLEEING AS MAKING A TACTICAL RETREAT.
FOR MORE OPPORTUNITIES AWAITED HER ON EARTH THAN IN THIS PLACE OF OGRES AND FAIRY FOLK.
AS FOR THE SQUADRON, IT WAS A VICTORY.
AND TO BE FAIR, IT WAS OF THEIR OWN MAKING AND NOT THE ONE I'D INTENDED TO FEED THEM.
THEY DID IT.
THANK YOU, SQUADRON, THIS IS A BRIGHT DAY INDEED.
WELL, IF YOU WANT TO SHOW GRATITUDE, GET US OUT OF HERE.
BOTTOM LINE, THIS WORLD CAN TAKE CARE OF ITSELF AGAIN NOW--
YEAH, IT'S THE ONE WE'VE LEFT BEHIND THAT NEEDS US.
WHAT SHE SAID.
HMM.
YES, HYPERION?
NOTHING. I--ER...
YOU LOOK TROUBLED.
OF LATE I AM. I ADMIT IT...
...AT THE SQUADRON'S CHOICE OF ACTION.
SEND THEM BACK HOME, TYNDALL.
AND SEND ME WITH THEM.
MISTRESS THUNDRA?

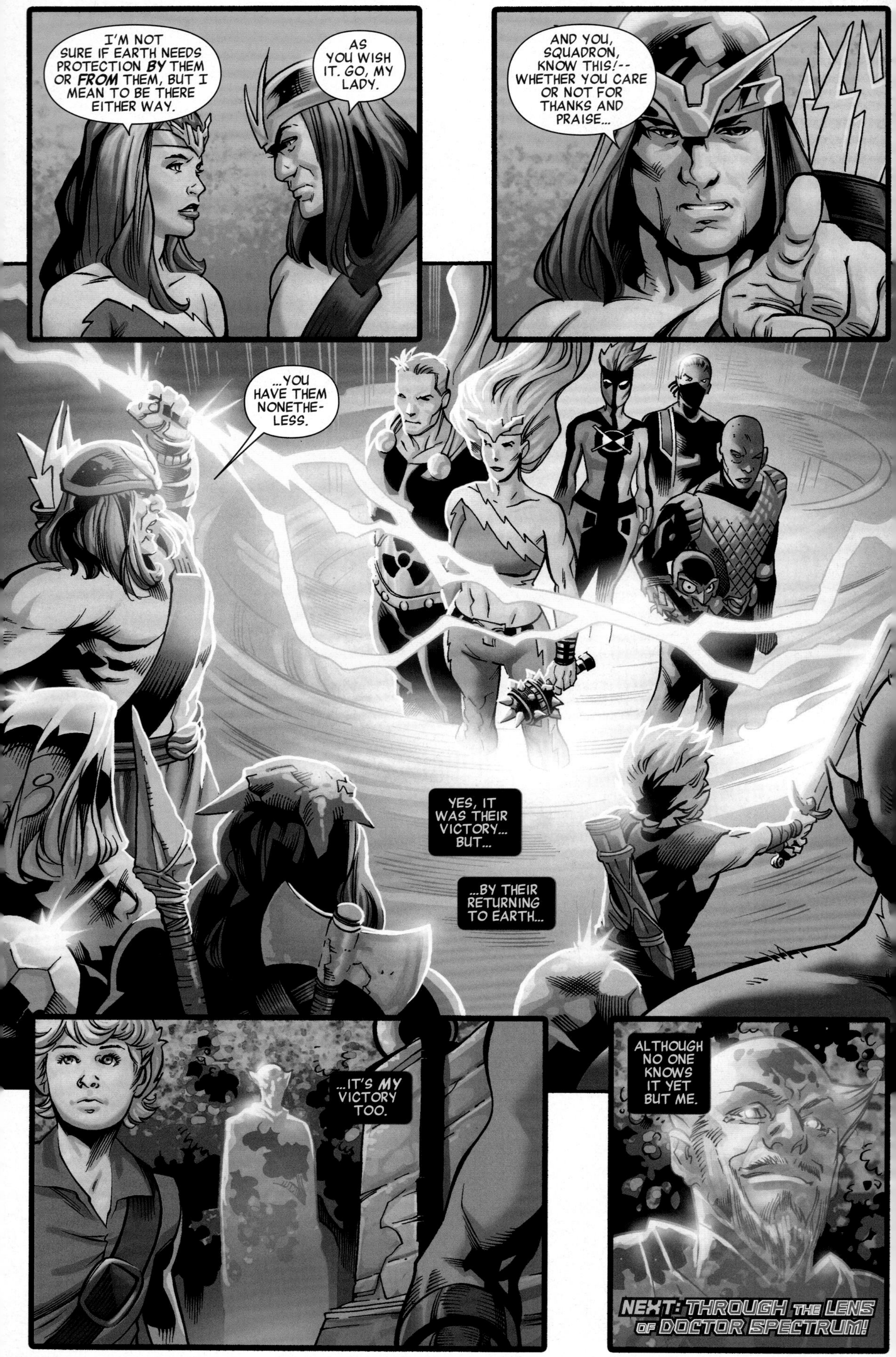
I'M NOT SURE IF EARTH NEEDS PROTECTION BY THEM OR FROM THEM, BUT I MEAN TO BE THERE EITHER WAY.
AS YOU WISH IT. GO, MY LADY.
AND YOU, SQUADRON, KNOW THIS!-- WHETHER YOU CARE OR NOT FOR THANKS AND PRAISE...
...YOU HAVE THEM NONETHE-LESS.
YES, IT WAS THEIR VICTORY... BUT...
...BY THEIR RETURNING TO EARTH...
...IT'S MY VICTORY TOO.
ALTHOUGH NO ONE KNOWS IT YET BUT ME.
NEXT: THROUGH THE LENS OF DOCTOR SPECTRUM!

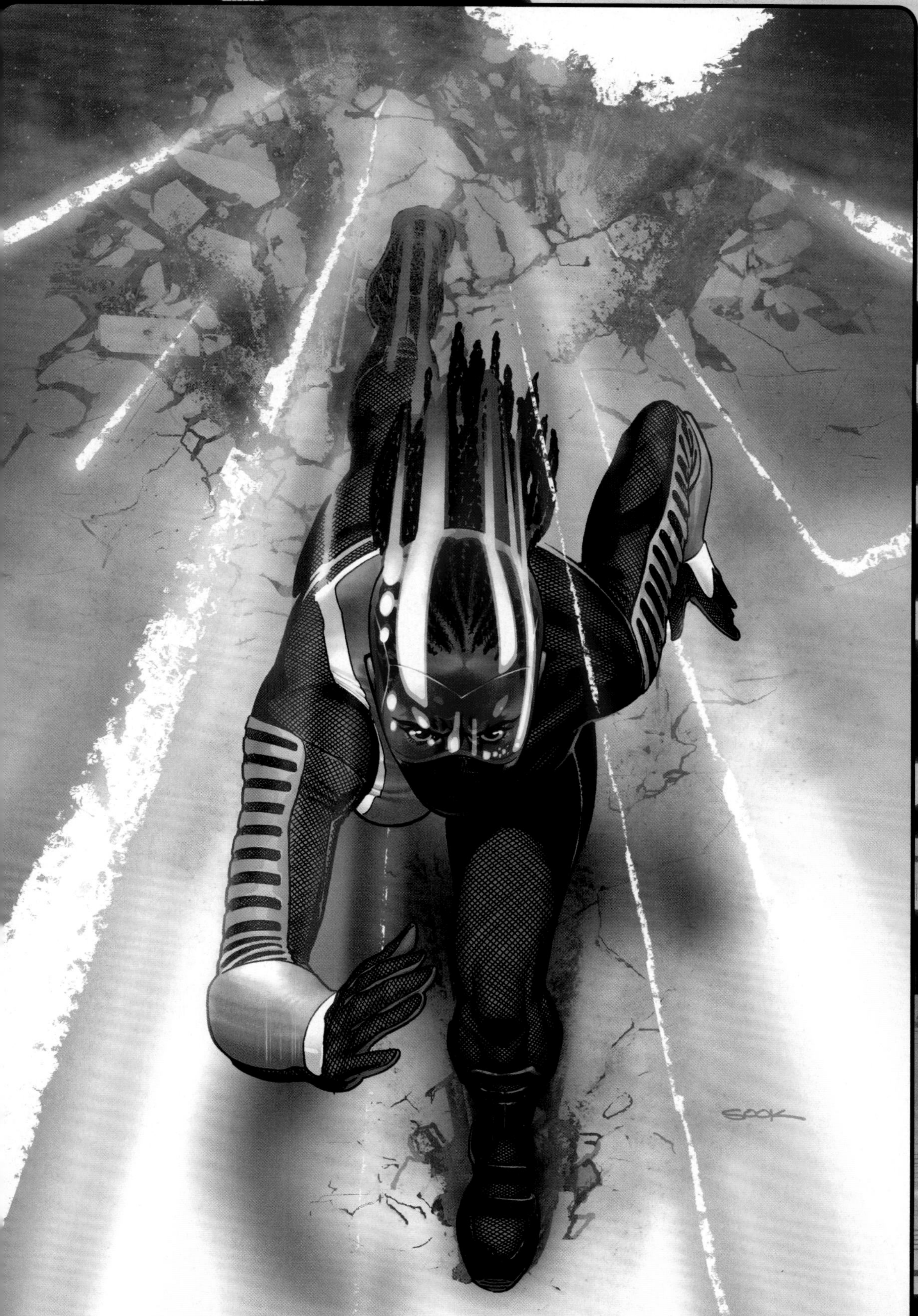
SOOK

#5 VARIANT BY **RYAN SOOK**

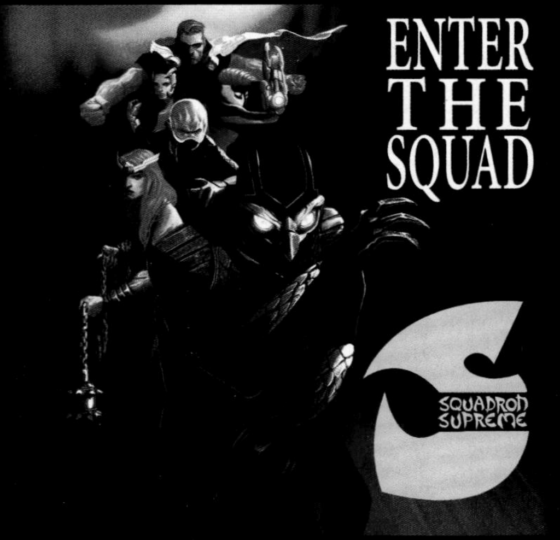
ENTER
THE
SQUAD
SQUADRON
SUPREME

⟶ #1 HIP-HOP VARIANT BY **MIKE DEL MUNDO**

#1 ACTION FIGURE VARIANT
BY **JOHN TYLER CHRISTOPHER** ⟵

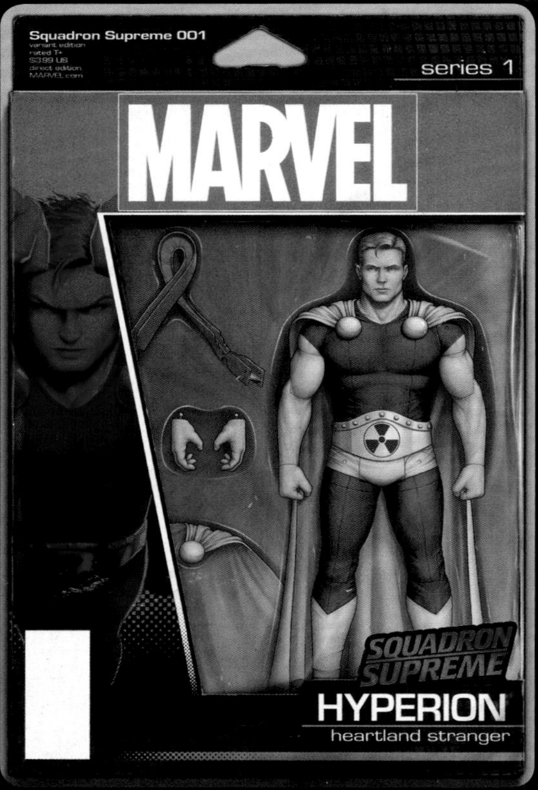
Squadron Supreme 001
variant edition
rated T+
$3.99 US
direct edition
MARVEL.com
series 1
MARVEL
SQUADRON
SUPREME
HYPERION
heartland stranger

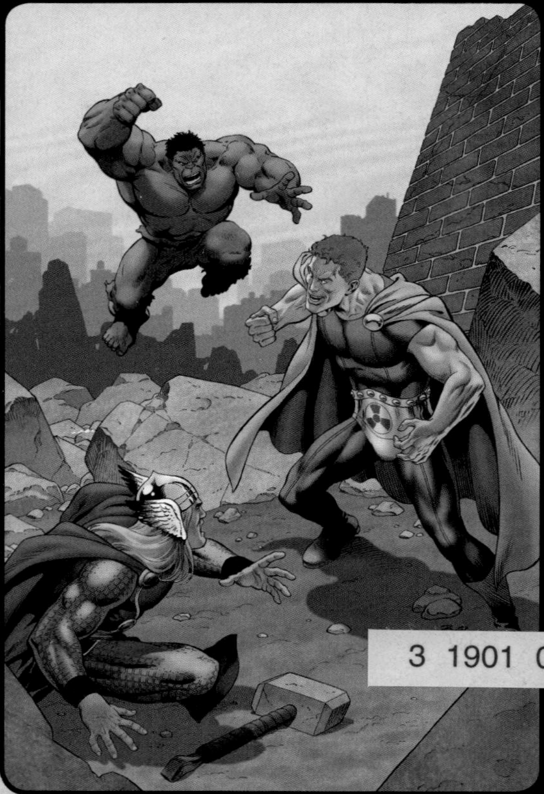

⟶ #4 VARIANT BY **BOB McLEOD**